The Necessary Blankness

Mary Allen

The Necessary Blankness

*Women in Major American
Fiction of the Sixties*

University of Illinois Press
Urbana   Chicago   London

Publication of this work was supported in part by
a grant from the Andrew W. Mellon Foundation

LIBRARY OF CONGRESS CATALOGING IN PUBLICATION DATA

Allen, Mary, 1939–
    The necessary blankness.

    Bibliography: p.
    Includes index.
    1.   American fiction—20th Century—History and
criticism.   2.   Women in literature.   I.   Title.
PS374.W6A4   813'.03   75-38780
ISBN 0-252-00519-8

To Women

Acknowledgments

I would like to thank Professor Carl Bode of the University of Maryland, who inspired me to wing out with my own thoughts and to do so before any more of life went by. The indispensable aid of librarians everywhere helped that work along. The late Professor John Lovell of Howard University made it possible for me to complete this project, and his warm encouragement was life-giving. To other teachers, colleagues, and friends for their stimulation and wisdom, which in many cases I may have tucked away as my own, I hereby give grateful acknowledgment. And finally, I deeply appreciate my family, who have all along supported my efforts at intellect as well as if I had been a man.

"... what was she going to do with herself?
This question was irregular, for with most women
one had no occasion to ask it. Most women did
with themselves nothing at all; they waited, in
attitudes more or less gracefully passive, for
a man to come that way and furnish them with a
destiny."

Henry James—*The Portrait of a Lady*

Contents

Introduction

Women matter to me. Much as I sometimes wish it were otherwise, featuring myself carried away by the lofty ideas of human history, there are few things I care about as deeply and as irrationally as what happens to them—a woman waiting for a phone call; a woman wondering what to do with her life; a woman realizing she is old. If these are the cares of men, then they matter to me, too.

I am no feminist in any formal sense of the word, but I have always been conscious of something wrong in the way women feel about themselves. Perhaps I experience only the human condition and figure it to be woman's plight. As a child I remember my distaste of Saturday morning housework, projecting then the life of a woman as eons of collecting the same scum around the toilet bowl. Years went by before I discovered that men also do nasty little jobs and are not forever involved in profound projects and adventure. For those are what I wanted, and something dark and ugly then made me angry to have been born a woman. I have long since been enlightened as to the abundant benefits granted us ladies, and with some shame admit how being a woman can be an excuse for a variety of mental and physical limitations. Knowing the tendency for such reasoning, I feel a special urgency for women to develop themselves more independently of the destinies that come from outside them. In spite of my desire to be as fair as possible to the authors discussed here, it is with these biases that the following study is informed.

In my early reading of fiction I recall few great ladies, but whenever a likely woman appeared I cheered her on and hoped she might be more than someone's sweetheart. It never happened. I remember that first shudder in considering the creation of Eve. Of all the books I have since read of women in literature, the most powerful for me, and I think still the best, is Simone de Beauvoir's *The Second Sex*. But it was hardly exhilaration I experienced in reading her definition of woman as the Other, rather, the painful sense of a truth I had feared but had never seen so plainly in print. Hers is a complete study of women's biological, sociological inheritance, and their treatment as myth in literature, always as appendages, with no concrete means for organizing themselves, "no past, no history, no religion of their own."[1] From her study of authors of various nationalities she concludes that only Stendhal gives us heroines who have destinies of their own, a rare event in any literature.

A check to the convincing argument of Kate Millett's *Sexual Politics*, a study of misogyny primarily in literature, is *The Troublesome Helpmate: A History of Misogyny in Literature* by Katherine M. Rogers, which reminds us that if women had written as much fiction as men have produced there would be as much misandry as misogyny. Literature is, after all, inclined more often to a description of disturbances than of contentment. Medea declares that if women had the gift of song as men do they could give a long account of men's treachery to them. Rogers interprets all forms of image-making of the feminine as types of misogyny, the medieval pedestal version of women as damning as any other. Like Simone de Beauvoir, she sees that women in literature are primarily creations which reflect the ideas of men. "Woman is created in man's image, not God's." Literature is a particularly effective medium for misogyny because it can be dealt with subtly, even subconsciously, since outright statements of misogyny are generally unacceptable. In the Western Christian tradition, since sexuality has from the beginning been associated with sin, and femininity has always been associated with sexuality, woman was initially tainted, and it is of course the Bible, along

1. Trans. and ed. H. M. Parshley (New York: Alfred A. Knopf, 1953), p. xix.

with the writing of the Romans and Greeks, that provides the greatest influence on English writers.[2]

Rogers traces a line of misogyny that continues through each literary period. The whore remains a standard figure, one of the most effective means of presenting misogyny, supported by the greater part of society's smug superiority to her. By the eighteenth century the rivalry between the sexes develops into sadistic exploitation by whichever party is the stronger.[3] The nineteenth century offers the much acclaimed saintly mother gratefully devoting her life to the virtuous raising of many children, exemplified by such writers as Dickens. With the decline of the father (and the advent of Freud), the twentieth century is the age of mom, and misogyny in literature carries on with more justification than ever.

It is not my purpose here to detail the history of misogyny or to make a study of its appearance in American literature, although that is a natural tendency in examining women in fiction, and there is abundant material for a *Sexual Politics* of American literature. It is necessary, however, to realize the extent of misogyny before looking at individual women in current fiction. Leslie Fiedler's *Love and Death in the American Novel*, with its fascinating and indispensable interpretation of women in our literature, notes at the outset "the failure of the American fictionist to deal with adult heterosexual love."[4] The absence of love, which is replaced by violent sex reflecting a puritanical rejection-fascination with the subject, is readily apparent to any student of American literature. According to Fiedler, the early gothic novel, with the maiden in flight from the artist-intellectual seducer, develops as a result of the failure of love. More noticeable than seduction, however, is the male's attempt to escape the woman, both as a puritanical reaction to sex and emotion and with the general urge for freedom, especially freedom from society. Natty Bumppo delivers the bride to someone else, taking as his true bride the spirit of the forest.[5] The virgin as an unattain-

2. (Seattle: University of Washington Press, 1966), pp. 4, 47.
3. Ibid., p. 160.
4. (New York: Dell, 1966), p. 12.
5. Ibid., pp. 142, 210.

able blonde goddess is the image most natural to our early writers, who, like their descendants, are never able to create convincing sexual heroines. Woman is also developed as the voice of moral authority, the village morality so repugnant to Huck Finn. Only with Henry James comes the creation of richer and more complete women. But generally our heroes are individuals, that is to say men, who confront the wilderness or other violent challenges to prove their worth. The familiar image of the Hemingway hero requires, for support of his ego, a woman who operates as a meek animal patiently waiting to fill the needs of her master. Faulkner develops her antithesis in Addie Bundren, who becomes among the "gallery of anti-mothers . . . the most icy and terrible,"[6] in a century by now overpopulated with frightening moms.

Little has yet been said of women in the literature of the present era. On first contact with the fiction of this period, particularly the fabulous tales, few individuals, men or women, stand out boldly because of the large casts of two-dimensional characters who are interchangeable or who constantly shift their identities. And the more realistic accounts of life also blur individuation. But even when characterization is not the writer's first concern, his attitude toward women is usually quite apparent. And we might well consider what the view of women in American literature is during the rise of the women's liberation movement. I find it distinctly reactionary. A chilling trend suggests that women should keep silent and content themselves at home.

The authors included in this study are those who seem to me the best writers to have come of age in the sixties and who deal significantly with women or a concept of the feminine. A few works of the late fifties are mentioned by way of background, and Updike's *Rabbit Redux* of 1971 receives considerable attention as the sequel to *Rabbit, Run* and as a possible indicator of the direction the future may take in the characterization of women. Regrettably, no major black writer emerges in the sixties to add to the image of women presented here the note of strength found in black women characters, most of whom are forced to provide for themselves, in fiction all the way from that of Charles W.

6. Ibid., p. 331.

Chesnutt and Jean Toomer to the writings of Ernest J. Gaines.[7]

What new strain might be expected in female characters of current American literature, which has offered so few richly developed women in the past? An expanded woman, if not an ennobled one, would seem essential to a truthful portrayal of the times. In a literary age dealing with the outcome of perhaps the greatest freedom we have ever had—certainly in terms of sexual activity for women, with the Pill made legal for public use in 1960—male characters are bombarded with choices to the point of paralysis. Women, however, continue to consider only a few (with occasional exceptions in the fabulous tales). But the need has never been greater for them to discover options: with the widespread emphasis on population control and the success to date of the program, along with the increasing longevity of the American woman, she will no longer spend the major part of her life raising children. The question of what she will do with her extended and freer life is crucial.

Before looking at the particular characteristics of women in the literature of the sixties, we should consider the general tendencies of the period and those traits which male and female characters share. It is a diverse era, producing a fascinating collection of bizarre tales, works of social realism, and documentary fiction. Wild plots are in fashion, with an emphasis on the mythic, allegoric, and symbolistic. In his preface to *The Red Hot Vacuum*, Theodore Solotaroff refers to this decade as "a kind of howling forum where all manners of ideas, styles and standards"[8] contend for attention. According to one study, what differentiates the novel of the sixties from that of the fifties, with the comfort of its existential philosophy, is the transcendence of questions of morality and social action through some extreme experience. There are few journeys in the sense of progressive action, although there is frequently an aimless movement through space, such as Benny Profane's "yo-yoing" up and down the Manhattan subways in Thomas Pynchon's *V*. Settings are stationary, with the

---

7. See, for example, *The Autobiography of Miss Jane Pittman* (New York: Bantam Books, 1971).

8. (New York: Atheneum, 1970), p. ix.

static institution, frequently an asylum, as the obstacle of human experience. Even though this literature is deeply pessimistic, it is not thoroughly nihilistic; one resolution remains—the simple affirmation of life over death.[9]

A general term for much of the writing of the sixties is *black humor*, a concept difficult to define, of long-standing use in literature, which entails a comic-revulsive reaction to things grotesque. The hero of black humor resembles the hero of the absurd, although no particular philosophy is involved, by demonstrating the one stance possible and admirable—to look at grim truth and somehow laugh at it (bitter though the laughter may be). Bruce J. Friedman, who has edited an anthology of writings by black humorists, admittedly makes no claim to a clear definition of the term *black humor*: it is "as hard to define black humor as to define an elbow or a corned beef sandwich," but there is a fading line between fantasy and reality, a nervousness, and "isolation of a frenzied new kind." Essentially, the material stems from that of the daily newspaper, which has usurped the ground of the satirist. The black humorist must thus move beyond this area into a greater darkness. And perhaps the best way he can examine the society is to show us its throwaways—junkies, fags, and hunchbacks.[10]

The blurring of the line between fact and fiction is one of the special concerns of writers of the sixties, whether treated as black humor or otherwise. Philip Roth concludes in his much publicized article, "Writing American Fiction," that the American writer in the mid-twentieth century has his hands full "trying to understand, and then describe, and then make *credible* much of the American reality. It stupefies, it sickens, it infuriates, and finally it is even a kind of embarrassment to one's meager imagination. The actuality is continually outdoing our talents, and the culture tosses up figures almost daily that are the enemy of any novelist."[11] In this case, Barth's and Pynchon's fantasies are not

9. Raymond Michael Olderman, *Beyond the Waste Land: A Study of the American Novel in the Nineteen-Sixties* (New Haven: Yale University Press, 1972), pp. 15, 18–22.

10. "Those Clowns of Conscience," *Book Week*, July 18, 1965, pp. 2, 7.

11. *Commentary*, 31 (Mar. 1961), 224.

so far from the documentary detail of Joyce Carol Oates, whose treatment of the kind of macabre violence reported in the news has linked her with the tradition of literary naturalism. All of the authors included here to some extent employ black humor, from the bawdiness of John Barth to Sylvia Plath's grimaces at herself. A specific type of writing related to black humor, referred to as *fabulation*, with its reliance on fantastic plotting, is discussed more thoroughly in chapter one.

In considering female characters it is a temptation to say ah-ha, look at the vapid female who suffers such-and-such a malaise, before realizing that her male counterpart is afflicted with much the same thing. Failure is common to all. The grotesque, particularly in a dwarfed state, is a familiar figure. But the weakened and impotent male, prominent throughout the twentieth century, is not necessarily matched by women figures. They are not crippled in the same sympathetic ways. And with the diminishing of male power, female power naturally seems greater by comparison. Father is dead, hence the rise of mother. In many cases fathers have committed suicide, an act not made a dramatic part of the plot but revealed as a dim event of the past. The intense search for identity which occupied earlier heroes has been replaced by the assumption of an absurd world into which the hero is born. Most forms of heroism are simply irrelevant to him, although he acknowledges the loss of something vital. But few American heroines of the past have made an intense search for self, and while they have no knowledge of how to do so now, they have not mellowed as the heroes have and are more likely to crack.

The most noticeable quality of women in the literature of the sixties is their blankness, certainly one of the most pronounced qualities of women in the literature of many periods. But in the past those women who fit this pattern—which is not to discount exceptional characters of ancient fiction to the present, particularly those in foreign literatures—were more colorfully embellished by the ideas of colorful men to the degree that their own lack of character was not so obvious. Men now project a kind of horrible blankness of the age onto the image of women, an idea epitomized in Pynchon's V. Thus, the casualty of the bland hero is the bland heroine. As one woman of current fiction laments, what does a woman do when she is married to a schlemiel?

Men and women do share an emptiness. Even the chameleon-like characters, in their multiple identities, have no identity. But there is a noticeable difference between the lack of distinction in the male and in the female character. His is considered a loss, in the past often a tragic loss. Something must be done to register the great wrong of a man's losing his core of meaning, even if that means reconciliation through laughter. But a woman's blankness is accepted by both men and women as her natural condition (although many women are horrified as they recognize this situation). Men follow various forms of activity to relieve their emptiness, and if their goals are not heroic, there is at least some validity in movement itself. John Updike's Rabbit Angstrom may never truly escape in his flight down Route 1, his visits to a prostitute, or his forays into the woods, but he must register a complaint against the mediocrity of his life: he has lost the splendor of his high school days as a basketball star. But his wife Janice has lost very little. She just vegetates as she always has. Who can suggest what to do with her?

In both the realistic and the satiric literature many of the same ideas operate. In *Cabot Wright Begins*, James Purdy's satire of American women who have nothing better to do than passively encourage rape, Cabot Wright is wildly active as the rapist. However distorted their dreams may be, men dream and women do not, bearing out the concept of idealistic man versus practical woman. This concept is parodied by Purdy, but it is not contradicted throughout the fiction of the sixties. In Philip Roth's *When She Was Good*, Roy Bassart constantly projects his fantasies of everything from an ideal job to a perfect baby daughter, while his wife Lucy bitterly plods through the practical. In Joyce Carol Oates's *them* the brother and sister, Jules and Maureen Wendall, distinctly differ in this respect: he lives on fantasies of romantic love, and she prostitutes herself, claiming she has never in her life had fantasies of love. Sylvia Plath makes such a contrast between men and women the theme of her story "The Wishing Box." Every morning a wife resentfully listens to her husband's dreams of the night before and is excluded by not being a part of the dreams and because she herself has no capacity for dreaming.

The husband tries to help by asking her to visualize a goblet and to describe it. After her failure to do this she frantically reads everything she can find, "anything to keep from facing the gaping void in her own head of which Harold had made her so painfully conscious."[12] She believes that only in death, which she inflicts upon herself, will it be possible for her to dream.

Another quality of the women of the sixties is their unfortunate lack of humor. While male characters of the period have mellowed from the earlier version of the intense hero seeking an identity to one who faces his failures with greater grace and humor, there is no counterpart among heroines, who are unable to see the humorous, to accept incongruity, or even to use laughter as a disguise for fear and anger. Women's hardness appears to be related to their inclination to madness, which is much greater than it is for their male counterparts. The use of insanity as a staple of literature to show the sensitive hero declared insane by a "sane" society is not the artist's purpose here in creating crazy women. There is no idealism in female madness, which is closer to a clinical version of insanity than to the quixotic one of the person "possessed." When a woman goes mad, like the madman she is distinctly at odds with her society, but not in a way either attractive or acceptable to the reader. Her breakdown is a shattering that reveals the ugliness, not the imagination, of her inner being. Referring to a hero as a madman is not at all like calling a heroine crazy.

A male view of sanity has much to do with women's "insanity," both as its possible source and as the standard by which a diagnosis is reached. In *Women and Madness* Phyllis Chesler points out that in the sixties the number of women in mental institutions increases dramatically, primarily as a result of the emergence of newly useless women trying to escape from repression, to the point where adult female patients significantly outnumber male patients. At the same time, according to 1960 and 1970 membership figures of the American Psychiatric Association, 90 percent of all psychiatrists in America are men. When these doctors diagnose women who act out the female role it is for depression, suicide attempts, anxiety, and paranoia, while women

12. *The Atlantic*, 214 (Oct. 1964), 88.

who reject the female role are diagnosed for schizophrenia, promiscuity, and lesbianism, the more aggressive activities, some of which would be acceptable in males. There is clearly a double standard of mental health.[13] A woman who refuses to stay at home and do housework may be diagnosed as mentally unfit. And yet one study reveals that while men complete far more suicides than women do, housewives make up "the largest single category of both attempted and completed suicides."[14] Since asylum life resembles the traditional family treatment of the female adolescent in its requirement of celibacy and submission, according to Chesler, the experience of incarceration (as it is often described) is probably more destructive to women than it is to men because it forces them into the very conditions many of them are attempting to escape, while the male rejecting an aggressive role will be more comfortable in a situation where he is required to be passive.[15] If this is true, such attitudes toward mental illness in women and the treatment of it can lead only to further madness.

Women are doubly doomed in current fiction. They are usually dreadfully bleak characters whose neuroses fester during the idle hours at home, but there is something wrong with them if they want to get out. Male writers (and women writers do not successfully counteract this attitude) suggest that women are best left to their traditional roles of wife and mother. The stereotype of the professional woman, epitomized in Kesey's Nurse Ratched, is that of the power-crazed neurotic who could have attained a position of authority only through cruel and bizarre means. The only alternative to this power figure is the stupid or incompetent woman. James Purdy portrays some women artists, but their work is inferior, simply a means of escaping a more "feminine" role.

13. (Garden City, N.Y.: Doubleday, 1972), pp. 33, 56, 62, 67. Chesler's source for figures on institutionalized women is given in her Appendix, p. 312: "Reference Tables on Patients in Mental Health Facilities," U.S. Department of Health, Education and Welfare, Public Health Services, Health Services and Mental Health Administration, National Institute of Mental Health: 1964–1968.

14. Quoted in ibid., p. 48. The study is Normal L. Farberow and Edwin F. Schneidman, "Statistical Comparisons between Attempted and Committed Suicides," in The Cry for Help (New York: McGraw-Hill, 1965).

15. Ibid., pp. 35–37.

The most familiar distortion of that role is prostitution, a recurrent subject of recent fiction. John Barth, whose treatment of prostitutes is unusually sympathetic, although at times comic, sees no alternative for the whore. Updike romanticizes her. Only Joyce Carol Oates understands the desperately practical aspects of prostitution. For the poor, such a thing as a humorous or romantic version of it is a cruel lie.

Women in the fiction of the period are exceptionally materialistic, particularly Purdy's middle-aged vampires, sucking up the wealth of America's men. But there is no suggestion from him or from anyone else that women might earn more than pin money of their own. Their only means of income is through men, either by marriage or by prostitution, which operate in the same way. When wives do not have money, they naturally nag and blame their husbands. Idealistic as most humanists are regarding money, authors of fiction find women the easy butt of an attack on materialism without taking into account that most of them have never had the pleasure of making the ample salaries taken for granted by many men. Betty Friedan's *The Feminine Mystique*, whose bias is clearly that no housewife is happy, does effectively make the point that there is no substitution for the satisfaction of having a pay check, something the housewife never knows. Her hobbies, which do not provide income, can never give her the self-esteem or the status that her husband expects from his work, in this country where people are, for the most part, valued not merely in terms of what they possess but by their capacity to earn. And yet the very affluence that has padded the egos of men has made it unnecessary for their wives to work. The wife is necessary as an ornament to the affluent man, but she is not essential to a job because of any ability, as he attempts to be.

Women are also destined to fail in motherhood. A woman is damned if she has children and damned if she does not. No period has been more aware of the sins of mothers; the literature shows the culmination of an awareness that results in a Sophie Portnoy. Mothers are generally manipulative—bitch mothers as the terms have become so naturally linked. On the other hand, women who practice birth control are considered inhumane. The post-Pill paradise of Updike's *Couples* is as dismal a picture of sterility as any in the sixties, in a community where sexual activity is rampant—that freedom from hangups we have been waiting for —without fear of conception or the bother of child care. Women who do have children neglect them, hoping they will keep out of the way so their own affairs can be carried on more smoothly. Although many varieties of female stereotypes are found in this period, even the bitch, usually a mother, is often some form of *tabula rasa*.

The arrangement of authors in this work was at first conceived with point of view in mind, beginning with the fabulators, whose fantasies give a distance to women characters and make greater use of pure myth, progressing to the first-person accounts of women. This does not mean that male writers necessarily make up the first group and women the second—Philip Roth, for one, is unusually skilled at giving a woman's point of view—although the pattern most naturally works out this way. The fabulators make use of more comic effects, and from there we move to the grimmer practicalities of Joyce Carol Oates. But the number of comic devices does not determine an attitude toward women. John Barth, for instance, whose world rollicks with the comic, has one of the most sober and sympathetic approaches to women, while Sylvia Plath uses humor unsparingly in the treatment of her own disintegration. The bitch figure appears more prominently in the first chapters of this study, with the less powerful woman treated by John Updike and Joyce Carol Oates. *The Bell Jar* brings the bitch and the passive woman together in the same figure.

It is of interest to see how male and female writers differ in their treatment of women characters. The similarity of their views is surprising to me, particularly as they present the hopelessly vacant woman. Women writers are not as likely to portray the bitch, however, not merely in deference to themselves, but because women feel that men have the power, while men feel that women are in control (at least they are considered to control men's emotional lives, if not the larger power structures of the world). The great difference between male and female writers is not in what they see, however, but, as we might expect, in how they feel about what they see. It is a very different thing for a man to rhapsodize about the delights of a lovable prostitute and quite another for a girl to decide to become one—a vastly different matter for a man to contemplate a woman's blankness and for her to be blank.

My own reaction as a woman to these literary characters at times brings rage and dismay, a sickening recognition of frustrations. I prefer the powerful neurotics of Philip Roth to the bovine women of John Updike, just as I prefer Medea to Ophelia. I resent the fact that women characters are so often reduced to merely the petty or the physical, and that it is necessary for them to remain blank to survive and to be accepted. That intelligence and strength in a woman are fatal. Charles Newman puts it very well in an article about Sylvia Plath, who he says is one of the few women writers to join the theme of womanhood with that of modern civilization: "While we have granted the woman some sophistication and sympathy in our fiction, we have been loath to permit her genuine despair. Male protagonists can wallow in the absurdity of existence. Women are considered bitches whose rejection of the world is considered presumptuous."[16]

The future should bring an increasing number of stories from women and about them. We need to examine in literature the reasons for a Sophie Portnoy and an Esther Greenwood. Why are professional women never sympathetic characters? Is John Updike right in his devastatingly realistic view of the American couple in *Rabbit Redux*—that men and women can exist together only when that woman is a Janice Angstrom?

16. "Candor Is the Only Wile," in *The Art of Sylvia Plath: A Symposium*, ed. Charles Newman (Bloomington: Indiana University Press, 1970), p. 44.

one

Women of the Fabulators:
Barth, Pynchon, Purdy, Kesey

The comic literature of the 1960s explodes into a fantastic world
of sexual activity, an activity as remote from love as it has always
been in American literature. In the writing defined by Robert
Scholes as fabulation, with its particular delight in design which
tends "away from the representation of reality but returns toward
actual human life by way of ethically controlled fantasy,"[1] sexuality often appears as an innocent and giddy escape from a
dehumanized existence. The sexual act may become decadent,
perverted, and frequently cruel, but it is usually comical. In a
world gone crazy, well into an age without gods which also
demonstrates a growing disenchantment with science and facts
in general, romantic love is parodied as people clutch each other
frantically—men and women, men and men, women and women.
When these choices are not available, people cling to animals or
objects, all in a bizarre struggle to make connection.

In *The Fabulators* Scholes stresses the joy of storytelling of the
ancient fabulators, a term used in Caxton's fifteenth-century
translations of ancient fables for the spinners of fabulous tales.
One fabulator, in the eighth fable of Alfonce, is a disciple who
soothes his king by a tale to lighten his spirits so that he might
fall asleep.[2] The modern fabulator may not soothe his audience,

1. *The Fabulators* (New York: Oxford University Press, 1967), p. 11.
2. Ibid., pp. 7–8.

but he does show a delight in the fantastic, and it is this characteristic, shared by Barth, Pynchon, Purdy, and Kesey, which is the basis for the rather loose use of this term here, as a way of distinguishing these writers from the more realistic ones to follow.

The delight in the fantastic for the modern fabulator rests in a surface activity, which is a way of blocking out an underlying vacuum. Sexual activity itself carries no warmth or power to bind, and in this event woman more than ever serves in her stereotyped role as object. (Men may be objects too, but they are not relegated to a merely sexual function as women are.) The attempt to make such superficial connections serve as the significance of life is frequently the source of the humor.

No one views the animalistic posture of man as more absurd than does John Barth. His is a great and swiving world, as is Thomas Pynchon's, but under a gigantic energy both writers lean to nihilism. The vast extent of prostitution eventually leads to the mating of people with machines, which figure heavily in the writing of this period, particularly in relation to women. Kesey's Nurse Ratched is a form of machine, and Purdy's women, obsessed with things, are little more than the objects around them. Barth, like Pynchon, extends the quest for connection from the merely physical attachment of objects to the mythic level, but at the same time such a quest must be parodied. For Barth the vision of the heroic, which may be read seriously in *Giles Goat-Boy*, is through union with a woman, while Pynchon's *V.* suggests a mechanical principle of the feminine. But whether through participation with a woman or in the vision of her as a principle, the significant thing is the fabulation of the woman in the mind of a man.

Barth's mythic woman is a mother archetype in *Giles*, following the familiar Oedipal pattern. Jung's study of the mother archetype, which shows it to be perhaps the most compelling of all archetypes of the collective unconscious, embodies a variety of aspects, many of them represented in the literature of this period: personal mother, grandmother, stepmother, mother-in-law, nurse, and governess. The concept of the Great Mother, represented in the field of comparative religion, embraces everything from the

Virgin to our feelings of devotion for Church, University, Nature, to include our way of perceiving all hollow objects.[3] The Great Mother is the primary archetype to appear in the writings of these fabulators, although mainly in her negative aspects. Virginia Hector of *Giles* is of these the most benign, and Kesey's Big Nurse is, in the words of Leslie Fiedler, "the biggest-breasted, whitest mama-figure in all American literature."[4] Purdy's matriarchal society is made up of clutching middle-aged matrons who control the weaker men. For Kesey and Purdy, the most awful characteristics of women are shown in their middle age, when they seem particularly qualified to represent what is worst in America. The mad pursuit of sexual experience gives way during this time as these women become less desirable physically and increasingly emphasize material things— manipulating, consuming, and imitating them. In this they are much more distasteful than men who do the same kinds of things. Power, which can be so fearful in men, is much more disgusting in women.

These men and women of the fabulators are often afflicted with the same vacancy of soul, and their attempts to fill the vacuum with sexual activity are ludicrous for both. Barth's and Purdy's men, particularly, lack distinction. But they seek an identity tirelessly, even though the attempt is not with the intensity of earlier heroes. (Barth, especially, makes great fun of the search.) With women, a lack of identity is pitiful, but assumed. For the male protagonist the disparity between a former heroic concept of what a man should be and his present inadequacies is the very basis of humor. But if a woman were at one time held in higher esteem than she is now, it was as the focal point of men's ideals, not through deeds of her own. She is thus not expected to seek an identity actively but to have it thrust upon her.

Of all the fabulators, and exemplary among all writers of the sixties in his sympathetic view of women's peculiar problems, is John Barth. He realizes what it means for women, and for men,

3. Carl Jung, "Psychological Aspects of the Mother Archetype," in *The Basic Writings of C. G. Jung*, ed. Violet Staub de Laszlo (New York: Modern Library, 1959), p. 333.
4. *Waiting for the End* (New York: Stein and Day, 1965), p. 131.

to attempt to live up to the roles determined for them. If he were inclined to the development of the complexities of character, and the role of women in society today, Barth might be the very person to lead literature into a new era of female characterization. But he claims to be shamelessly uninterested in addressing himself to social problems, and since he says he knows little about reality, "it will have to be abolished. . . . reality is a nice place to visit but you wouldn't want to live there, and literature never did, very long. . . . Reality is a drag."[5]

The pessimism of Barth's first two novels and the carefree bawdiness of *The Sot-Weed Factor* are basically not didactic. Instead, their expression of relativism allows for unlimited choices, for the most part without the confinements of moral distinctions. But *The End of the Road* does suggest in the death of Rennie Morgan that she is a tragic victim of the two men who make her their battleground of both intellectual and physical prowess, a disaster which serves a severe moral judgment on them. Rennie is clearly remade to fit her husband, who paradoxically slaps her around when she claims she has no will of her own. Barth's sympathies are with her. This is not to discount the fact that before her husband attempted to form her she *was* the blob she describes herself as being. Barth suggests no solution for her condition, but he is far from sanctioning the way her husband and her lover capitalize on her undefined nature.

In his work of the sixties Barth apparently changes so much that it is at first difficult to see whether this sympathy for the condition of women like Rennie Morgan continues to be important. *The Sot-Weed Factor* of 1960 announces a newly hilarious and abundant view of an absurd world, not a tragic one. The enormous energy of this parody, which is probably closer to the ideas of *Candide* than to any other of its many literary analogues, gives the sense of survival just as Voltaire's characters continue to come alive after they are assumed dead. Barth's people are shunted off but appear again under new disguises; it is best for them to acknowledge the world's absurdity and then to laugh in

5. John Enck, "John Barth: An Interview," *Wisconsin Studies in Contemporary Literature*, 6 (Winter–Spring 1965), 11.

order to survive, a basic tenet in the stance of the comic hero of this period. But this funny book has a great deal to say very seriously and sensitively about the status of women. Here again Barth sees women as victims.

The humor in the relationships between men and women in *The Sot-Weed Factor* relates back to a brilliant scene in Barth's first novel, *The Floating Opera* (1956), which sets the tone for an attitude toward sex (and almost inadvertently toward women) which is crucial in understanding his other works and the literature of the decade generally. The fifty-four-year-old protagonist, Todd Andrews, reveals the decisive incidents of his past which led to his present suicidal condition, four of which events convinced him of his animality (and thus, apparently, of a nihilistic view). The first of these was the loss of his virginity at the age of seventeen to Miss Betty June Gunter, who was "better informed" than other girls of his neighborhood. Barth parodies the ideal of virginity (a central issue of *The Sot-Weed Factor*) by having Todd claim that as Betty June talked to him she "broke the seal of my mind,"[6] as she is very soon to initiate him sexually. With her he becomes an animal. She regards boys as puppies, and Todd is seen "pawing her flat chest" (127); he later considers himself to have gone from colt to stallion through his alliance with her. His initiatory sexual experience with her sets a mood for his entire future with women. As they make love, he glances up at a huge mirror on the ceiling which reflects what to him is the most absurd act a man can perform, and he explodes with laughter: "Nothing is intrinsically funny, to be sure, but to me nothing is so consistently, profoundly, earth-shakingly funny as we animals in the act of mating. Reader, if you are young and would live on love . . . then don't, I implore you, be so foolish as to include among the trappings of your love-nest a good plate mirror. For a mirror can reflect only what it sees, and what it sees is screamingly funny" (131). The point is not that he laughs at the girl, who is, as we later learn, hurt and justifiably angry. Nor is she disgusting or in the least immoral, merely serving a necessary function for him, allowing but not coercing him into a sexual alliance. The

6. John Barth, *The Floating Opera* (New York: Avon Books, 1965), p. 126. Further page references to this edition are included in the text.

scene does, however, establish an attitude toward sex that reverberates throughout Barth's later writing.

But if the act of love is absurd, even though the girl herself is not specifically ridiculed, she nevertheless considers herself absurd. Barth is sympathetic to Betty June's anger, which she still harbors years later when Todd meets her as a prostitute who wants to kill him for having laughed when they first made love. As if being properly punished for laughing, he now suffers an infected prostate which gives him such pain he can only writhe on her bed, utterly incapable of lovemaking. Betty June by now may have discovered absurdity for herself, but she never laughs about it as he does. In his pain he is aware of "the tight smile on Betty June's lips (she hadn't laughed)" (144). This inability to laugh becomes one of the characteristics that most strikingly distinguishes female from male characters in the sixties. The overtones that develop from this scene—whenever sex is made ridiculous—cannot help but make women appear foolish or perhaps unnecessary, especially when men see humor and they do not. But as long as men are the aggressors Barth never makes fun of the women who participate as pawns, even when his men laugh heartily. It is all the more noticeable that Barth does not laugh at women, because he laughs at nearly everything else. He does not suggest that women are more complex or nobler than they are generally given credit for being, but he is seriously distressed at their incapacity. Even in making fun of the idealization of virginity, it is Eben Cooke and other men who have built up the idea who are satirized, not the female virgin who is more likely to be the victim.

Barth makes the most of an interesting device used in the literature of an era where styles of dress and sex roles have changed to the point of confusion between men and women—the direct switch of the customary male and female roles. Thus, Eben plays the role of the virgin, and Joan Toast is the worldly aggressor in the sexual encounter. For Barth, aggressiveness in women is often merely humorous, while other writers treat it more bitterly. But the power women exert in his fiction is shown only in the initial stages of their relationships with men. As commodities, women are soon wasted and abandoned. Like Betty June Gunter, the women in *The Sot-Weed Factor* do not see anything humorous about the place of sex in the world, for it is the standard by which they are valued and devalued.

In *The End of the Road* (1958) Rennie Morgan represents Barth's view of the blankness of women, a blankness the more unfortunate because of her awareness of it without the ability to change the condition. Rennie's manners are borrowed from her husband Joe, all performed under his careful scrutiny. She admits, "I lived in a complete fog from the day I was born until after I met Joe,"[7] and that she would "rather be a lousy Joe Morgan than a first-rate Rennie MacMahon" (63). A statement like this may pass unnoticed when spoken by a woman, but if it were the sentiment of a man of one race or status in regard to that of another male, it would probably draw protest. Rennie's condition is a common one, and even though both she and her husband are aware of it, neither they nor Barth can suggest other possibilities for her.

Rennie resembles Jacob Horner in the relativism that allows both of them to change almost without limits. But Horner, it appears, has chosen his relativism to prove something; he may pass the phase and choose again to believe. His doctor treats Horner's cosmopsis, the disease of having too many choices, as a serious disorder. But Rennie's relativism is her very nature. All she will ever do is adapt to someone or something else, just as she bends first to her husband and then to Jacob. In giving such a woman a tragic death (in a pre-sixties novel), Barth is the only major novelist of our time to treat a woman's blankness this seriously. A compassionate treatment is also given to the other woman associated with Horner, Peggy Rankin, a forty-year-old "pick-up" whose pilgrimage to the beach in search of a lover is pitiful at what is considered a hopeless age for romance. It is easy to see how this poor soul should be treated with more kindness and respect by men, but beyond that it is difficult to imagine how her life might be improved. This very dilemma is what Barth portrays most movingly. While the philosophies of Joe Morgan and Jacob Horner may make for more fascinating thought, it is

7. John Barth, *The End of the Road* (New York: Bantam Books, 1969), p. 57. Further page references to this edition are included in the text.

the plights of Rennie Morgan and Peggy Rankin which elicit our deepest sympathies in this novel.

The Sot-Weed Factor is such a collection of literary steals, such a conglomerate of changing identities, and such a bawdy account of early Maryland, that simply to sift the book out is a considerable job indeed. With a little of *Don Quixote,* much of Boccaccio, *Tom Jones,* and numerous other sources of the questing hero, Barth makes a mockery of innocence, particularly Candide's version of it, and at first it appears that Cunegunde is a direct analogue for Joan Toast. But with her the tone changes from the consistent comedy of Voltaire. With the exception of Mary Mungummory, Barth's women are a serious matter. They are as victimized in *The Sot-Weed Factor* as they were in the earlier non-comic novels.

As the traditional roles are switched with Eben Cooke as virgin, the satire is aimed at an idealized, male version of virginity. And since for Barth it is much easier to laugh at men than at women, Eben is truly comic. The female virgins of the book are never so funny. In this satire on innocence, particularized in the virginity of Eben Cooke, Barth suggests the same lack of alternatives that Voltaire offers in *Candide*: virginity is foolishness, but free love brings its venereal disease. Voltaire maintains a comic tone by making survival a main value of his story, and we are never drawn to sympathize with any of the characters. But Barth's comic tone for his male characters gives way to a more tragic tone for the woman, both in her virginity and in her promiscuity. In either case she is a victim.

The whores—Joan Toast, Mary Mungummory, Anna Cooke, and others—have far more interesting lives than the virgins, but they age quickly and usually die young. On the other hand, Pocahontas, the super virgin, is humiliated by the public knowledge and discussion of her impenetrable hymen and must endure the attempts of the men who would prove themselves sexually able by penetrating her. Readers of *The Sot-Weed Factor* have noted that Eben Cooke is an American Adam,[8] and indeed he suggests

8. See, for example, Richard W. Noland, "John Barth and the Novel of Comic Nihilism," *Wisconsin Studies in Contemporary Literature,* 7 (Autumn 1966), 239–57.

a primary American concern with innocence of a general kind. But Barth's emphasis is on the problems of literal sexual innocence, first in Eben's comic evasions of the whores who pursue him, and then much more seriously in the sexual initiation of Pocahontas, an altogether violent act. The deflowering of Pocahontas gives a new soberness to the subject of innocence, which is treated lightly with Eben. Even when women do approach Eben to relieve him of his innocence, they have no way of sexually violating him with the sheer force that characterizes men's treatment of women. In the realm of psychological damage, to be sure, women equal or surpass men in inflicting pain. But since *The Sot-Weed Factor* does not examine the minds of its characters, surface action is the main indicator of the conditions between men and women. And men being more powerful physically, they thus inflict more pain. The female virgins elicit sympathy, while Eben's plight of virginity is comic.

In contrast to Eben's ideals of love, and he believes he loves Joan Toast, her worldly understanding presents not only a humorous contrast to him but a serious statement of her position as a woman and of how she is expected to relate to men:

> "Howbeit, what with men forever panting at us like so many hounds at a salt-bitch, and begging us put by our virtue and give 'em a tumble, and withal despising us for whores and slatterns if we do; or bidding us be faithful to our husbands and yet losing no chance to cuckold their truest friends; or charging us to guard our chastity and yet assaulting it from all quarters in every alleyway, carriage, or sitting room; or being soon bored with us if we show no fire in swiving and yet sermoning us for sinners if we do; inventing morals on the one hand and rape on the other; and in general preaching us to virtue whilst they lure us on to vice—what with the pull and haul of all this, I say we women are forever at sixes and sevens, all fussed and rattled and torn 'twixt what we ought and what we would, and so entirely confounded, that we never know what we think on the matter or how much license to grant from one minute to the next. . . ."[9]

9. John Barth, *The Sot-Weed Factor* (New York: Grosset & Dunlap, 1966), p. 68. Further page references to this edition are included in the text.

Eben's naive response to this statement is Barth's method of emphasis: "It had not struck me ere now, what a sad lot is woman's" (69). This familiar idea is offered with real compassion. The status of whore is the ultimate conclusion of this condition, which in the primitive, swashbuckling early days of Maryland appears an almost inevitable route for a woman. Barth adds to the stereotype of the good-hearted whore the sheer violence and humiliation that come to such a woman, good-hearted or otherwise. By listing a catalog of names for whore, in the amazing naming contest between the French and the British prostitutes which lasts for seven pages, he reminds us by this quantity of names the extent to which women, who are inevitably used sexually, are then maligned:

> "Whore!" shouted the first.
> "*Bas-cul!*" retorted the other.
> "Frisker!"
> "*Consoeur!*"
> "Trull!"
> "*Triquenelle!*"
> "Sow!"
> "*Usagère!*"
> "Bawd!"
> "*Viagère!*"
> "Strawgirl!" [466]

and so on. The varieties of prostitution that range from primitive patterns of survival to the most casual and repetitive affairs give *The Sot-Weed Factor* the flavor of the 1960s, with its freedom of sexual activity that is so often desperate or simply empty. But if the frequency of sexual acts during our own time does nothing to dignify the increasing number of participants, it does alter the concept of the formerly reviled whore, who no longer appears so unlike other women.

One reason why the absence of love is understandable in Barth's bawdy world is the confusion of identities of both male and female characters. The masks of identity shift so rapidly and when Eben Cooke thinks he is loving one woman she to be another. Perhaps there are no true identities, and if not, deep affections are unlikely to develop. Like other writers of the sixties, James Purdy in particular, Barth shows the void in both men and women. But the cosmopsis that paralyzes Burlingame, and eventually Eben, does not affect women the same way; their lives usually remain limited to the difficult choice of attempting to remain virgin or how best to be whores. Otherwise, the defining features of a woman's life are gained from the men she is attached to, and because their identities have become so nebulous there is little to be gained from them.

Since Barth sees a woman as fated to be used by men in this great orgy life, although she may also be expected to serve as the muse to the poet, a woman can be most successful by becoming a clever, businesslike whore. Such is Mary Mungummory, formerly known as the Traveling Whore o' Dorset, one of the few comical women in *The Sot-Weed Factor*, and at the same time one of the most admired of its characters. This version of the good-hearted prostitute, whom we first see as somewhat dilapidated after several years of successful prostitution, is one of the funniest and happiest characters in the novel. Her sobriquet was the pride of her younger years, when she went by wagon from one plantation to another practicing her trade. Age has inevitably curtailed that career, and she has now taken up the procurement of girls for a living, becoming one of the first great madams. Mary's "red-brown and wrinkled" face and "her grey hair as tangled an an old brier-thicket" (428) suggest the scruffy survivor beloved by all. She has a humor rare among women and is considered the "most Christian lady in the Province of Maryland" (619).

The conquest of women parallels the conquest and rape of the new land, as everything becomes a matter of business—property values and commodity. The need for territory includes the need for a whore-wife-housekeeper, but the demand is greatest for the whore. Because in most cases women are a sexual commodity, they are obviously most valuable when young and beautiful, which is for a very short time. Wild living takes its toll on the ladies far sooner than it does on the men, and in a twinkling they pass from desired, pretty things to decaying, pockmarked waste products.

Most of the men in *The Sot-Weed Factor* use whores, but it

is not only in this connection that Barth shows the corruption of
the bond between men and women and particularly the victimization of women. The naive Eben, who idealizes the woman, in
doing so uses her for his own poetic needs quite as certainly as
another man takes advantage of her physically. On first meeting
Joan and apparently intending to give her his highest praise, he
says, " 'I love thee for my savior and inspiration! . . . ne'er till I
embraced thee have I been a poet, but a shallow coxcomb and
poetaster!' " (70). Later he makes the claim to McEvoy, Joan's
pimp, that he would " 'not cross the street for a whore . . . but
I shall cross the ocean for a principle! To you, haply, Joan Toast
is a whore; to me she is a principle!' " (75). But McEvoy suggests
a deeper motivation for Eben's reaction to Joan: " 'Think not ye
love Joan Toast, Mr. Cooke: 'tis your *love* ye love, and that's but
to say 'tis yourself and not my Joan' " (73). Eben never treats
Joan cruelly and remains devoted to her to the story's end when
he discovers he has "luckily" married her by mistake. But she dies
bearing his child (conveniently so, for he survives to continue
life with his beloved sister). Thus, while Barth's novel is not
based on a natural disaster as was *Candide*, it does show women's
biological heritage to be one more element in the conspiracy
against them exemplified throughout the book.

Barth's satire at this point is twofold: his barb is aimed generally at any idealistic and impossible version of love, and particularly at men for their way of romanticizing women, who
do not so idealize men although they are often completely dependent upon them. Beyond his satire is the serious treatment
of the sexual violence done to women, for which they have only
one means of revenge—venereal disease. As a kind of justice for
Eben's exploitation of women as ideals, he is afflicted with the
pox. But it is women who most often suffer physically, victimized
by men's brute strength.

The most vivid example of wholesale brutality to women is
the pirates' rape of the passengers of the *Cyprian*, the boat which
transports "impoverished young ladies" (270) who are willing
to prostitute themselves in the colonies. What could be a scene
of joyful bawdiness, which this novel is quite capable of deliver-
ing, becomes a horrible attack: "Girls assaulted on the decks, on

the stairways, at the railings, everywhere, in every conceivable manner. None was spared, and the prettier prizes were clawed at by two and three at a time" (271). During this assault, the oldest member of the pirate crew relates an account of an even more violent incident of mass rape in which sixteen hundred virgins, pilgrims bound for Mecca, were taken by his band, leaving the deck of the ship looking like a butcher's block. On the *Cyprian* some of the victims recover their spirits, but one forgotten woman remains stuck high up in the rigging of the ship, like a fly in a web, possibly even dead from "the bite of her black spider" (281). Barth's technique here, as elsewhere, is to follow a comic version of abuse to women with a sympathetic image. If the concept that virginity is dearer than life appears comical in application to Eben, it is bitterly illustrated in this case as women lose their honor and very nearly their lives as well. On a previous occasion a girl was forced by thirteen brigands, "with a taffrail at the small of her back" (156), until at last they broke her spine and heaved her over the edge of the ship. One rogue's claim is that no woman pleased him unless he could stare at the sharks who would have her when the rape was done.

Another treatment of rape, as a special form of prowess, is the Pocahontas story, related in the *Private Journal of Sir Henry Burlingame* as the account of Captain John Smith's adventures. In keeping with the pornographic flavor of the novel are Captain Smith's favors to the Indians—pornographic materials the likes of which they have never seen. They accept these goods, in return granting Smith his life. His heroism is proven by the magic potion he creates which will allow penetration of the impregnable Pocahontas, the Chief's daughter. Before anyone can marry her he must prove his ownership, and Smith is forced to compete. Pocahontas, whose name in that language signifies smallness and impenetrability, has the problem that "her privitie was that nice, and the tympanum therein so surpassing stout, as to render it infrangible" (169). At the age of sixteen she has the shame of being a virgin, as well as of being unmarriageable.

The humiliation of the men who fail to seduce Pocahontas is complete as Barth, playing on male egotism and proclivity to violence at the expense of women, turns men's violence back upon themselves: "Labour as they might, none had been able to deflower her, and in sooth the most had done them selves hurt withal, in there efforts; whereas, the proper thing was, to injure the young lasse, and that as grievouslie as possible, the degree of injurie being reck'd a measure of the mans virilitie" (169). Only the magical potion saves Captain Smith from death as he appears before the altar where Pocahontas is tethered. His clothes are torn from him, and behold, an erection of eleven inches! Before an awed crowd he deflowers Pocahontas (who is mercifully in a swoon) so masterfully that for the next three days she hovers between life and death. Smith, who escapes from marrying her by sharing the secret of his virility with the Chief, forever after brags of his great achievement. Pocahontas pitifully follows him around as if when he took her body he also automatically won her soul.

On the subject of the American Indian, Barth has been considered one of our most important writers. Even more clearly on this subject than in his treatment of the white settlers he shows male brutality and the victimization of the female, this time by altering the story of Pocahontas to make her as nearly a blood sacrifice as possible without actually having her killed. Interpolated into the account of Eben's virginity, comically treated, is this dilemma of Pocahontas, the not-so-funny female counterpart in the experience of virginity. Far from being squeamish about sexual purity or infidelity, Barth focuses on the physical brutality of the sexual encounter, and this naturally shows the woman to be the more likely victim. Pocahontas's virginity brings upon her an act no less painful than the venereal disease contracted by Joan Toast through prostitution, not to mention the humiliation Pocahontas suffers as a virgin, which equals the infamy of the whore. In this archetypal American experience Barth's emphasis is more on the victimization of women than on the victimization of the Indian, who joins with the white man in establishing these first brutal patterns toward woman as a commodity to be plundered.

One woman whose early life promises something better than the lives of Joan Toast or Pocahontas is Anna Cooke, Eben's twin, by a fact of nature given the unique beginning of equality with a man. Eben and Anna are closer than any two people in

The Sot-Weed Factor, bound by platonic and incestuous love, or at least the suggestion of the latter. Anna's life is unique also in that she is not "kept to her dolls and embroidery-hoops" (16), the usual training for girls (nor is Eben restricted to the male activities of hunting and fencing). Because their father Andrew is so preoccupied with his merchant-trading, the twins are "seldom subjected to any direction at all, and hence drew small distinction between activities proper for little girls and those proper for little boys" (16). As it turns out, Anna not only grows into a beautiful girl but is less timid, quicker and better coordinated than her brother. Barth's suggestion that a woman need not be a weak pawn if she is only trained to do more apparently either contradicts his view that women are the automatic victims of men and nature, or suggests that none of the victimized women he shows had Anna's kind of early training. But as we see Anna develop into womanhood, the pattern of victimization overwhelms the positive effects of her early, non-feminine training. (The effects of not being taught a manly role, however, remain with Eben, making him nicer but more naive than other men.) Anna is left behind as Eben begins his adventures, her life narrowing as his expands. He casually meets her from time to time, but she is now like other women of the street. There is little doubt that her maturity will bring the destructive effects of being a sexual object. We are left to wonder only what form her seductions will take, that is, if she will toughen up as a prostitute, not whether or not she will become one.

As the comic pattern of the book is to reverse male and female roles, Anna becomes knowledgeable in the world while Eben remains innocent. When they meet at the age of twenty-eight, he says she looks thirty-five (presumably he looks much younger). This early physical depreciation is the common point at which the woman in literature passes from desired commodity to waste product. Eben continues to love her, as Candide did his Cunegunde, but neither he nor Burlingame, who also loves her, nor Barth, can spare her the diminishing returns of her life, which is so unlike that of a man. If not age or disfiguration from venereal disease, then pregnancy, the sign of a malignant sexuality, and finally childbearing, the conspiracy of nature, take their painful toll. Joan Toast dies in childbirth as did Eben's and Anna's mother.

In *Giles Goat-Boy* Barth also portrays and sympathizes with woman as a commodity. Anastasia Stoker is both the serviceable sex object and the muse to the would-be hero. As Joan Toast was Eben's inspiration, Anastasia is elevated to a mythic hope for Giles: "In Anastasia I discovered the University whole and clear. Mother of my soul, its pulse throbbed around us; my Father's eye it was glowed near, whose loving inquiry I perceived through My Ladyship."[10] The word *through* is a meaningful one, for like so many women of literature, Anastasia is most valued as a backdrop upon which a man's concept of himself is imposed or a transparency through which it is projected. Barth is astutely aware of this fact, and in *Giles*, which is based on myth, he examines the woman as mythic heroine, a play on the Christian view of self-sacrifice. Women in *Giles* are more comically treated than in *The Sot-Weed Factor*, but still they are never wholly the butt of the joke as the heroes are.

Giles is another hodgepodge of sexual activity, with various combinations of people, animals, and objects in intercourse, making sexual experience more absurd but less cruel than it was in *The Sot-Weed Factor*. The goat, Billy Bocksfuss, is first attracted to the goat Hedda and in anguish watches this love being "tupped" by an Angora. The animal's desire for monogamous love is humorously posed against the indifference of the members of New Tammany College who so casually carry out their multiple affairs. The goat-boy progresses to love of humans but continues to be painfully torn between the goat and the human worlds. His keeper Spielman would have him stay with the goats, but the first "human lady" he meets, the "cream-haired weeper" (53), draws him toward the human world with her. The animal part of Giles is obviously what makes him superior, but his heroism must be developed with humans.

If woman is the Other, in *Giles* she is more than ever an other, because the point of view is that of a goat. But the fact that she is distant does not diminish Billy Bocksfuss's attraction to her—if

10. John Barth, *Giles Goat-Boy* (New York: Fawcett World Library, 1967), p. 731. Further page references to this edition are included in the text.

anything it increases it. And when Virginia Hector is discovered
to be his own mother, this cream-haired lady who is also the virgin
mother of his lover Anastasia, the attraction is complete with
Oedipal desire, which can be lived out unknowingly because
identities shift. The Oedipal theme is emphasized by a parody of
Oedipus Rex called *The Tragedy of Taliped Decanus,* a focal
point of the novel, in which the faculty members are satirically
represented. The giddy satire is complete with the mock-heroic—
the cream-haired lady, as the contemporary mother, offers her
son a peanut-butter sandwich. Oedipal attraction, incest, and
romantic love all merge as Virginia Hector, Anastasia, and Giles
attempt to unsnarl their actual relationships to each other. By
the time this is accomplished sexual encounters have long since
occurred, of course, and any attempt at simplification is impossible and irrelevant. But none of Oedipus's horror at discovering a
marriage with his mother is here; Billy Bocksfuss is delighted!
He hesitates briefly before consummating his love with Anastasia
when he learns that she might be his sister, but soon they make
spectacular love in the belly of WESCAC, creating the most
fantastic combination of elements possible.

   Giles offers the possibility of a more heroic message than is
found in *The Sot-Weed Factor,* but it is also much lighter in tone.
For the first time women are ridiculed, however only in their
lesbian activities. Perhaps lesbianism carries a taboo too heavy for
even the comic Barth to ignore. But more likely, when women are
not in the society of men, thereby no longer victims, their own
foolishness and aggression emerge, and like the male characters
they are funny and disgusting. When Anastasia allows herself
to be serviced by everyone, fool martyr that she is, she elicits
sympathy at least in behalf of her generosity. But when she is
discovered making love with Hedwig Sears, in a hilarious scene,
Barth at last ridicules her equally with his male characters. It
takes some time for the naive narrator Giles to understand what
is going on, but he does see the incredible change in this usually
serene, self-sacrificing woman, now aggressive and flustered, trying to get what she wants. Since Anastasia's concept of herself
has been that of generous giver, she is indeed startled by the discovery of her own lust. But she returns to her role as martyr to

the sexual needs of others and is never made fully the figure of satire. Hedwig Sears is the only woman shown to be totally ridiculous. We last see her as a mental patient, chasing men in Swiftian fashion, as she tears off her clothes and attacks a student named Croaker, whom she finds in the lobby of a motel making love to a soft-drink machine.

Even in company with the very funny Mrs. Sears, Anastasia never laughs. Her soberness could be a sign of dehumanization as it is in the case of Kesey's Big Nurse, but for Barth, who quite delicately treats a woman's discomfort, her sobriety rather indicates his own usually sober attitude toward women. Giles, the would-be hero, whose trials are by far greater than Anastasia's, never appears to suffer, either in extreme conditions or in his growing awareness of the nonheroic nature of his world. On the other hand, Anastasia, whom Giles is surprised to discover weeping, reveals a deep and moving unhappiness that is hardly funny. The reason she gives for her sorrow is that she does not have what both the animals and the human males are given—"heats." She weeps for having no orgasms. " 'Human women don't have *heats*, You know, George . . . but we're supposed to have *orgasms*, and for some reason I don't' " (666). Perhaps Barth means for this condition to be funny and fails. But the tone indicates that Anastasia's sexual deprivation is a sympathetic condition, not something to laugh at—a woman, foolish as she is, who gives herself completely to others who never consider her needs.

Giles's concern with the heroic is unusual in an age when a cool acceptance of defeat and obscurity is much more fashionable.[11] He daringly asks how one can bear not being a hero. The journey toward Grand Tutorhood is a confusing and at times hopelessly difficult task, but there does exist a pattern for becoming a hero, even if it may be an outdated one. The pattern for a woman to become a heroine, however, makes a most interesting contrast: it is a parody of the Christian virtues of self-sacrifice and generosity as applied to a woman's sexuality. Barth shows this to be Anastasia's adaptation to a standard outside herself which provides

11. In creating Giles, Barth inadvertently followed the qualifications for the mythic hero as outlined by Joseph Campbell in *The Hero with a Thousand Faces* (New York: Pantheon Books, 1949).

very little satisfaction for her. Even in the context of heroism, the woman is not given a positive, self-actualizing role but a complementary one. And yet Barth's sympathies are with Anastasia for her genuine desire to make others happy, which is one very credible female attitude toward sexual experience. Anastasia's explanation to her Uncle Ira, who does not believe a word of it, tells just why she sleeps with everyone who asks: " 'So finally I just told the plain truth: I said that what I enjoyed about the boys was just what I'd liked about playing with the maids when I was little: that it seemed to make them happy without hurting me' " (186).

The possibilities for the hero and the heroine are so vastly different that Giles may become (or discover that he is) the Grand Tutor, and the best Anastasia can do is to lie with him in the belly of WESCAC or, like her mother, to give birth to someone who might be a hero. The adventures of Giles are often jovial and freewheeling. Even his imprisonment is not serious, for we know it only to be another obstacle for the hero to overcome. Once again, Barth's treatment is more comic for the male than for the female character, for whom the outlook is so much more limited. Anastasia's altruism brings little satisfaction for her and leads only to countless affairs with men, women, animals, and machines, all of which merely wear her down and make a nobler level of activity impossible. The hero also has such failures, but not as inevitably as these. Being serviceable (sexually or otherwise), Barth shows, is far from being heroic. The value of Anastasia's serviceability soon depreciates, whereas the concept of a hero is to establish a mystique to live on after his death. In *servicing*, Anastasia is reduced merely to the function of the animal that Giles was in the beginning. And he exhibits an indignant male view toward extensive sexual (animalistic) activity for a woman: " 'You're too affectionate. . . . You let *everybody* service you, whether they deserve to or not' " (424). Imagine a woman making a similar accusation to a man.

The animal in Giles gives him freshness and nobility, but references to human females in animalistic terms make them merely ludicrous. Giles sees women as "udderless," and he compliments Mrs. Rexford as "a Hedda among lady girls" (652). While he is in awe of human women, his term "lady girls" distinctly sets them apart as a special breed of humans, not as equals or even as people. This appears to be so because Giles is not entirely human himself, but the attitude persists as he becomes more human. Giles speaks as though he would like women to be more animalistic, but he is disappointed when he discovers them to be so. He wants women to remain ladies, without sexuality, and is ashamed when his beloved Anastasia responds to his physical demands.

Anastasia may never say no, being an ultra-passive female, but she never says *yes* to anyone—"With her sex, perhaps, but not with her heart of hearts" (668)—until she meets Giles. Only this goat-man seems capable of love in return. Giles wonders why love seems impossible for others, particularly for the faculty members of the famed West Campus, who suffer the paralyzing effects of "higher learning" on the emotions. He is to be the humanizing element for them, and one of his quixotic aims is to revive esteem for Anastasia. His idealized stereotype of woman is pitted against the crude and vulgar view of Peter Greene.

Mr. Greene met his wife Sally Ann in a funhouse, where she was whistled at and followed by someone who saw her when the wind blew her skirt up. After marrying Peter, Sally Ann agreed with him that a woman's place is in the home. "There she gave orders to a staff of domestics, took up the piano and painting on glass, read long novels, and tatted the hems of pillowslips" (280). Greene considers his marriage perfect, although he is soon distracted by Anastasia. In the meantime, Sally Ann has spells of faintness, oddly imagining her life to be empty. In the presence of men, Greene offers clichés about women which are the expected things to say. When a girl comes out of the administrator Stoker's office he quickly categorizes her:

> "A durn floozy's what she is," he insisted. "Tease the bejeepers out of a feller."
> "Not sweet and modest like your wife, I suppose."
> "I should hope to kiss a pig!"

· · · ·

> "When a man's sunk down to the likes of O.B.G.'s daughter,
> it plain unstarches him for good girls like Chickie Ann and Miss
> Anastasia" [470, 472].

The double standard of sexual behavior for women is naturally
assumed.

Peter Greene is not one of Barth's truly funny characters, for
the position he represents is too predictable and dimwitted to
surprise us into laughter. But his type is effective in presenting a
familiar and recognizable attitude toward women and the standard that makes their denigration automatic. Harold Bray's position is a similar one. He may only be expressing an unpleasant
truth when he announces in his speech that the co-eds at New
Tammany College believe that a bright smile may make up for
a dull intelligence. Or he may be expressing an expectation of
his own. Dr. Eierkopf thinks much the same way and stresses the
commodity value of a woman by asking if anyone wants " 'a
woman? . . . An aspirin, then? Or a sandwich?' " (372). For
Ira Hector an involvement with a woman demands a price, and he
admits " 'a *few* investments don't pay off' " (439), referring
to another man's wife who would not have him.

What seems a contradiction to the commercial value placed
on women is Anastasia's own generosity with herself, the idea of
giving, as opposed to buying or selling. Giles suggests that the
hero is he who gives himself away free. But as it works out for her,
what she gives is taken as an expected commodity and then used
as a source of derision. Barth is only partially satirical here, for
he deplores the crassness of the receiver while he admits to the
genuine kindness in giving. For Anastasia, as well as for Giles,
heroism is extremely difficult in a world not attuned to it. Both
Giles and Anastasia seem capable of love, but as they unite in a
bizarre arrangement with the mother of them both, it is difficult
to believe in such a possibility. The love between them may be
sincere, but their situation is so absurd that a serious love affair
would be as out of place in the novel as it appears to be in the
society.

Giles's special capacities for affection are his because he is part
goat; the men around him have only the capacity for lust. And
Anastasia is uncommonly generous in every respect. But Giles

discovers that he is allowed to do anything he wants with her, "not because she was a passed martyr to the needs of others, on the one hand, or on the other a self-deluding nymphomane, but because she simply had not the will to assert her wishes over another's" (519). When Giles realizes this he knows he must use a special divination to be able to understand her. But if she is, after all, without will, then deeper probing can reveal nothing. This is a disappointment but at the same time a relief to him, and certainly no deterrent to the romance. From the earlier satirical position of Oedipal love, Giles has evolved to a more normal (although perhaps incestuous) and limited love with a generous and beautiful but evidently vacant woman. And despite his knowledge of her many affairs, the very human desire for purity in his lady persists. He wonders how such a "splendid fair student lady girl" (162) could have lent herself to the forces of darkness.

Anastasia Stoker, who is "submissive to everyone" (173), was married on the basis of her submissiveness. Her husband is her particular master, and she never volunteered to marry him but merely agreed to his wishes. With her Uncle Ira who raised her, and spanked her often, she saw herself simply as a disobedient child (not knowing his erotic motives), a perception that led to her belief in the importance of pleasing others. Anastasia, however, is no martyr in the masochistic sense, and while her willingness to be used sexually may not satisfy her own biological needs, it brings her no pain. She genuinely enjoys being able to give pleasure, as naive to cruelty as Giles is when he asks the chancellor why he beats his wife. The goat in Giles and the childlike in Anastasia make them superior to the more sophisticated New Tammany College faculty members and allow their simple but valid questions to be raised.

When Giles finally consummates his love for Anastasia in the belly of WESCAC, the experience is defined as one too sublime for communication, a touch of satire on the idealization of romantic love. But perhaps Barth suggests that a fine union of two good people is possible, even though it must be treated lightly in the context of this novel. Mother soon breaks up the event by arriving with her peanut-butter sandwiches. To punish mother, the machine partially eats her, which is no more fatal than the violence of *Candide* usually is, just a mild warning to mother not to interfere.

From the semi-fantastic Anastasia, Barth in his fabulation extends his characterization to the purely abstract in *Lost in the Funhouse*, which includes in several stories an illusive and faintly defined "She," who first appears in "Night-Sea Journey" in the imagination of the sperm considering his mysterious and frightening voyage to the unknown. The technique of using smaller-than-life figures, the dwarfish or the nonhuman, for instance, causes the woman or the feminine principle to look gigantic and frightening by contrast. In these stories Barth shows the feminine idea to be much more formidable than it is in his earlier works.

For the sperm-narrator in "Night-Sea Journey" and for the boy protagonist of "Lost in the Funhouse," love is an impossible hope. The sperm fears unity with the great She—he will be buried in her side and transformed or die in the attempt. Thus, his creed is to "Hate love." (More noticeably here than elsewhere the purely sexual is referred to by the word *love*.) The female is considered as a giant womb, particularly awesome to the male reduced to his smallest sexual unit. In extending the idea of male fragility to this point, Barth is well within the trend of the period to show the lesser male in opposition to a monstrous female.

A similar pattern exists in "Lost in the Funhouse," with the huge figure of Fat May the Laughing Lady, who bellows her recorded laughter outside the funhouse in ridicule of the boys who go inside. As in other literature of the sixties, the mechanical is associated with the feminine. And here again is Barth's virginal boy, who approaches the funhouse hoping its chaotic tumbling will offer the girl he is too timid to find outside. She might be lost in the dark, and if he is very lucky the hot air will blow her skirt up. (The whole point of the funhouse is that the girls might be upended.) But the unnamed boy is fated to construct funhouses for others and to operate them secretly, although he would rather be among the lovers who make use of them. Fat May, who mocks him, is one of Barth's few grotesque female images, and for the first time his sympathies clearly lie with the boy. But whenever Barth shows an even partially realistic woman, and not a completely abstract "She" or a wooden model of a woman, his sympathies return to her.

Barth also treats mothers less harshly than most writers of the period, although he does acknowledge the smothering mother in "Ambrose His Mark," also of *Lost in the Funhouse*. Ambrose is embarrassed by the mother who hauls him about for years, breastfeeding him anywhere, but the picture of this unappealing woman is more pathetic than bitterly satirical. The uselessness of her life, once her days of nursing are over, is painfully apparent as she passes her Sunday afternoon in a hammock, able only to lie passively now that she no longer carries her boy around, chainsmoking and dabbling at the Sunday crossword puzzle. To wean Ambrose would be to do away with her only necessary function, and this she refuses to do. As if to punish her, a bee stings her on the nipple.

John Barth is capable of making a joke of almost anything, avoiding didacticism, but he is never at his funniest when writing about women. The comic strain gives way to pathos or painful awareness when the focus shifts from a male to a female character. As Barth represents women's sexual repressions or excesses, pity overtakes his humor in the dawning of how little is left for a woman when she is not taken seriously as a sexual partner. The bitch mother is noticeably absent from his work. And if the world has reached a point where sex is a great joke, as it appears to Todd Andrews, women are the sad losers for not being able to laugh. Many of them cease to exist when love, their domain, is gone. In a physical world they are the victims of brutality, and in an intellectual contest they are merely the battleground upon which ideas are established. This understanding of women mitigates Barth's satire to sympathy.

Pynchon's version of women is broader, funnier, and much more critical. He stands out among contemporary writers in developing the most extensive mythic view of woman in *V.*, it would seem, but the woman V. eventually turns out to be a horrifying symbol of the inanimate. The varieties of women encountered in the search for V., however, range from the noble and the ideal to the vulgar. V.s pop up everywhere throughout the novel in the

form of everything from the halo of light surrounding a gas lamp
to the many names that lead to the woman V.—Victoria Wren,
Vera Meroving, Veronica Manganese, Hedwig Vogelsang, Venus,
the electronic woman Violet—to the place Vheissu. Stanley Edgar
Hyman suggests as well the V of a woman's spread thighs.[12]
    Pynchon's professed interest in Henry Adams is the basis of his
V. for virgin to symbolize traditional humanistic values in contrast to the machinery of a new age. The search for V. is appropriately removed to Europe, repository of the past, but the shift
back to the sordid milieu of New York and to various scenes of
violence in other countries, concluding on the matriarchal island
of Malta, suggests a diseased state everywhere which breeds only
the inanimate. The correlation between older countries and mystical elevation of ideas is dispelled as exploitation and mechanization take over on a world front. The virgin and the dynamo
become one as V. thrives on the violence she seeks throughout
the world, revealing her own disintegration into the inanimate.
Finally, as the Bad Priest on Malta, crushed by a fallen beam,
she is dismantled by children who remove her wooden legs, false
teeth, and wig (revealing a tattoo of the Crucifixion on her bare
scalp), and who cruelly knife out a sapphire from her naval.
    While Henry Adams's contrast of the dynamo and the virgin
is a saddening theme for him, Pynchon unites the symbols, however pessimistically, for his comic purposes. Some of his funniest
moments—and he is a brilliant comic—are those in which people
express genuine tenderness for machines. One of V.'s most vivid
scenes is Benny Profane's midnight discovery of his girl friend
Rachel Owlglass fondling the gearshift of her MG and muttering
soothing words to it. She refers to the carefully washed car as
" 'You beautiful stud.' "[13] Unable to abide such a demonstration,
Benny ambles away in silence. Women have apparently learned
from men, who know so much more about machines than they do,
just how to love them. A few nights before Rachel's amour with
the MG, Profane discovered his missing roommate also in the

    12. "The Goddess and the Schlemihl," in *Standards: A Chronicle of Books for
Our Time* (New York: Horizon Press, 1966), p. 140.
    13. Thomas Pynchon, *V.* (New York: Bantam Books, 1968), p. 19. Further
page references to this edition are included in the text.

dead of night, in an alley on his motorcycle, fondly racing the engine.

The association of people with machines, by now a belabored literary topic, in V. goes beyond a mere criticism of materialism, suggesting first a genuine affection for an object and then a transformation in which the person becomes like the machine. Pynchon holds Rachel up to ridicule for her love of a car, and yet he suggests to us all, if we dare admit our attachment to particular objects (not merely to all material possessions), that this dramatization touches on something only too true. The affection for the machine is so genuine that the scenes with people and cars are comic not so much for their absurdity as for their suggestion of actual feelings. Pynchon also plays up the fact that the beloved automobile is our greatest killer, but as the animate and the inanimate merge in comic scenes, the tone is as genial as it is critical, showing people to be no less dangerous than machines. Rachel meets Benny Profane covered with lettuce leaves on his way to dump the garbage and mocks him by saying he may be the man of her dreams. But taking a peek under the lettuce, she changes her mind and roars off in her MG. Profane reflects that here is an inanimate object that has nearly killed him, not making clear whether he refers to Rachel or to her car.

The search for the true V. represents a desire for a principle that transcends such materialism, but eventually the female principle is shown to be inanimateness itself. As Pynchon, Purdy, and others show, the American woman may be the likeliest subject of complete mastery by the machine, enamored of it but unable to control it. Not all ideas of women are embodied in the inanimate, however. The levels of V. go from the profane, Mrs. Buffo for a start, to the sublime in the Madonna image. These contrasts are achieved partially through the shift from one country to another and in the contrast between Profane's often crude search for women and Herbert Stencil's quest for the mythic V. Yet Stencil, in effect, does not want to find V., for his ideal would vanish and be replaced by something more vulgar, which we see exemplified in Profane's life with The Whole Sick Crew in the contemporary scene of New York. The juxtaposition of the profane and the sublime concepts of V. is a source of the book's comedy, especially when diverse incidents occur simultaneously. But gradually the vividness of the vulgar begins to take precedence over the more ideal version of V.

The first comic imposition of the divine upon the vulgar is the practice of naming all the barmaids in the Sailor's Grave bar the holy name of Beatrice. Stereotypes of women are presented at the outset (although the book shows such a variety of women that the final effect is not one of simple stereotyping) for business purposes, as Mrs. Buffo, the crusty old owner of the Sailor's Grave, reasons: "Just as small children call all females mother, so sailors, in their way equally as helpless, should call all barmaids Beatrice" (4). It is further Mrs. Buffo's policy, for the benefit of her male clientele, to install foam-rubber beer taps in the shape of large breasts, especially for use during that time of day designated as Suck Hour. The plan is a great success for the drinkers, but it backfires on Mrs.Buffo when she is toppled into an ice tub during the onslaught. This motherly, proprietary woman perpetuates the supremacy of the female breast symbol with no offense to herself because she, like other Americans, is primarily concerned with business.

The use of females as sex symbols in advertising is noted in Pynchon's writing as one of the most powerful ways in which women are linked with materialism, even though men create most advertisements. But while James Purdy's writing relies heavily on women's succumbing to such images of themselves and in a complete capitulation to advertising in general, Pynchon's women follow a more willful direction toward materialism than as the victims of the psychology behind advertising. Even where the symbol of women becomes crudest in V., they are never shown as the innocent victims depicted by Barth. (*The Crying of Lot 49*, on the other hand, does deal with the innocent female victim.) A woman like Mrs. Buffo is the counterpart of the American businessman, just as Rachel Owlglass, enamored of her MG, is equal to the man infatuated with his motorcycle who precedes her. The result is that the women of V. are as corrupted but at least as interesting as their male counterparts. They are as involved in political intrigues as the men, intrigues which are equally baffling to everyone.

V. is threaded through with numerous plots: political plots on an international level and various personal plots. The sensation of plotting is so pervasive that no one or nothing is above suspicion. The character V. is eventually linked with many occasions of international plotting that result in violence. Simpler women than V. plot on a simpler level, but few remain innocent, or if they are, there is no way we can be convinced of their innocence. One of the first to be exposed is Victoria Wren, who locks up the old man Godolphin in her room. Her experience of men has brought her to abandon the schoolgirlish tendency of describing "every male over the age of fifty as 'sweet,' 'dear,' or 'nice' " (183), adjectives that apply no more to them than they do to her.

Pynchon never deals directly with clichés about women (which Barth handles so skillfully through the innocence of Eben), but a foreign point of view regarding the status of a wife is enlightening as to the American attitude toward the matter of women as possessions, legally gained by marriage. The islet of Luderitzbucht has what is referred to as a woman-pool, from which a man may order any item he wants. But when the American narrator of the story finds the charming Sarah, who serves the feminine function of "bringing a man's discontent into focus," and he wishes to keep her, he must illegally force her to stay because no legal method can do it. "During the day he manacled her to the bed, and he continued to use the woman-pool at night so he wouldn't arouse suspicion. Sarah might have cooked, cleaned, comforted, been the closest thing to a wife he'd ever had. But on that foggy, sweating, sterile coast there were no owners, nothing owned. Community may have been the only solution possible against such an assertion of the Inanimate" (253). The man's concept of the proper wife leaves him destitute in a situation where he may not use some kind of force or the more frequent American practice, bribery. Benny Profane, back in America, knows he must have money to get a woman, and he looks for work only to buy a girl. There may once have been an idealistic notion that women inspire men to their great creations, but now "the eyes of New York women do not see the wandering bums or the boys with no place to go. Material wealth and getting laid strolled arm-in-arm the midway of Profane's mind. . . . the only reason anybody wants to get rich is so he can get laid steadily, with whomever he chooses" (198).

Unlike these materialistic versions of women, Herbert Stencil's quest is a mythical one. His purpose is to find the mysterious V., made known to him through his father's papers, which reveal that perhaps the dignified Mr. Stencil was not as faithful to Herbert's mother as the young man had always believed. This slur on the most idealized version of V. at an early stage in the novel is a clue to our perception of her as a purified being, which is constantly being threatened by actuality. Mr. Stencil never fully explains his connection with V., but his journal entry from Florence in 1899 makes their relationship ambiguous, at the same time broadening the concept of V. " 'There is more behind and inside V. than any of us had suspected. Not who, but what: what is she. God grant that I may never be called upon to write the answer, either here or in any official report' " (43). This reluctance to write the answer suggests either that Mr. Stencil has some ominous knowledge of V., so sinister it cannot be spoken, or that he prefers to keep V. intact as an ideal, which by defining he would destroy. The younger Stencil takes up the second cause, and the V. he seeks is the most ideal version of woman in the book, but rather as a principle of motion, or the quest, than as anything resembling an actual woman:

> Work, the chase—for it was V. he hunted—far from being a means to glorify God and one's own godliness (as the Puritans believe) was for Stencil grim, joyless; a conscious acceptance of the unpleasant for no other reason than that V. was there to track down.
>
> Finding her: what then? Only that what love there was to Stencil had become directed entirely inward, toward this acquired sense of animateness. Having found this he could hardly release it, it was too dear. To sustain it he had to hunt V.; but if he should find her, where else would there be to go but back into half-consciousness? He tried not to think, therefore, about any end to the search. Approach and avoid [44].

It gradually becomes apparent that none of the many V.s is the virgin of Henry Adams. The V.s add up to the dynamo itself as they are found in combination with machines and other forms of the inanimate. By the conclusion of the novel on Malta, V., who now appears to be made up almost entirely of artificial matter, merely splinters into fragments. All surface. If Stencil's version of the mystical woman represents a more idealistic period of the past, the mechanical V. is modern man's projection of the mechanical and the nihilistic into a ghastly symbol of the feminine.

Pynchon's most obvious attack on the attention to surfaces is his treatment of a woman having a nose job, which he relates in graphic detail by showing how first the nose must be broken free of the face. Girls preparing for the marriage market pack the surgeon's office in January, since it takes four months for a nose job to heal and they want to be ready by June. "This meant many pretty Jewish girls who felt they would be perfectly marriageable were it not for an ugly nose could now go husband-hunting at the various resorts all with uniform septa" (35). Rachel suspects that something more than cosmetic reasons takes these girls to the doctor, however; the traditional hook nose of the Jew must be changed to the sign of the WASP of the movies and advertisements. In changing their looks, the girls become more like each other. As they are standardized, the monotonous round of affairs becomes even less interesting and the search for important and unique relationships less promising, a concept which John Updike, for one, develops in *Couples*. One relationship has little more value than another. The variety of women in V. results from the various fantasies of men, but a projection of reality in New York among The Whole Sick Crew indicates a sickening sameness about women.

The idea of Heroic Love is satirized in the portrayal of Mafia Winsome, wife of Gouverneur "Roony" Winsome, who cannot even attract her cat Fang as she dangles her empty bra before him. Like the men of V., she fantasizes her theories of the opposite sex, incorporating them into her novels. But as women are characteristically shown during this period, she has no capacity for the ideal; her "vision" sinks to an absurd level of physicality, a mockery of the ideal which men like Herbert Stencil are still able to envision. While Pynchon's women aptly follow men in their love of the machine, they do not attempt to imitate their quest for something beyond the tangible. Mafia's ideal of Heroic Love is "screwing five or six times a night, every night, with a great many athletic, half-sadistic wrestling holds thrown in" (113).

On a superficial and methodical level women are associated with the spiritual through their attentions to religion. Always satiric, Pynchon shows Victoria Wren to have turned her religious beliefs into a rationale for sexual activity: "Whether she had taken the veil or not, it was as if she felt Christ were her husband and that the marriage's physical consummation must be achieved through imperfect, mortal versions of himself—of which there had been, to date, four" (152). Women are more obsessed with the physical than men are in V., and in such cases as Victoria's, hypocrisy is a cover for lust. On the other hand, Benny Profane need not use any religious pretensions to conceal his desires. His frankly admitted sexual drive leads him to approach at random any girl he thinks he can get. On one occasion he selects an employment agency (he must have money to get the girl) by following the fold in the newspaper on his lap which is created by his erection. At the agency, before inquiring about a job he tries to arrange something with the first woman he sees. But even Profane's craving for women to gratify his immediate needs never replaces the suggestion of something higher, which is also imagined in feminine form, just as Stencil quests for the ideal.

The most fascinating and perhaps the most erotic liaison in V., certainly the most important one for the woman designated as V., is her alliance with Mélanie l'Heuremaudit, a fifteen-year-old French ballet dancer. Like Barth's Anastasia, V., after a variety of sexual experiences with men, at last finds satisfaction with a woman. (Barth, who is usually so serious in dealing with women, treats the lesbian incident comically. But Pynchon, who is usually so comic, develops it more seriously than other events in V.) The chapter entitled "V. in Love" shows the ultimate corruption of romantic love as V. reaches her consummate experience in a lesbian affair. One reason for considering V.'s attachment to be a significant one is her mystical age of thirty-three years, with its symbolic suggestion of momentous event. Pynchon satirizes what V. considers her grand passion by reducing it to the shallowness of mere tourism: she finds "love at last in her peregrinations through (let us be honest) a world if not created then at least described to its fullest by Karl Baedeker of Leipzig . . . populated only by a breed called 'tourists' " (384). But he goes on to deal with the lesbian affair through an extremely violent expurgation.

In this Freudian period of history, Pynchon defines homosexual love as narcissistic. The lesbian liaison is enacted only in a room full of mirrors. But none of the involvements are less than this. Even the most exalted view of V. is narcissistic in being a projection of one person's ideas on the mystical image of another, primarily of men's image-making of the feminine. V. and Mélanie accept the narcissism of their relationship to a point, recognizing their own foolishness as "lovers." V. mocks their passivity: " 'Do you only lie passive then, like an object? Of course you do. It is what you are. Une fetiche' " (381). The affair under mirrors may be as ludicrous as lovemaking appears to Barth's young Todd Andrews when he sees himself and Betty June making love under a mirror. But the bitter humor in V. soon ends in one of the most shocking scenes of the book, which Pynchon significantly reserves for the destruction of this lesbian affair that he apparently views as more insidious, even, than people's love affairs with machines. Mélanie is given a brutal death, dramatically on stage, as she is impaled on a pole to which she was to have been fastened and protected by a metal chastity belt which she forgot to wear. The heavy symbolism of this scene her death, so utterly phallic a destruction—puts sex back into its violent but heterosexual place, freeing V. of the lesbian alliance and making her available to men again, her life cleansed. The cruel and symbolic punishment of Mélanie for her failure to preserve her chastity—more important, to preserve it for men—is a powerful indictment of V. as the aggressor in love, as it is to all lesbianism. Pynchon never damns male homosexuality with any such violence—it is more foolish than awful, not hideously out of order as is V.'s affair with Mélanie.

Tony Tanner points out that Pynchon's characters in V., however cosmopolitan the book may be, are American in the sense that they live *through*, not *in*, an environment. The lesbian affair which takes place amidst a setting of reflections is one way of emphasizing the superficial. The movement of V. shows characters in reaction to the many places they visit, but with little sense of attachment to any place.[14] The Whole Sick Crew of New York characteristically drift in their environment and use it but are not truly aware of it. Pynchon seems intent on presenting the surface quality of the action, which exists more in its appearance than with any dramatic force. The symbol V. works this way for the book as a whole, for what at first appears as the culmination of a deep and complex concept of the feminine turns out to be little more than surface. Many have the superficial V. in their names, but it turns out to signify nothing particular about them. Changing colors reflect a varied and enticing surface, but beneath them is ice.[15] V. is finally discovered to be a void, like Vheissu, which is a dream of annihilation, a disturbing vision projected into the principle of the feminine.

The female protagonist of *The Crying of Lot 49*, Pynchon's second and more concise novel, charmingly named Oedipa Maas, makes a more direct attempt to define herself than any woman in V. But her clever name announces that here is a woman who represents first a concept and then a vague substance to be molded. The book opens delightfully, zeroing in on the center of meaning in a housewife's day: "One summer afternoon Mrs. Oedipa Maas came home from a Tupperware party whose hostess had put perhaps too much kirsch in the fondue. . . ."[16] Pynchon projects in such an image a whole study of the American woman whose afternoons are filled with only the excitement of such as the Tupperware party. Even the attempt at intoxication is deadening. Oedipa remains a mass of unenlightened material.

The main movement of plot in *The Crying of Lot 49* deals with the search for a mysterious and possibly traitorous system operating to undermine the culture of the United States. Oedipa ineptly but earnestly tries to discover what is going on as she works out the estate of Pierce Inverarity, her former lover, for whom she has been named an executrix. Her efforts entail such irrelevancies as the search for the sources of words to a Jacobean

14. "Caries and Cabals (Thomas Pynchon)," in *City of Words: American Fiction 1950–1970* (New York: Harper & Row, 1971), p. 158.

15. Ibid., p. 170.

16. Thomas Pynchon, *The Crying of Lot 49* (New York: Bantam Books, 1967), p. 1. Further page references to this edition are included in the text.

play written by a Randolph Driblette. About the time Oedipa goes hunting for this material in San Narciso it is quite clear either that she is the pawn of a traitorous group or that she is a foolish and lost woman who can be driven to anything. In reading this novel we are never quite clear as to (1) whether there is a Tristero System planning the overthrow of the American society, (2) whether the plot is simulated only to baffle Oedipa, or (3) whether that plot, as others, is purely a result of Oedipa's imagination.[17] The third alternative is the most probable and interesting one in regard to her characterization. It is likely that there are real plots, but they stimulate her paranoia in the creation of new plots of the mind. In any case, the focus of the novel is very sympathetically with this woman who tries so desperately to comprehend the mysteries around her. It is quite true that no one of her acquaintances fully understands the complicated underground system that is suggested, but the unfortunate Oedipa lacks even the most basic means to communicate in her society. She is totally an alien to the technology she is immersed in, including the forms of the media she uses daily: "She knew even less about radios than about Southern Californians, there were to both outward patterns a hieroglyphic sense of concealed meaning, of an intent to communicate" (13).

Herbert Stencil and others of V. are all disturbed by their inability to comprehend the strange forces about them, particularly the symbol V. But Oedipa's bafflement is a result less of a complicated and questing imagination than of an ignorance of practical realities. While Stencil's ideals seem foolishly unrelated to his experiences of reality, he has, at any rate, had various and concrete experiences which broaden his understanding of the vulgar. Oedipa has had almost no experience of any kind, particularly any that would help her relate to the technology of her society. She suggests, half tauntingly but much in the spirit of her own ignorance, that people do not invent things any more. " 'I mean, who's there been, really, since Thomas Edison? Isn't it all teamwork now?' " (61). Kate Millett makes the point in *Sexual Politics* that one way American women are shut out from their society is that they have no conception of the basic processes of

17. Tanner, "Caries and Cabals," p. 176.

the machines on which we are all so dependent.[18] And yet Oedipa
becomes the heiress of America. Pynchon reminds us that women
live longer than men do and inherit the large fortunes in this
country, even though they are oblivious to the means by which
money is made and to the processes by which products are developed. Women are merely the consumers. Oedipa is left in her
ignorance at the end of *The Crying of Lot 49*, bidding at an auc-
tion for some mysterious inheritance of America in the form of a
stamp collection, which will be as impossible for her to decipher
as is everything else she deals with, an incapacity shown with
particular conviction in a female character.

Among the fantasies that perpetuate Oedipa in her uneventful
life as a housewife is that of a Rapunzel waiting for someone to
request that she let down her hair. Pierce Inverarity senses that
he is to be that man, and at his insistence she literally lets down
her hair, which, after the pins and curlers are pulled from it,
tumbles down in a "dainty avalanche" transformed "through
some sinister sorcery, into a great unanchored wig" (10). The
magic of the tale is lost as the rich image of Rapunzel's hair,
signifying the sexuality of the past, gives way to the wig's ugliness
and artificiality.

In Oedipa's fantasy of Rapunzel she defines herself as a captive
maiden not imprisoned in a tower by a vicious keeper but as the
victim of a mysterious force: "What really keeps her where she
is is magic, anonymous and malignant, visited on her from outside
and for no reason at all. Having no apparatus except gut fear and
female cunning to examine this formless magic, to understand
how it works, how to measure its field strength, count its lines of
force, she may fall back on superstition, or take up a useful hobby
like embroidery, or go mad, or marry a disk jockey" (11).

Pynchon insightfully reflects on exactly how many women per-
ceive their lack of control over their lives. The familiar stance of
the male protagonist may be his discovery of a determinism that
can be inverted to an existential point of view. But Oedipa's sensation of helplessness is first romanticized and then brought to
bear on the only choices she imagines herself to have. These
seemingly foolish choices are not merely a mock-heroic version of

18. (New York: Doubleday, 1970), p. 41.

what a heroine might aspire to, but a literal version of the situation of many women. If the Tristero System is a metaphor for all that Oedipa cannot understand, the ways suggested for her to combat it are the only realistic answers she has to any problems. The first suggestion for coping with the mysterious force, "to fall back on superstition," is what she apparently does in believing herself a Rapunzel. Another method of falling back on a superstition for Pynchon's women is religious activity, which they are shown to accept as true spirituality more readily than men do. But such superstitions are obviously not a way of gaining control of the mysterious forces in this society, here and now.

The second option for Oedipa, the "useful hobby" of embroidery, is, like any triviality raised to importance in a barren life, simply ludicrous. Housework is another such useful hobby, since machinery does the essential labor. But women like Oedipa know of nothing outside their homes that makes sense to them, and they continue in their meaningless activity. Her option to marry and have a home is the obvious one for Oedipa; through her disk jockey she can fill her own emptiness. However meager Mucho's ability may be, he has more of a vocation than she does, and a shift to his problems is a relief from the struggle with her own vague dilemma. Mucho is confronted by failure in his occupation, but at least it is a failure more tangible and interesting than her own. He bounds home in the evening greeting her with " 'Today was another defeat.' 'Let me tell you,' she also began. But let Mucho go first" (3).

Oedipa's alternative for conducting herself against the mysteries around her by going mad shows a familiar pattern for the housewife that reveals the correlation between a woman's idleness at home and her lapses into insanity. Oedipa never goes completely mad, but the underlying hysteria builds with the perpetuation of her frustrating life. Pynchon supplies her with a capacity for real human love, but the complex systems around her, to which men are more attuned than she, incapacitate them for human love in return. Men are not in full command of the systems either, but Oedipa's femininity makes her a particularly apt symbol for conveying the confusion and mystery brought on by the patterns of modern American life. Her loneliness is a profound statement on a society which has gone beyond the traditionally softer feminine qualities and in its mechanical complexity has lost its humanity, moving toward a mass madness, which Kesey illustrates with his Combine.

In addition to being the dupe of advertising, Oedipa is caught by the romantic notions of the screen. She acts out a scene for a movie director named Metzger in which she is required to put on as many layers of clothing as possible. Far from a glamorous image, she sees herself in the full-length mirror as a beach ball. Metzger attempts to fondle her breasts but cannot find them beneath all the clothes—an apt image of materialism as a deterrent to romance.

While lesbianism is a peak but fatal experience in V., one which Pynchon heartily condemns, male homosexuality in *The Crying of Lot 49* is simply another of the elements that isolate Oedipa from her environment. The complex and mechanized aspects of the plotting she tries to uncover are all distinctly of male orientation. But on a sexual level she finds a demasculinized society which leaves her loveless. (One male lover, Nefastis, will make love with her, but only during the evening news program, preferably when the news is about China.) Oedipa's loneliest moment, one that is particularly revealing of the state of the sexes in this decade, occurs as she finds herself alone in a room of homosexuals: "Oedipa sat, feeling as alone as she ever had, now the only woman, she saw, in a room full of drunken male homosexuals. Story of my life, she thought, Mucho won't talk to me, Hilarius won't listen, Clerk Maxwell didn't even look at me, and this group, God knows. Despair came over her, as it will when nobody around has any sexual relevance to you" (86). This scene, while revealing Oedipa's paranoia and her characteristically feminine habit of demanding that attention be paid to her appearance, is a pathetic one. When she is not recognized sexually, even though it is so often women's plea that they be recognized otherwise, Oedipa in a sense ceases to exist. Not being heard or seen, she is a form of invisible woman.

From the concept of the feminine in terms of mythic heights and vulgar lows in V., Pynchon moves on in *The Crying of Lot 49* to a sympathetic portrayal of woman as a forsaken mass. He uses the extremes of caricature but tends toward realism in this novel, which, like V., shows a strong connection between women and objects. Oedipa Maas, the consumer, stands out as the lonely woman in a society whose complexities are far beyond her understanding and to which she contributes little except as a consumer, a pawn of advertisers as of everything else.

The most conspicuous and odious women consumers are James Purdy's middle-aged matrons, always in the process of gathering goods around them, without which they have little to identify themselves. Makeup and various other products created to add beauty and comfort to life are the means of the desperate, aging woman to assuage her despair at being fat and forty. Purdy's few younger women are merely weaker versions of the same, and even in their youth are never desirable. The factor of age is particularly important because these women are obsessed with commercial concepts of youthful beauty. And as time depreciates their value as commodities, they consume more.

Purdy's aging woman, in the period of her life when her children no longer need her, reaches new heights of panic and possessiveness. In "Why Can't They Tell You Why?" a young boy hisses at the mother who clings to him. Purdy shows the transition from the middle-aged woman's possessiveness of children to her total obsession with things (especially houses) or people she can treat as things when her children leave home. If a woman is not a possessive mother she may be a neglectful or absentee parent, leaving an orphan bitterly reflecting on his loss. In either event, Purdy displays a sharp contempt for these unappealing creatures, as he does for most things American. Women exemplify the most disgusting outcome of the capitalistic experiment.

In an early story, "63: Dream Palace," a "greatwoman" referred to simply by her married name of Grainger is a powerful rendition of the acquisitive Purdian female. At first glance she is a splendid creature, given some dignity by her affluence. But we soon discover that only by means of her house and her money can she entice people to surround her. Admitting that only her money keeps her alive, Grainger is certain that when it has drained away she will die. Purdy shockingly emphasizes the fact that American women are wealthy and live long but have little to offer aside from what they own. Their status is gained only through the use of a man's name and his money. In a strangely up-to-date story, in view of the growing practice of women to use their maiden names, entitled "Don't Call Me by My Right Name," a Mrs. Klein hates her new married name so much that one night at a party she announces to her husband that she will no longer use it. He is utterly baffled by this kind of talk, simplistically imagining divorce as the only solution. For the first time in their marriage he hits her, knocking her to the floor, to both his and her amazement. What is most damaging for her is the dawning that her identity, in the form of her maiden name, has been taken from her. At last she halfheartedly agrees to go home as Mrs. Klein, her problem unresolved. In another case, a woman as desperately clings to her married name, registering like Mrs. Klein a horror of being without an identity. Purdy recognizes the peculiar form of this problem of women, but he suggests an awful truth: what *would* Mrs. Klein be without Mr. Klein to give her a name?

Many of Purdy's male characters are as blank as these women, to a greater degree than is true for most authors. But the question of their need for enrichment is, again, much more crucial than it is for women, whose blankness is considered inevitable. The issue with the boy Malcolm is such a case. He is a sort of cipher waiting on his park bench for someone to come along and give him a self. And Cabot Wright, who becomes a rapist for want of something better to do, has little to distinguish him aside from his repetitive and empty activity.

Many of Purdy's women have an announced profession, but usually one from which they are in semi-retirement and which is more a neurotic compensation for the lack of an interesting personality than an expression of one. They are never truly creative. Purdy, deploring the useless, middle-aged female consumer who does nothing but spend her husband's money, is equally appalled by the women who attempt careers. Women are especially disgusting in their aggressiveness: the singer Melba, for one, who is responsible for Malcolm's death, and the midget Kermit's wife, who, although a brilliant steno, can never keep her position, "owing to her wish to meddle in the higher business of the offices where she is employed."[19] Women simply cannot do things well. And so, to compensate, they send their men on quests—financial, creative, or perhaps even sexual. In "63: Dream Palace" the author Parkhearst Cratty's wife Bella is the stereotyped consumer-mother-bitch who prods a man on to do what she is obviously incapable of doing. Her husband is found wandering in the park, "not daring to go home to his wife Bella. He had done nothing in weeks, and her resentment against him would be too heavy to bear."[20] It does not occur to Parkhearst that Bella has not done anything either. No one expects her to produce.

Purdy vehemently damns marriage, showing it as either a bitter struggle in which each party loses or, in the more placid cases, a situation in which one partner or both have made such sacrifices and compromises as to obliterate their own personalities. Cratty's marriage pursues him "like a neverending nightmare" (120), and he cannot free himself from the obsession that everything is over. Bella's power over him is enhanced by the suggestion of an Oedipal problem as she is frequently taken for his mother.

Malcolm presents the crucial problem of identity for a young male virgin, a familiar figure in the literature of the sixties, which includes fewer female than male virgins. The boy has had no meaningful contact with people and finds no particular value in being alive; he sits on a park bench every day just waiting. But he is more innocent and appealing in his emptiness than any of Purdy's women, more a pitiful victim, quite unlike the predatory female consumer who attempts to make up for her void by accumulating things. Mr. Cox, the astrologer, approaches Malcolm in his innocent stupor with the suggestion that he meet Girard Girard, a billionaire. Through this connection we are introduced to another of Purdy's monstrous collectors, Madame Girard.

Like Purdy's other powerful women, Madame Girard has come to her power through a man's money. Among other reasons given for the diseased state of marriage, the wife's greed is perhaps the

19. James Purdy, *Malcolm* (New York: Farrar, Straus & Cudahy, 1959), p. 20. Further page references to this edition are included in the text.

20. James Purdy, *Color of Darkness* (New York: Bantam Books, 1970), p. 120. Further page references to this edition are included in the text.

most obvious. Although marriages are disastrous, Mr. Cox tells Malcolm, " 'Everybody is married, Malcolm. Everybody that counts' " (39). From the legal issue of a wife or husband as property to be bartered for, used, and paid off, Purdy transcends to the more compelling psychological manipulation husbands and wives practice on each other. And Madame Girard is a master manipulator.

She is first seen with a riding whip at her feet, in one of Purdy's less than subtle touches. Her present project, before meeting Malcolm whom she will want to possess, is suing her husband for the remainder of his wealth. In such a getup as we first see Madame Girard she resembles a clown more than a woman, not that she is blessed with humor but that her outfit reveals her outrageous consumerism. By contrast, Malcolm, another vacant person, has no inclinations to materialism to fill his hollowness. He is desired by everyone, while quite understandably no one likes Madame Girard. As was the case for Grainger of "63: Dream Palace," Madame Girard's money is her only attraction.

She appears not at all disturbed by her husband's infidelity as long as she gets his money, advising him to commit his "routine adulteries" (150). She now has in mind her next prey, Malcolm. The age factor here is crucial, since a middle-aged woman involving herself with a boy of seventeen invariably has sinister overtones. To the orphan Malcolm, Madame Girard is a grasping mother, a threat of seduction, and above all a collector of things. She pays $10,000 to have his picture painted, literally making an object of him. Purdy uses the age gap, with the woman much older, to make her sexual needs the more grotesque.

One of the most repellent things about Purdy's marriages is that the woman usually proposes, and aggressiveness is always ugly in women. In *Malcolm* the handsome midget Kermit's wife, a whore, coerces him into marriage and then makes him miserable. She eventually runs off with a Japanese wrestler who has "the real equipment" (48). Frequently Purdy shows the impotent man, crippled as this midget is or weakened by extreme age, and terrified since his parents deserted him, left with only a vicious woman to rule his life. Women are clearly at fault in failing marriages, their husbands the long-suffering victims. Eloisa Brac, another "friend" of Madame Girard's, is married to a former burglar who she claims is now the burglar of her better qualities. Their marriage has never known a day of rest. Brac claims that life with Eloisa equals the misery of his life in prison.

Malcolm is the only unattached person in the group, and confronted by a host of awful marriages, he is the inevitable prey for one more doomed alliance. Again the woman proposes, a young singer named Melba who snaps him up as she meets him, admitting that in another five minutes she would have married someone else. The importance of timing to a marriage is just one more sign of its superficiality. In the same way that a person buys a bad product under the influence of a flashy advertisement, Purdy's men fall into the marriage trap. Malcolm is the most desired product on the current market, and the powerful female consumer swoops in for the kill. Such manipulation is fatal to Malcolm, whose hair turns white a few days after his marriage, which shortly leads to death.

Purdy's least monstrous female character is Alma Mason of *The Nephew*, one of his few realistic works. This pitiful and unattractive middle-aged woman, in these respects typical of Purdy, lives in an earlier, more idyllic time in America. Not as vicious as his other women, she is like them in being devoid of interesting characteristics of her own. Most discussions of *The Nephew* focus on the lack of identity in the nephew, Cliff Mason, who never once appears in the book. His lack of a strongly defined character is a major issue, a mysterious waste or a problem to be solved, whereas the lack of character in Alma is based on an expectation of her limits as a cloistered woman, a pitiful but expected fact. She represents a thousand Alma Masons in the world, all those characterless nice ladies who live entirely through other people. Usually children serve the function, but since Alma is childless, and unmarried, she lives through the image of her nephew. Because she has no opportunity to manipulate the boy (he joined the army to get away from the town and from her), she is less offensive than most mother figures. The basis of conflict in the novel is the debate between Alma and the older brother she lives with as to Cliff's nature and his relationship to them. Which one of them does he write to? When a telegram arrives announcing that the nephew is missing in action, Alma is free to fabricate her particular version of him and his relationship to them without the hindrance of his actual presence.

Alma is more likeable than Purdy's later women because she has no wealth or power to bolster her. But she is weak and unable to face realities, even when acquaintances inform her that she is using her nephew to fill her own emptiness. Another thing that sets Alma off from Purdy's other women is her innocence, not merely the naiveté of any provincial person in the early forties, but the innocence of so many women of the past who were protected from "harmful" knowledge. Her brother Boyd has a much more informed and realistic view of the nephew, not only because Cliff once confided in him but because of what Purdy suggests is an essentially more truthful male point of view. Manly knowledge and forthrightness versus female naiveté and self-deception are presented as a natural condition. We expect Alma to prefer her own pretty version of things to the unpleasant truth.

The picture of Alma standing each day at the window watching for the mailman is typical of her and of women like her as static images. The passage of time only hardens the picture, which becomes more pitiful with age. In this twilight of her life, as a result of the news that her nephew may be dead, Alma partially comes to life with her plan to write a memorial to Cliff. But even this is a futile effort, for she knows less about him than any one of her neighbors does. Like so many women, she is simply not aware of what is going on, or will not admit to it, and her failure to grasp reality makes her lonelier than those around her, who are all more perceptive than she is. As the product of an earlier time period she suffers the same kind of alienation as Pynchon's Oedipa Maas experiences, although the fault appears to be more with Alma than it does with Oedipa. And without money to glamorize her life, Alma is Purdy's bleakest woman, merely a burden to those around her—nicer than the more materialistic women of later decades, but unappealing all the same.

All of Purdy's important themes are brought together in what is probably his most important work, *Cabot Wright Begins*, a fabulous tale peculiarly representative of the comic violence in the literature of the mid-sixties. The victims and, despite the rapist, the victimizers of this age are the women, who epitomize the monotony and boredom of standardized urban life. More comically than previously, in *Cabot Wright Begins* Purdy pursues the theme of the older, richer woman, in this case Carrie Moore, who controls her husband's activities. Bernie Gladheart, like Malcolm, looks for a home and a savior, who turns out to be the female predator with money and a mansion. Carrie, twelve years older than Bernie, cleverly discovers the two things he wants most —encouragement and praise—and gives him a "wagonload" of each. And with her understanding of these needs, she is "a church open only for him, with services in full operation twenty-four hours a day."[21] Bernie is totally in the power of this mother figure, a sophisticated woman quite expert in her capacity for collecting husbands. Since Purdy's male characters have usually been deserted by their natural mothers, they are particularly susceptible to these surrogate mothers, who take over the manipulative but never the beneficent aspects of the role.

Like most of Purdy's women, Carrie is overweight and plain, but sexually demanding. Another manipulator and consumer. Bernie is her fourth husband, one of her many dispensable products. She refers to him as her "change-of-life baby" (19), a swipe at the perverted role of mother and the breakdown of the family. Sending Bernie to Brooklyn to investigate and write up the life of the notorious rapist Cabot Wright, however, although a manifestation of Carrie's control over him, is not necessarily calculated to destroy him but to relieve the boredom of her own life.

The life Bernie leaves behind on his pilgrimage to Brooklyn suggests no tragic loss as far as his marriage is concerned, but in leaving Carrie he relinquishes his only home. In this perhaps lies the source of so many disastrous marriages: the need of orphans for a home, even when the price is marriage, which is bound to be destructive. After Bernie's departure Carrie continues to see the Bickles, closest acquaintances of the Gladhearts, at whose parties everyone regularly indulges in a "perfunctory type of sexual encounter," to-dos that are "sordid rather than exciting" (25). Such manifestly dull sex is explained by the fact that everyone

21. James Purdy, *Cabot Wright Begins* (New York: Avon Books, 1964), p. 14. Further page references to this edition are included in the text.

is growing middle-aged, an obsession with Purdy that sets him apart from the many critics of the society who see younger people as the generation of the spiritually dead. The ugliness of middle age results not from lamenting the passing of better days but from never having had good days and knowing that there never will be any. No good times are shown for the young or the old. But by middle age, signs of physical decay add their touch to the dismal condition.

Carrie, in her forties, is a lively nymphomaniac. Showing her to be oversexed as well as unattractive completes Purdy's satirical purpose of making her undesirable and comic. As one of the proprietors of a matriarchal society, she obtains, consumes, and discards items, including husbands. Marriage, disgusting as it is, remains absolutely essential in Purdy's society. Carrie would not be without a husband, equating being single with wearing no makeup. But the "best thing about marriage was the increased opportunities it afforded to meet a number of men sexually in relaxed homelike surroundings" (53). Whenever Purdy uses the terms *home, family, mother,* or *husband* and *wife,* he is bitterly satirical as to the lost values of such concepts, bitter toward the person in a mother's role because she manipulates, but much angrier at the mother (occasionally the father) who deserts the child, creating another orphan.

The climax of Purdy's reactions to women comes with the bitingly humorous allowance of Cabot Wright's multiple rapes, the ultimate in excessive, perverted sexual activity. None of the victims appear to have been hurt, and in fact they encourage the rapes; such useless products of the society are these women that they might as well be used this way as for nothing. Cabot Wright, who is merely alleviating his boredom, does the ladies a favor as he serves the sexual needs they dare not openly admit.

The psychedelic wilderness of the sixties, which gave us everything in our national life from a rash of political assassinations to a moon landing, is on the other hand paralleled by a growing ennui. The fabulous tales of the sixties are in one way an attempt to escape that boredom while at the same time it is one of their themes. Purdy convincingly captures the bizarre and the boring through this tale of the rapist who exemplifies both forces, expressly bringing our attention to the latter in Cabot Wright's interpretation of American life in the sixties: " 'Wasn't boredom the only experience I could latch on to, considering what Wall Street had for me? Next to dying, boredom is the most. I knew only boredom was possible then, because there is no time for pleasure today, you can just allow yourself that second-and-a-half to hear the message, which is always an ad' " (147). And if American women are the super dupes of advertising, having become through their marriage to products the master products themselves, then Cabot Wright's rape of them is the appropriate act for him to register his disgust. " 'I raped everyone through boredom, so maybe then I chose the thing I felt would bore me most, dumb dames' " (147). Such "dumb dames" resemble the heroines of John Updike (unlike Purdy in being very fond of women), who accepts them as stupid replicas of one desired object.

Cabot Wright is a married man, and as can be expected in Purdy, the marriage is an unredeeming failure. Mrs. Cabot Wright, the former Cynthia Abigail Adams, is as bland as the products she uses. Employed as a dress designer to supplement Cabot's salary so that they might maintain their costly apartment overlooking the Statue of Liberty, her refrain "Where does the money go?" so irritates Cabot that he finds a copy of the question in an advertisement and pins it on the wall in front of her. Mrs. Cabot Wright's language, her looks, and her thoughts can all be documented in current commercials. One of Purdy's few younger women, she is if anything more plastic than her older but equally materialistic counterparts. The middle-aged woman, who is disgusting through a physical description, is at least occasionally vivid. But the younger, more attractive woman, who is not described physically, is quite forgettable.

Cynthia Wright is hardly interesting enough to attract our attention (Cabot is sufficiently bored with her) except as a stereotype of Purdy's modern, urban, young wife. Like many other young women of the period, she is bound to objects and portrayed as inhuman for not wanting children. Although she is a lackluster character, there is one bizarre scene with her which hilariously exemplifies women's consumerism, as she goes berserk in the supermarket. This clever piece of satire successfully dramatizes a particular female obsession with products and the possibility for madness which underlies such an obsession:

> The ice-cream hostess, Miss Glenna De Loomis, attempted to salvage as many of their Dairy Maid frozen products as possible, but Cynthia then began to throw the articles at the fluorescent lighting fixtures. Just before the police and rescue squad came, she had moved back to fresh fruit and vegetables and had managed to throw in the air nearly all the pomegranates, persimmons, apples, peaches, and Jerusalem artichokes she could get her hands on. Then in a rush toward the front of the store, she had overturned three entire shelves of detergents and cleaning fluids [123].

After Cynthia is taken away and locked up, Cabot gaily lives out his new-found freedom, gaining much respect for the "courage" he showed during his domestic crisis.

The subtlest satire of *Cabot Wright Begins* is directed at the women who are so bored that they want to be raped. When Carrie sends her husband to investigate Cabot Wright, after reading the notice in their Chicago paper, "Noted Rapist Released from Prison: Cabot Wright Returns to Brooklyn," she registers the same kind of morbid interest that the victims of rape experience. Carrie suspects the real nature of the crimes through a "queer feminine doubt that he had been motivated to his deeds—more than 300 rapes in Brooklyn and Manhattan—by the overpowering lust attributed to him by the press" (12). When Carrie discusses Cabot Wright with Zoe Bickle, for the first time in their close acquaintance the other woman is really interested in what she has to say, revealing the same suspicious interest in rape. Like the rapist, and the victims of rape, these women are chronically bored. The partner-swapping at their parties is a dull venture, and yet the need for excitement is still fantasized in sexual terms, Cabot Wright and his activities being the only stage of sexuality left to interest them.

Zoe Bickle, a brazen woman intent on discovering Cabot Wright for herself, makes a pilgrimage to New York and arrives in his room by way of the skylight, through which she falls "by accident." To her surprise she finds a clean-cut, mythical American youth. His link with advanced technology is much more redeeming than women's use of products: his only addiction is a hearing aid by which he takes in everything, including the boring chatter of the women he is about to rape. Purdy cleverly satirizes the attitudes of these women in the jargon of Wall Street and the press, as well as through the mystique of this modern hero, which is revealed in a manuscript Zoe discovers, written about the rapist: "The popularity of Cabot Wright as a criminal may have stemmed from two facts. He was employed in Wall Street in a well-known brokerage, and he was no respecter of age, raping girls, young ladies, middle-aged matrons, and even elderly women. Anyone who was a woman could be next. . . . He didn't kill, he didn't bruise, he didn't cuff or buffet. He used, everybody insisted afterwards, some form of hypnotism. He raped easily and well" (81).

The clever inclusion of the American myth of heroism into the activities of the rapist is based on the daring and expertise involved in the crimes, the sheer quantity of acts performed, and most shrewdly, the democratic and fair way the rapes are executed. This version of the hero displays the destruction involved when such American ideals go awry. But it can exist only in a society where women are passive and then vengefully seek the punishment of the seducer with their hypocritical outrage. Purdy reminds us here of the significant legal problem of determining whether rape has actually occurred and the potential it gives the plaintiff for maligning an innocent man. The alleged victims of Cabot Wright allow and enjoy the "rape" and then scream for his arrest. This kind of nastiness is a new dimension for Purdy's already distasteful women, and one reason why the treatment of rape in *Cabot Wright Begins* takes on such an interesting slant.

While women appear to be victims, they are the victimizers in this novel just as they are in Purdy's others, by pushing their men into quests that idealize the rapist and by being so lethargic that only rape can awaken them. Cabot's victims may well be lumped into the round number of three hundred; one woman is like another, and there might as easily be three hundred more. His activities do not deviate so far, after all, from the random sexual exchanges of the society in general. But in naming his acts as rape the women have a double advantage—they first take their pleasure and then their revenge.

Cabot Wright is a hero not only to women but to Bernie Gladheart and presumably to other American males. Bernie is aware at the outset of his pilgrimage to Brooklyn of a closeness to Cabot simply from reading about him. This timid husband, so at the mercy of his older, more powerful wife, sees in Cabot's example the supreme form of violence against women, the controllers. The rapist daringly and successfully lives out Bernie's own desire for retaliation, accepting imprisonment as the price of such heroism.

Repulsion for the women who desire rape, for career women, and for the perverted parent resounds with increasing bitterness in *Cabot Wright Begins*. The most disgusting of career women (being the closest to advertising) is Goldie Thomas, a "top-notch model," daughter of a despicable mother, the former silent movie star Zenda Stuyvesant, as a result of her liaison with the former matinee idol Horace Ross. Zenda chose for Goldie the name Thomas, that of her fourth husband, thinking it would do her daughter the most good, another occasion of a woman using a man's name for the status she cannot gain by herself. Purdy caustically represents this mother who on the pretext of helping her daughter is only corrupting her, having little to project on the child but her own shabby life. Her most perverse act of motherhood is the manipulation of Goldie's seduction. Jealous of the girl for her youth and apparently for her virginity, Zenda, in the grasp of Cabot Wright, begs him not to rape her by suggesting he try her young daughter upstairs instead. Cabot goes ahead with Zenda, who is not displeased after all, and as he pumps the "origin of life into the old girl" (172) he finds out about the daughter. Zenda protests that he will ruin Goldie's career, and sensing her actual desire that he do this, Cabot is able to carry out his own purposes while at the same time soothing Zenda's conscience with the rationale that when Goldie is ruined she can pose for middle-aged women's ads. " 'Take it from me,' he said, 'middle-aged women are in and besides run the nation' " (172).

The greatest revenge on Purdy's middle-aged women (and raping ages them) is that they become ugly. And the more disgusting Zenda becomes to herself, the greater is her jealousy of her youthful daughter. Fortunately, she is tied and gagged while Cabot rapes the young Goldie, which ostensibly frees her of complicity in the act. "As the mother lay in her thongs, though her cheeks blushed as her mind told her they should, she realized she was not entirely unhappy about what was happening to Goldie. Her daughter had always been such a snot—Zenda was thinking this even as she heard the peculiar light and heavy sounds above indicating speeded activity by a sex criminal . . . her daughter's career, Zenda feared, was over" (173). As if this were not enough punishment for Goldie, the career girl, her beauty is later obliterated in an automobile accident.

The outlook on sexual activity in *Cabot Wright Begins* ends where John Barth's began in *The Floating Opera,* as the young boy saw the mirrored version of his lovemaking and found it ludicrous. Cabot reads in a newspaper editorial that " 'the true sexual orgasm in America takes place today in the popcorn bag in the movie theater on your right . . .' " (179). From this he goes on to discover the comedy associated with orgasm, bringing himself to an erection through paroxysms of laughter, without any need of a woman. As in the case of Alexander Portnoy, the most intense sexual pleasure is autoerotic. Cabot Wright declares that laughter is the supreme reaction to the absurd condition. " 'After all, laughter is the greatest boon Nature has bestowed on miserable unjoyous man' " (222).

A stance of laughter is the most noticeable feature of Kesey's hero McMurphy in *One Flew over the Cuckoo's Nest* and that which distinguishes him most sharply from the Big Nurse. Like Purdy's monstrous and humorless middle-aged women, Nurse Ratched is a power figure, the super female power figure of the sixties, representing at the same time the horrors of mechanization and those of motherhood. Unlike most fabulous tales, Kesey's develops some of the male characters with a degree of individuality and realism while his super female is thoroughly a caricature, but the dominating center of the book. Aside from a couple of good-natured whores who provide a relief for the inmates of the asylum, in the same way a bottle of booze and a fishing trip do, the matriarchal nurse is the idea of malignant woman, symbol of all that is wrong with the mothers of her patients. Toward her the inmates may direct all of their hostilities for their mothers and for women in general, who hover as the power figures outside in the Combine.

Even as caricature, Nurse Ratched exudes a truly terrifying sense of both the mechanical and the maternal. There is nothing subtle about her, and Kesey never probes her mind for complexities. Without any redeeming qualities, she serves most effectively as the total authority figure and as a scapegoat for everything that the men hate. This image of the feminine is obviously capable of arousing hostilities in the men that no male authority figure could so inspire, eliciting along with a loathing of the subtle controls of mothers and other women a hatred of all authority.

The nurse's noticeable anatomy cannot be avoided. Endowed as a super sex object with huge breasts, she has perverted herself into a machine. Like some of Pynchon's characters, she has become the machinery she has embraced. As the narrator Bromden imagines it, she carries tools in her wicker bag instead of lipstick and other womanly things. Her purpose in life is to serve the Combine by seeing that these men are adjusted to run like well-oiled machines. Pynchon's characters are often comically related to their machines, but Kesey's machine woman is a much more frightening creation. She has no tender affection for her tools, which she uses to mold the men's brains. And while there are many scenes which are laughable in the men's reaction to her, she has absolutely no sense of humor.

Like many characters who at first appear to have complete power, Nurse Ratched can soon be recognized as a frightened and empty person who must have machines to reinforce her power. She has little more security in her own identity than Anastasia Stoker, Oedipa Maas, and Mrs. Cabot Wright have, but she exhibits the militant side of the same deadly void. It is no surprise to discover that the inmates of the asylum are the sane and sensitive ones and that the Big Nurse, who may represent a majority, is a robot (although capable of hysteria) representing the insanity of the standardized life of the Combine. In contrast to the caricature of the nurse, someone like Bromden is developed with much more complexity. Kesey interestingly combines a flat female character with several partially developed male characters in the same novel, not only to produce the shock effect of his robot woman but as a suggestion that the modern woman has much less depth than the man.

Nurse Ratched's pronounced appearance, which announces a sexuality she has obsessively denied, is an even greater source of the men's resentment of her than her authority over them. She has denied the expected femininity in favor of the "wheels and gears, cogs polished to a hard glitter, tiny pills that gleam like porcelain, needles, forceps, watchmakers pliers, rolls of copper wire"[22] that Bromden sees in her bag. The movements of her face, as she attempts a mandatory smile, an almost impossible gesture, occur with grinding and machine-like awkwardness. When Mc-Murphy shocks her by appearing in the hallway clad only in a towel (a sexual mockery is the obvious way to offend), she shakily attempts to match his gaiety: "Gradually the lips gather together again under the little white nose, run together, like the red-hot wire had got hot enough to melt, shimmer a second, then click solid as the molten metal sets, growing cold and strangely dull" (90).

The clacking of machinery is matched by her abrupt, frigid approach in the white sterility of the hospital setting. Rampant sexual activity may be a sign of the decay of both love and genuine sensuality, but abstinence from it is a despised solution. Without the strict moral and practical considerations of the past, there are now few convincing reasons for a retreat from sexuality, which becomes a damning perversion in anyone. The nurse announces such a denial by pulling tight clothes over her enormous chest, and McMurphy reacts by ripping away her dress to expose the large wasted breasts.

Because the emblem of mechanized society is a woman (the male army officers of *Catch-22*, for example, similarly represent the absurd mechanization of military life), many interesting complications are added to the standard robot figure of authority. The Oedipal problem, for one, is of primary consideration, especially

---

22. Ken Kesey, *One Flew over the Cuckoo's Nest* (New York: New American Library, 1962), p. 10. Further page references to this edition are included in the text.

as the nurse's mammary glands recall the forbidden mother and in this case the unattainable sex object, although the inmates are not in any healthy way attracted to her. They wish to destroy her, and the most natural way to do this would be sexual violation. (McMurphy admits defeat in considering an actual seduction, however.) She calls forth their hostility not only to mother and sex object but to the woman teacher, predominant in the system of elementary education in this country—another of the forces that make up the matriarchal system that oppresses these men. It is no wonder so much hatred lies under the surface order of this asylum before McMurphy stirs it to action, a hatred repressed so completely in Harding, for one, that he can only speak of his administrator as a " 'strict middle-aged lady, but she's not some kind of giant monster of the poultry clan, bent on sadistically pecking out our eyes' " (56–57). McMurphy answers with a definitive description of the bitch stereotype:

> "No, that nurse ain't some kinda monster chicken, buddy, what she is is a ball-cutter. I've seen a thousand of 'em, old and young, men and women. Seen 'em all over the country and in the homes—people who try to make you weak so they can get you to toe the line. . . . She may be a mother, but she's big as a damn barn and tough as a knife metal. She fooled me with that kindly little old mother bit for maybe three minutes when I came in this morning, but no longer. . . . Hooowee, I've seen some bitches in my time, but she takes the cake.
> ". . . she's a bitch and a buzzard and a ball-cutter, and don't kid me, you know what I'm talking about" [57–58].

Although most of the inmates agree with McMurphy, they have neither his daring nor his ability to express themselves. In word as well as in deed he is their hero. Like a Paul Bunyan he makes great boasts, and his stance of laughter would assert a control over all situations. Bromden relates that McMurphy knows "you can't really be strong until you can see a funny side to things" (203), and McMurphy tells Cheswick, " 'Man, when you lose your laugh you lose your *footing*. A man go around lettin' a woman whup him down till he can't laugh any more, and he loses one of the biggest edges he's got on his side' " (65–66).

Harding does remind them that laughter is not weapon enough against matriarchy—only one thing is—sexual assault. But if Mc-Murphy does not defeat the nurse through laughter, he very nearly does so, and his capacity for the humorous clearly announces his superiority over her.

With McMurphy to draw negative attention to the Big Nurse, we see repercussions of their own bitch mothers in several of the patients. Already mentioned is Harding, whose mother is weightily present whenever we hear from him, although never in clear detail, in his super-polite attitude to the nurse. As a result of Harding's homosexuality, which makes him excessively shy and inhibited, he never possessed his wife but forced her into acts which brought on the guilt that resulted in insanity. Billy Bibbit, a terrified, stuttering young incompetent, has been thoroughly castrated by his mother, whose influence hovers over him constantly and keeps him from any free act. This thirty-one-year-old virgin is the extreme example of the debilitated male who faces the nurse. When invited to go on a picnic with the whores, he refuses because of what his mother would think. Always embarrassed to give his age, he barely comprehends what chronological age means. Mrs. Bibbit, "a solid, well-packed lady with hair revolving from blond to blue to black and back to blond again every few months" (246), will not admit that she is old enough to be the mother of a "middle-aged" man. His subjection is complete, and the lifelong trauma, brought into focus by Nurse Ratched, finally drives him to suicide. Another casualty of a woman is Ruckly, whose mind was garbled by an error of therapy and who can react to any question only with a violent " 'Ffffffuck da wife!' " (125).

As completely as the Big Nurse appears to be in power, she is ultimately quite vulnerable. Perhaps it is going too far to sympathize with her—Kesey never does—but while there is never anything likeable about her, the difficulty and loneliness of her position should be acknowledged. Alone in authority, she is also alone as a woman against an intelligent, diverse group of desperate men. She may be reasonably confident in her methods of control, but she recognizes a cleverness and a power in McMurphy that unnerves her. Only through reliance on the absolute power of machinery— the fog-making devices, shock treatments, and the lobotomy—is she able to maintain her shaky authority.

While we never get a look into Nurse Ratched's heart (assuming she once had one), certain probable factors of her past are worth considering. The fact that neither the patients nor the reader can ignore her large breasts is sign enough that her body was always her primary attribute. Still at the age of fifty she is first of all a sex object. She obviously detests this fact, which must have caused complications for her when she was younger as it does now. Given her noticeable anatomy, she was that girl of our high school days who elicited catcalls if not bodily attacks and was given names to describe her endowment. Nurse Ratched's sex life was evidently a destructive one, resulting in her disgust of her body. Not really the antithesis of the typically timid spinster, she is a form of the stereotype of the spinster with no love life who takes out her frustrations on the people around her, in this case badgering men, probably in retaliation for the way they have treated her. Far from being ugly and unwanted, as an attractive and shapely girl (if her experience is at all typical of the American woman) she was in demand for her physical charms and for those alone. McMurphy's claim that he could not make love to her even if she looked like Marilyn Monroe is an interesting allusion in light of the movie star's exclusive role as sex symbol and her consequent suicide.

The final blow of the nurse's authority over McMurphy (before his lobotomy) that finally tempers his flippant attacks on her is her power to keep him in the institution as long as she wants, a version of maternal possessiveness. She does finally destroy many of the inmates, but not without self-destructive consequences. Without humor and without comrades, she is far from the satisfied villainess whose schemes are complete. Her lapses into hysteria reveal a chronic fear and instability. But because she is more purely a caricature than the male characters, her feelings are not considered. The final blow of justice to her, after her administration of the lobotomy to McMurphy, is that "her face was bloated blue and out of shape on one side, closing one eye completely, and she had a heavy bandage around her throat" (268), as if she too had been lobotomized.

Nurse Ratched is entirely necessary as a scapegoat. When Mc-Murphy asks Harding what he thinks is wrong with her, they speculate as to whether or not she is the source of their troubles in the asylum. Bromden relates that they "talk for a while about whether she's the root of all the trouble here or not, and Harding says she's the root of most of it. Most of the other guys think so too, but McMurphy isn't so sure any more. He says he thought so at one time but now he don't know. He says he don't think getting her out of the way would really make much difference; he says that there's something bigger making all this mess and goes on to try to say what he thinks it is. He finally gives up when he can't explain it" (165). McMurphy appears to clarify the problems of the other patients in the way he directs his attack at the Big Nurse and by representing a familiar version of strength, which goes beyond any particular identity of his own, just as the nurse functions as a clear-cut version of the things they hate.

Aside from the nurse, only a few other women are mentioned in *One Flew over the Cuckoo's Nest*, most of them mothers whose authority she reflects. The women in contrast to these bitch mothers provide a comforting but not very convincing alternative, the generous-hearted whores who exist as a brief respite to the prisoners from the frigid powers of the Combine and a few other "good women," notably of other time periods or different races: Bromden's grandmother, the gentle Japanese nurse who has been crushed by the Combine, and the Negro girl Bromden met in a factory who begged him to take her to a better life. But these are minor and unconvincing figures beside the nurse, who in caricature represents much that is frighteningly real.

The exaggeration inherent in fabulation allows for such vividly defined concepts of women as these. By means of the fantastic, in addition to Kesey's super ball-breaker, various other striking types are set. Among them are Barth's Pocahontas, the victim; Pynchon's V., the mechanical principle; and Purdy's Madame Girard, the acquisitive matron. Through the freedom of caricature attitudes may be trumpeted rather than modified to the more complex version of reality. Fabulation may not help us to know the intricate inner side of female characters, but it clearly brings into focus many beliefs about them.

two

Philip Roth: When She Was Good She Was Horrid

Philip Roth writes brilliantly of obsessives—Eli, the fanatic, and others compelled by orthodox forms of Jewishness; Alexander Portnoy, obsessed with masturbation to compensate for everything his mother has outlawed and the puritanism of his heritage generally; the bisexual hangup of Alan Kepesh, blossoming into a female breast, metaphor of repressed desires. And in both his comic and his sober writing Roth reveals an obsession with women's power over men. Being intensely concerned with his characters' morality, as most Jewish writers have been, he shows the great wrong of a woman's wielding her power in the name of goodness. Like the characters of Kafka, who greatly influenced Roth, most of his men are so emotionally bound to those in power that even though they hate and fear them, they do in fact believe them to be right, and thus, good. It is through this quality of appearing "good" that the woman obtains her power. As one of Roth's most penetrating critics, Theodore Solotaroff, points out, Roth is preoccupied with a woman's power over a man "by a kind of moral one-upmanship that attaches his virtue, indeed his humanity, to his willingness to satisfy her needs, however unending or corrupt these may be."[1]

Portnoy's Complaint gives the super caricature of the Jewish mother, perhaps of all mothers. This is the home-life version of the ball-breaker, who is not unlike the middle-aged castrators of

1. "Fiction," *Esquire*, 78 (Oct. 1972), 82.

James Purdy and the epitome of female monsters as the career woman, Nurse Ratched. All the ugliness of the type gushes forth with Mrs. Portnoy, all from her sick son Alexander's point of view. There is clearly enough power in Roth's development of this type to indicate more than a mere literary interest in it. But through the detachment of caricature, the method of the fabulators, and the technique of allowing the analysand the couch to himself for the entire course of the book, a one-sided and prejudiced treatment of the subject of mother is granted. The revealing last line of the novel, which is the psychiatrist Dr. Spielman's only comment—" 'Now vee may perhaps to begin. Yes?' "[2]—calls for a more complete accounting, which would necessitate a modified version of mother that is not as simplified as the stereotype which has guided Portnoy's complaint.

We realize early in his soliloquy that Portnoy has never considered the possible reasons for his mother's obsession with perfecting and possessing him. If he has been used by his mother, at this point he is no less guilty of using her as the incorporation of all that is distastefully Jewish as well as everything that is wrong with him. As Portnoy the child imagined her incapable of doing wrong, Portnoy the obsessed adult sees her incapable of doing anything right. The safe distancing of Mother Portnoy in caricature can enlist the unqualified outrage of Jew and goy alike for all wrongs committed by mothers, without the problem of considering her point of view. The caricature clarifies and thoroughly denigrates, while freeing the reader from any conflicting sympathies that might occur had she been given a more realistic treatment. The obviousness of the satire from an author who is not everywhere heavy-handed indicates Roth's awareness of the means by which such stereotypes are projected, in this case through the eyes of the self-pitying son. And while Roth treats his comic version of woman glibly and with relief, the bitch type represents a deeply felt view of women's power, which is a major concern of the two long non-comic novels preceding the story of Mrs. Portnoy.

In parodying the *Reader's Digest*'s idea of "The Most Unfor-

2. Philip Roth, *Portnoy's Complaint* (New York: Bantam Books, 1970), p. 309. Further page references to this edition are included in the text.

gettable Character I've Met," *Portnoy's Complaint* reminds us how closely most mothers fit such a description, which is particularly ironic given the complexes Roth deals with. But by reducing mother to comic imbecility one may strike back at her for being the pervasive, guilt-producing force that she is. A comic treatment of the Oedipal obsession (suggested to Roth by Kafka's use of the absurd) is both refreshing and effective for Alexander Portnoy and for Roth, giving the appearance, through distance and exaggeration, of a control over a problem that otherwise might be overwhelming. Only through caricature, however, is Roth able to undermine the concept of woman's power.

Portnoy's sense of his mother's omnipotence is a first sign of his own limited view, an understandable one for the inexperienced child judging his parent. All of his female teachers and all women of authority resemble his mother; from that womb he came, and to it he must return. After a time of escape with his fantasy woman, the Monkey, her sexual indulgences no longer intrigue him. Completing a cycle of escape through other types of women, he returns to his true obsession in the form of Naomi, the Jewish Pumpkin, who resembles his mother and accordingly renders him impotent. All things reside in mother, who can do anything— she, with the power to suspend peaches in jello and foretell a rainstorm by one drop on the window!

The link between mother's power and her goodness, which becomes the downfall of a Portnoy, is created in no subtle way by Sophie Portnoy. Obvious as her methods are, the boy is too much the believer to detect any fallacy in her thinking. She invests her son with the idea that she is "too good," a term which becomes synonymous with the concept of mother and her authority. "It was my mother who could accomplish anything, who herself had to admit that it might even be that she was actually too good" (10). Her goodness manifests itself in her constant concern for others (primarily her son) and in her capacity for self-sacrifice, so righteously based on holy doctrine. The mother becomes the saint, with her perversion of selflessness and suffering the claim to her child's devotion and the means by which she develops his guilt. Portnoy's mother is so good that she even befriends the old Negro woman who works for her. Roth's facile use of this treatment of the Negro is one of his least effective touches, one which might once have been clever but which in a contemporary reading falls flat. Nor are other specific ways in which Mrs. Portnoy's narrow, obsessive soul manifests itself either original or of particular fascination. It is her cumulative effect as an absolute power and source of goodness in Portnoy's eyes that is her significance. The caricature, like Portnoy's obsession, is shown through necessarily repetitious effects rather than through surprising and unique ones. This is the limitation not only of Mrs. Portnoy but of her son, and of the novel that relates his monotonous complaint.

Not only is Sophie Portnoy good, or "too good," as she says, but "she alone is good" (12). Only she clears the weeds from the graves of her relatives; only she is a good sport when losing at Mah-Jongg. Her very being encompasses a particular definition of *good*. For the boy, who has not discovered the perversion in his mother's use of this term, he continues, no doubt in great confusion, to wonder at the meaning of such goodness. He even maintains her integrity after she holds a knife over him (the castrator at work) to persuade him to eat. And for all his later attempts to dispel his early myth, no analyst can untie for him the mother-power-goodness construct.

The reversal to masturbation, that special secret kept from Portnoy's mother (despite her attempts to get at the doings behind the bathroom door), is a triumph against her obsessive demands that he be a good little boy. The act satisfies the sexual urges she would never allow him to experience in a normal heterosexual way, and the form of satisfaction is itself a further taboo. The pornography of these activities is an exotic way of disobeying mother and doing so in her near presence, adding further titillation to the excitement Portnoy finds in masturbation. The novel's first few pages are hilarious until the act, like any obsession, becomes monotonous. Unlike most of his contemporaries, obsessed with varieties of heterosexual sex, Roth persists with onanism even in his non-comic novels. This perfectly appropriate subject of *Portnoy's Complaint* is a less appropriate activity for the cerebral, dutiful Paul Herz of *Letting Go*, who has no desire to make love to his wife or to other women, but who reverts to masturbation as a way of demonstrating his manhood.

If all that is good is Jewish, and all that is bad goyish, Portnoy's rebellion seeks the opposite of his virtuous mother in his fantasy of the deliciously wicked *shikse*. His mother might control him, but he will control this dream woman, the very embodiment of America, "a *shikse* nestling under your arm whispering love love love love love!" (165). Gone are the heavy concerns, the goodness and the guilt, the power which Portnoy and other Roth protagonists associate with "character." "But who wants character?" Portnoy asks. "I want Thereal McCoy! . . .—Miss America . . . —this perfect, perfect-stranger, who is as smooth and shiny and cool as custard" (170). But simple bliss is not for Portnoy even when he actually meets his fantasy woman, since he is doomed to deny easy satisfactions. With his true passions linked to mother there is little left for anyone like the Monkey, whom he callously abandons with a cheerful goodbye as she prepares to leap from a hotel room in Athens.

The Monkey is a sometimes humorous caricature of Portnoy's "most lascivious adolescent dreams" (118), an amazing creature who initiates sexual perversions which equal Portnoy's own fantasies. She is never made believable, nor is she meant to be, although she shares with Roth's serious heroines an inclination to insanity and suicide, brought on by the sense of a personal void, which she in her quaint fashion attempts to fill with extravagant sexual pursuits.

The Monkey's effect is quite unlike that of the women who exert the real power in Roth's works and who are his central figures, however. For one thing, Portnoy, and any other observer of this phenomenal girl, can easily see into her wild obsessions and eventually steer clear of them. Portnoy understands her perversions because they are his own, and he scoffs at the idea of ever marrying such a person and having to pull her up from degradation. It is exactly the opposite quality—a stern moral posture (or what appears to be that)—which truly binds the Roth male to a woman, offering him the hope of being lifted from his own mire of corruption back to the blessed status of the good boy. Quite as obvious as the Monkey's perversions is her low mentality, something the Roth hero would never accept in a wife. Such a liability is made painfully clear when the Monkey is seen in social situations, such as the Mayor's party, which are so important to the conventional Portnoy. There is no way that this hillbilly from West Virginia can ever make Portnoy proud. She is "ineducable and beyond reclamation" (232), evidenced to Portnoy by her speech, her thoroughly visceral reaction to all experience, and finally by her handwriting and the illiterate note to her cleaning lady which is the decisive touch to this portrait of coarseness.

Roth's writing demonstrates a desire that his characters retain some form of the awe and dignity that inspired the Jew of the past, and the Monkey quite clearly has no capacity for refinement or noble aspirations. Public figures who represent only a slick and immoral approach to life particularly offend Roth, who writes in disgust of the way Eisenhower prayed every night, as related by Mrs. Eisenhower: " 'I muffed a few,' " he would say, and then, turning the failures over to God, he would roll on his side and sleep.[3] The posture of talking to God as one would to a valet represents a sacrilege Roth deplores and which is related to the way his characters seek something almost divine in women. Lucy Nelson's bitchery may be the focus of attack in *When She Was Good*, but Roth does sympathize with her outrage against the vapidity of her surroundings, which offer so little color and sense of wonder. Although Roth's writing often takes the form of tedious obsessions and vulgarities, he never allows a reconciliation with the banalities which are his subject.

If *Portnoy's Complaint* is the embodiment in caricature of Roth's realized obsession with women's power, his earlier books, *Letting Go* and *When She Was Good*, are the dramatization of this concern in a more realistic and complete way. Neither of the two heroines of the books is Jewish, and it is to the author's credit as one of our most versatile writers that he accurately depicts the rhythms of their dialogue and the details of their surroundings, which are so far from his native, urban, Jewish milieu. He does not attempt to show that all women are shrewish manipulators, as these two women are, but he does play up the fact that his conscience-stricken men seek out such women who will repeat the persecutions the men received from their mothers. Women

3. "Positive Thinking on Pennsylvania Avenue," *New Republic*, 136 (June 3, 1957), 11.

who are not dominating do populate Roth's world, but they never hold the interest of the author, his male protagonists, or the reader. Few of them are as colorful as the Monkey, and none of them are as convincingly developed as Libby Herz and Lucy Nelson.

Libby, wife of Paul Herz in *Letting Go*, holds a special appeal for Gabe Wallach, the narrator and central character of this long account of his interaction with the painful Herz marriage. Many readers of the novel justifiably question what the two men both see in Libby. As Gabe relates, "My first impression of her had been clear and sharp: profession—student; inclinations—neurotic. She moved jerkily and had the high black stockings and the underfed look. She was thin, dark, intense, and I could not imagine that she had ever once gotten anything but pain from entering a room full of people."[4] Nothing in this portrait indicates Libby's great appeal, and the impression of her throughout the novel does not change basically from this first account. *Letting Go* is not a love story, although it is very much a story of combinations of men and women, incapable of love, whose various obsessions draw them destructively together. Paul and Libby often refer to their "love" for each other, but their life together is a constant, nagging battle, fed by her gnawing lack of purpose and his obsession with duty. Even making love to her is a burdensome task for him. (For all Roth's pornography his men are squeamish about heterosexual lovemaking.) When Gabe discovers Libby's distress because her husband so seldom makes love to her (the pretext for his abstinence is to avoid the expense of a pregnancy), Gabe weakens, just once, and kisses her. But no sexual attachment follows, which is rare considering the ease with which couples in most contemporary fiction commit their adulteries. Gabe is bound to Libby throughout this long story, but it is with a peculiar psychological, not a sexual, dependence.

Perhaps one reason why many readers have questioned the likelihood that both of these men would be attracted to Libby is that sexual attraction, which we have come to accept as inevitably leading to culmination in our fiction, is not the primary source

4. Philip Roth, *Letting Go* (New York: Bantam Books, 1970), p. 6. Further page references to this edition are included in the text.

of her power over them. In fact, most often for Roth's people it is because of men's reluctance that liaisons do not culminate sexually. Libby desperately wants her husband to make love to her, and there is a good chance that she would sleep with Gabe if he urged her to. But both men are drawn to her for something else—a tense, demanding quality that gives her power but which also makes her vulnerable. She may be a woman of deep character whose potential is frustrated by her limited life. On the other hand, perhaps she shows only a surface promise of depth and is frantically vacant within. The men see her as the former, she herself as the latter.

The clue to Libby is in the first descriptive word Gabe applies to her, *neurotic*. She is by no means an unintelligent or an insensitive woman, and her comments regarding James's *Portrait of a Lady*, which is the issue of the first few pages of *Letting Go*, reveal a perception finer than Gabe's. Her husband Paul, who will teach the novel, has not even read it yet, and it is difficult to imagine a particularly perceptive reading coming from him, although Libby is certain that his intellect is far superior to hers. Libby's dismay at Isabel Archer's marriage to Osmond is one way of announcing her own marital problems, although as Roth's work dramatizes, modeled on James's *Portrait*, there is no simple thing one wants or gets from marriage. Gabe realizes, "Perhaps the truth was that Libby was a girl with desires *nobody* could satisfy; perhaps they weren't even 'desires' but the manifestations of some cellular disorder, some physiochemical imbalance that fated her to a life of agonized yearning in our particular world of flora and fauna, amongst our breed of humanity" (239). While he senses these qualities in her and is harshly critical, Gabe is attracted to her despite (or perhaps because of) them, drawn beyond his will to just such neuroticism as hers.

Paul's Uncle Asher has warned him that Jewish girls devour, but Libby, a Catholic, proves to be as devouring as any of them. The author frees himself of any Jewish stereotype in the creation of *shikse* bitches, but it is likely that they retain something of a Jewish quality that Asher refers to. Roth clearly despises the domination of women, but he is so well aware of this attitude, and of the weaknesses of men which make such domination possible, that the interactions of his men and women characters are truly convincing. Roth's women are by no means inferior in stature to his men, but they are less likeable. In Paul Herz's obsession with duty to his wife he is stiffly aloof, but as other of Roth's husbands, vulnerable and somewhat lovable all the same. In this the lines are drawn between Roth's men and his women, who are distasteful to most readers but who are loved by his men. Although Gabe later modifies his opinion, his first view of the Herz marriage is that "the impossible one to live with . . . was clearly the wife" (15). The feeling throughout the novel is that it is she who brings about the unhappiness of the marriage.

The theme of woman as the source of unhappiness in marriage is announced in the opening pages of the novel with a letter from Gabe Wallach's mother, written as she was dying: "Whatever unhappiness has been in our family springs from me. Please don't blame it on your father however I may have encouraged you over the years. Since I was a little girl I always wanted to be Very Decent to People. . . . I was always doing things for another's good. The rest of my life I could push and pull at people with a clear conscience" (2). This is an incredible statement. What woman on her deathbed or at any other time would admit to this crime, so indefinable that it need never be confessed either to herself or to others? But of course the "confession" is ironically balanced by Mrs. Wallach's reminder that what she did resulted only from her motive of doing good. To whatever degree Roth's heroines may be responsible for causing unhappiness, they are almost never dissociated with the concept of good.

Mrs. Wallach's letter reveals the fantasy of a Portnoy and perhaps of other Roth characters—the desire that mother (or her replacement) take the responsibility for their unhappiness. Roth is too perceptive an author to suggest any simple placing of blame for human misery any more than he suggests that Portnoy's complaint gives a complete picture of Mrs. Portnoy. His characters believe what they want to believe. It is peculiar that Gabe Wallach, ostensibly a perceptive intellectual and our enlightened narrator (perhaps an unreliable one), should never have observed any pattern of power in his own mother when he sees it so clearly in Libby. Although he appears more sophisticated than Paul and is surely more disciplined than Portnoy, like them he is obsessed with the notion of the woman as a figure of power and goodness. Thus, there is no sign that he takes his mother's confession seriously.

Libby, likewise, never loses the aura of her superior worth in the eyes of her husband, regardless of what she does. Even though Paul doubts his own manliness when he marries her, and Gabe sees him looking "as shabby and defeated as a man can who has been made a fool of by his wife" (17), neither of them is quite capable of seeing her as other than good. Nor can they do enough for her. In a perverted form of self-sacrifice Gabe goes through a torturous process to secure a baby for Libby. And among other things, Paul can never make enough money to satisfy her obsession to buy. On one occasion he comes home with a slashed hand, and her first reaction is to ask only if he was docked his afternoon's pay. Libby takes an office job for a day or so, but the sight of her over a typewriter is so pathetic to her husband and to Gabe that it seems quite out of the question for her to work.

The traditional duties of a man weigh heavily upon Paul, who is pathetically, and predictably, no freer when he leaves Libby to go to New York than he was with her, being hopelessly and unhappily bound. Even Libby's inability to have a child (due to a kidney ailment) is somehow flung back at him as his failure, perhaps for not making love to her oftener. Libby accentuates Paul's sense of guilt, but it is difficult to imagine his being much happier with anyone else. She is quite necessary to him, in great part as a focus for his unhappiness. Gabe once described him as a person who "actually found pleasure in saying to the world: Woe is me" (26).

There is more than one opportunity in *Letting Go* for Gabe to let go of his attraction for this neurotic girl who holds him with the same power she holds her husband. Gabe attracts women with no trouble, the first of these being a student named Margie who insists on moving in with him after their first night together. Like Paul, who was hastened into marriage by Libby's demands, the good-natured but weak Gabe offers no resistance, and Margie moves in with all her trappings. While she is ill he is reduced to errand boy, stalking the supermarket to collect supplies for her.

He soon realizes how little difference it makes whether or not she is sick, however, and gathers the nerve to escape "this sweet empty-headed girl" (28), who is not powerful enough to dominate him. His allegiance once again turns to the neurotic Libby.

Gabe's most promising alliance is with Martha Regenhart, a divorcée with two children, among whose squalor an almost successful love affair takes place. Martha is the sanest and the sloppiest person in the novel, capable of love, and healthy-minded particularly in contrast to the other characters. Her lack of self-consciousness is refreshing in view of the tedious vanities of the unhappy trio, each with a crippling sense of his own problems. Paul, Libby, and Gabe are more intelligent and literate than Martha is, but there is a sterility in the men's studies as there is in their lives. For all three of them existence is unduly grim. Martha is much the better for being less cerebral than they, but we know from her earthy simplicity that Gabe will not be attracted to her for long. Perhaps he is incapable of involvement to the point of marriage, but if he were to marry, the girl would probably be someone more like Libby. His rationale for breaking with Martha is epitomized in the way he sees her medicine cabinet, which is such a wreck he considers the perpetrator of it insane. "I flung open the medicine chest to be confronted again by that skull and crossbones. Big as life it said: DANGER. But *she* didn't seem to know there were children in the house! *She* apparently didn't read in the papers about all the poisoned kids! A mess! An unexcusable mess!" (281). Gabe, of course, is not as worried about the danger to the children as he is about the threat of involvement to himself.

Martha is what the other women in *Letting Go* are not: motherly, frowzy, earthy, and large. Gabe sarcastically alludes to her size: " 'It's great you're five nine, Martha, it's perfect you're hefty. The bigger they are the better they can enjoy the fall' " (385). Her fleshiness is the too obvious reminder to him of the sexual nature of their union. But it is not the sexual bond or a sexual trap that is the nemesis for Roth's men. They soon weary of the mere sex object. Their lives might be easier with the simpler, more physical women, but they always turn back to the complicated, suffering ones whose very misery suggests something

noble. Such women are seen as saviors who in turn must be protected and labored for. The affection and devotion of Roth's
protagonists appear to be proportional to the demands of the
woman, and since Libby's demands are almost impossible to fulfill she continues to exert a fascination for both her husband and
Gabe. They strain themselves with efforts for her as if in doing
so they might free themselves of the guilt and coldness which
characterize them both.

Martha makes her demands as well, but they are in more
concrete and realizable terms: she wants Gabe to pay the rent,
buy the food, and stay with her, marry her. Much has been said
in praise of Martha, but it is more by contrast with Libby that
her humanity appears in so favorable a light than that her actions
are particularly noteworthy. She hassles Gabe about money, about
the Herzes, about her children, and soon their affair takes on the
sordid and monotonous quality of the Herzes' continuous arguments, in a book which excels in the lifelike dialogue of people
who repeat their tedious quarrels for a lifetime. But there are
choices offered to all of the main characters—if the story is pat-
terned on James there must be—and especially with Gabe we
are kept wondering if or how he will let go of his old ways and
take hold of something new. The various women in his life offer
choices in the same way Isabel Archer's suitors offer different
lives for her. But instead of choosing one of them, Gabe remains
a Lambert Strether, observing and helping others to fulfill their
lives in preference to dealing with his own.

In light of the abuses of parenthood that abound in *Letting Go*,
Martha's generous affection for her children is particularly meaningful. " 'I love those kids. I'm glad I've got them, overwhelmingly
glad. I work nights and I hate it—you don't *know* how I hate it.
But I'm glad I've got those kids. They're *something*, damn it' "
(321). Martha's honorable motherhood weakens, however. Apparently as a way of favoring the relationship with Gabe, she
eventually allows the children she so ardently cares for to go with
her former husband, a man she describes as crude and cruel, an
unlikely replacement to offer the children a good home. And it
follows that after the children have moved in with him a tragic
accident takes the younger child's life, an act which serves as a

punishment to Martha for relinquishing her responsibility as a parent. The sacrifice of her children is further a foolish move for Martha because they were never the source of her problems with Gabe in the first place. In fact, he rather admired the way she handled them. Until she gives up her children, Martha is the only exemplary parent in a novel which has for a main concern the abuses of parenthood. But no longer the fully dedicated mother, Martha realizes that she has lost Gabe's respect without increasing her chances of marrying him. He is never explicit about his dwindling interest in her, but she suspects it is related to his idea of a woman's nobility, and she has now lost hers. " 'You don't feel the same, Gabe. I think you liked me noble better' " (465–66).

Roth attempts to create in Martha Regenhart the kind of woman, in contrast to Libby, whom both his protagonist and the reader will like and admire. She is warmer, more spontaneous, and more loving than anyone in the book. But Roth betrays his own distaste for her and his preference for more neurotic but intelligent women. The statement by Paul's Uncle Asher that he prefers women who are uncluttered by education, keeping "the thing in a pure state" (429), parodies a kind of purity which holds no charm for Roth. Martha embodies such an uninteresting purity. Perhaps she is not bright enough, too big, or too vulgar. Roth shows keen attention to the details of dress, that shell of a person which, as one James character points out, is indeed an essential part of the human being. Roth's men want women to be ladies, and they grimace at the discrepancies in a woman's style of dress and manner of speaking which indicate more than a surface disarray. This kind of clutter *is* significantly damning. Nothing about Martha disturbs Gabe so much as the way she dresses when the Herzes come to dinner: "When she rushed past me to answer the knock at the front door, it was not a woman that moved by but a circus—a burst of color and a clattering of ornaments" (308). Like her sloppy medicine cabinet, Martha is messy in a way that cannot be dismissed. Even her natural blond hair let loose and floating below her waist is repellent to Gabe, who prefers Libby's stark hairdo, pulled tightly back. Whether the appeal is to propriety, dignity, or discipline, the neurotic woman, who is neater and more delicate physically, is the one who holds the limelight. Just as Martha could not be at the center of a James novel, she cannot be a focal character for Roth, who tries to make her likeable but does not succeed.

Gabe's obsessive efforts to help the Herzes adopt a child are a way of projecting the worthiness of motherhood onto Libby as well as being an eerie projection of his own thwarted sense of family. His bizarre pursuit of the baby is merely melodramatic if seen only as an attempt to bring about the adoption for the sake of his friends. But when seen as a form of do-gooding to ease his own conscience and as a projection of a halo for Libby as a mother, the frantic chase to the child's home on New Year's Eve becomes a more symbolic quest. (Presenting Libby with a child may also be a symbolic form of the adultery that never took place.)

Motherhood when viewed from Libby's point of view is an obsession of another sort, a primarily materialistic one. It is no loss to her that she is advised not to attempt a second pregnancy (she had an abortion early in her marriage), for she is not willing to take that kind of a risk to become a mother. However, she would gladly purchase a child and possess it. Such a concept further defines Libby as less than the "good" woman her men imagine her to be. Nor is she "good" if the term has anything to do with a benevolent concern for other people; by her own admission, "out of the clear blue sky she began to hate people" (325).

The women in *Letting Go* all let go of their children: Libby through abortion, Martha when she turns her children over to their father, and Theresa Haug, who gives her child up for adoption by the Herzes. The reasons for abdication of motherhood are different in each case, but they add up to a general malaise affecting the bond between parent and child. Early in the novel distortions of this bond are shown in the relationships of the three main characters with their parents: Paul visits his dying father, who has never forgiven him for marrying Libby, and is so disgusted by the man that he almost stays away from his funeral; Libby's parents have blotted her name out of the family because of the marriage, a fact announced to her in a chilling letter of denunciation; and Gabe's father clings to his son, compulsively nagging at him to come home for visits. Mr. Wallach finally decides to marry a gaudy woman named Fay Silberman, a doomed alliance from its beginning, sheerly as a compensation for his not having Gabe nearby. Parents and children infect each others' lives, but Roth's primary attack is aimed at parents for the suffering they inflict. And Libby's destructive powers in marriage are a sign of her destructive potential as a parent.

Roth is equally adept at relating the states of mind of his male and his female characters. While at times we see his image of women only as his own fantasy or that of his characters, he keeps us aware that it is just that, and he has enough concern for his women to examine their minds for a necessarily different viewpoint. Gabe, as he narrates the story, sympathizes first with Paul and then with Libby. Roth takes us into the daily life of a woman alone at home—what she thinks about and what she does while her husband is at work. Most housewives in literature are notoriously bored, and few of them must any longer spend the day doing housework. When the husband goes the wife is faced with a desperate vacancy, and the activities she manufactures are usually meaningless repetitions to kill time until her husband returns. One favorite pastime is the shopping trip. The neurotic Libby, miserable as a housewife, is plagued by her craving for expensive things she cannot afford. After her husband leaves she nervously recites to herself, *"But I am sweet and good. I deserve as much as anybody—"* (355), which is what her husband believes her to be and what she imagines she should be, but far from what her feelings tell her she is. With all of the hours of the morning lying ahead, should she get dressed? Make the bed? What can she do after that? She lies down and hides her head in the pillowcase, one of the many suicidal impulses of the idle housewife.

Libby does not generally lack insight, but she convinces herself of an inferiority to her husband, the scholar and writer of the family. She only dabbles at bad poetry. In such a view of a woman's concept of herself Roth does not necessarily project a desire that women be incompetent but a realistic and sympathetic view of their actual *sense* of incompetency, particularly as they measure themselves in relation to the activities of men. Libby is awed by her hard-working husband (although she is oblivious to his lack of intellectual passion for his studies). Their days always begin with the important announcement that he must be off to his job. And what is she going to do? Paul even fixes her breakfast in his zealous attempts at duty, and as Libby sees her plate laid out in the morning (she makes no attempt to fix breakfast herself), she feels more useless than ever. It does not offend her that Paul takes over the duties usually expected of the wife, for she has no feeling for her role as homemaker. She must force herself to prepare dinner as if it were a major hardship; her thin little hands grating potatoes make a sad sight indeed. She says to her husband, " 'I don't want to stay at home! What's at home? What's at home but a lot of crappy furniture! . . . Oh I want a baby or something . . . a dog or a TV. Paulie, I can't do anything' " (246). The same sentiment is reflected in her reply to the question asked her by the representative from the adoption agency, what does she do?: " 'I don't do anything' " (346), the usual dismal comment of women. Roth is unusually sensitive to this question put to a woman and of the demeaning answer. The scenes with Libby at home during the day, doing nothing, are among the most painful and effective moments of this or any other recent novel that deals with the consciousness of a woman.

With the dread empty hours on her hands Libby looks forward to her appointment with a psychiatrist. After a traumatic afternoon in his office, she is hysterical by the time her husband comes home in the evening. We hear very little about his day, but we know how bad hers has been. Roth does not suggest that Libby or anyone else escape through a job any more than he suggests simple answers to other complex problems, but his documentation of what happens to a high-strung, intelligent woman who remains idle certainly suggests that some occupation is in order. While the adoption of a child for Libby is a central issue of the novel, it is obviously only an illusion of the three main characters that this or any other form of parenthood will be a cure for her despair. Libby is delighted when she finally gets a baby, but her pleasure is demonstrated in an abnormal obsession with the child —too much running to the baby's room to see if she is still there, with the same brittle tension that is her reaction to other things. Since the truest satisfaction in Libby's life comes from owning things, she would be better off making money than raising chil-

dren. But Roth, the humanist, could hardly suggest this. Becoming
a mother is surely the conventional answer to what Libby might
do with her life, but it does not represent a choice that has anything to do with her understanding of or suitability for motherhood.

The main characters in *Letting Go* are all locked in their own
obsessions, but Libby's misery is shown the most vividly. Her
husband and Gabe are both involved in work they presumably
have chosen for certain expected satisfactions, although these are
never demonstrated. Paul at least has the pride of doing his duty
by his wife, and if that does not bring pleasure, he never expected
that it would. Gabe has a life free of the painful marriages he
sees around him and is in demand as a lover and as a friend. But
Libby is narrowed into a style of life that offers nothing particularly suited to her, except perhaps that it gives her a position of
some power over her husband. Her admiration of him, however,
makes her despise herself by comparison. With little to do all
day but contemplate her own condition, she sinks toward madness. She tells the psychiatrist she is "nuts" and demonstrates it
by screaming that she will have only him as her analyst, even
though she cannot pay. Eventually she attempts suicide.

In showing the neuroticism that festers in idleness, particularly
as Libby feels increasingly inferior to the men around her and
lashes out more spitefully, Roth takes a closer look at the *creation*
of the bitch than most writers do, those who merely show her
devastating effects on others. Readers who know only of Roth's
caricature of Mrs. Portnoy, where no insight into her is given
because her son is so thoroughly obsessed with his own problems,
should look at *Letting Go* to see that he does attempt to get at
causes and complexities of the manipulating woman. It makes
Libby no less a shrew if we learn how she came to be one, but
Roth, while he exploits the type, at least makes us aware that
there are processes which lead to her condition.

Gabe's mother was not unlike Libby, someone difficult to live
with and impossible for her husband to know: "Anna had been
more than he could handle or understand, but he had asked her
to marry him; maybe that was *why* he had asked her. He did not
know. He had thought at the time and he thought still that he had

loved Anna" (503). The pattern of female dominance changes little from one generation to the next; Libby carries on with the same mysterious power that Anna possessed. And as a sign that the future is to repeat a similar process, Martha Regenhart's seven-year-old daughter Cynthia pushes her brother to his death from the top bunk of their bed, where he has crawled in with her. With more than a sexual innuendo the incident suggests women's power to effect men's ultimate destruction. Surprisingly, considering the constant tensions seen here between men and women, sexual problems are only secondary. Even with Paul and Libby, the fact that he rarely makes love to her is not the source of their arguments. In fact, Roth is unique among current writers for giving so little time, in his non-comic works, to explicit scenes of lovemaking. His heroes are not so easily satisfied. They seek the domination of women, which eventually may lead to total destruction as it does for Martha's unassuming young son. No one casts the slightest suspicion on Cynthia for the "accident"; they sympathize with her for having gone through such a traumatic event. After all, how could a little girl be anything but good?

When She Was Good presents the epitome of female self-righteousness in Lucy Nelson, a product of Liberty Center, a small town in the Midwest. This novel also emphasizes a noticeable contrast between leading male and female figures in the fiction of the sixties: the men are usually gentler, weaker, and more sensitive, while the women are rigid and dominating. As with Paul's attitude toward his wife Libby, Roy Bassart sees Lucy as "good" no matter what she does or how much he suffers because of her. Although he finally denounces her, he makes his statement from a distance, impulsively, and we rather expect to see him fall back into his irrational belief in her goodness. Roy may be less masochistic than his counterpart Paul Herz, for he does enjoy his pleasures, but both men have a weakness for the same kind of woman.

The lightness signified in Lucy's name, and she is a blonde, is translated in Roy's initial concept of her to the title of "Angel." He meets her as a friend of his cousin Ellie, and drawn to the "character" in her face he immediately offers to take her picture. Roy could find more perfect faces for his pictures any time, those with the look of fashion models, but typically of the Roth male he has little interest in shallow, pretty girls. He sees courage and strength in Lucy, especially in her suffering, knowing like everyone else in town of her drunken father and of how she daringly took steps against him. Above all, he is convinced of her worthiness. This image of Lucy is set immediately as Roy meets her (before she has talked to him), idealized by his concept of woman as angel, an image he joyfully imagines he can capture in a photograph. Under the effect of this illusion of Lucy as angel he is oblivious to the nastiness she soon displays. When he playfully asks her if she wants her picture taken she abrasively blurts out *no*, a prophetic reaction to him. Moments later she glares at him: " 'Just who do you think you're talking to, you!' "[5] To anyone but this idealistic man she is no angel.

Lucy's obsession with her own dignity is emphasized by shame of her family, as well as by a belief that women are superior to men (although she is furious that men will not take their place as *men* and be stronger). Her father's drunken uses of her mother set a pattern she refuses to forget, with the absolute rigidity that comes to characterize her. At the age of fifteen she gets the chance she has wanted, and when her father comes home drunk one night and for no apparent reason dumps his wife's Epsom salts on the floor, Lucy calls the police and has him put in jail, an act that immortalizes her. The ostensible cause of Lucy's fury is her mother's passive suffering, but she thrives on a reservoir of hatred for all that is weak and incompetent, especially in men. In marrying Roy Bassart, a kind and dreamy boy, she is in a position to demonstrate fully her scorn of such weakness.

One criticism of Roth's characterization of Lucy is that he gives little hint as to the sources of her viciousness. Life is lackluster for all of these midwesterners. Why then is it that Lucy is filled with so much more hatred than anyone else? But if the author cannot fully know the source of her anger, that does not negate his portrayal of it. After all, can we ever know what in nature makes these hard hearts? Many male writers give amazingly effective portraits of women, with a credibility that admits a lack

5. Philip Roth, *When She Was Good* (New York: Bantam Books, 1970), p. 99. Further page references to this edition are included in the text.

of comprehension. Lucy's hostility is not entirely inexplicable, however. Certainly ambition with no adequate outlet has something to do with it. Given the limitations of Liberty Center, and the author's antipathy to the tedium of a daily existence that offers no hint of enlightenment, Lucy's reactions are believable. In Liberty Center none of the inhabitants will advance far, but a significant and traditional difference separates Roy and Lucy: he is the male dreamer and she the female domestic. Dissatisfied with one job Roy moves on to another, always with the belief that he will find his true vocation. Lucy expects a great change to better her life as well, but she has in her past no concrete satisfactions to draw from and none to look forward to. Roy's dreams are of the past as well as of the future. After coming home from the army he strolls down to his old high school and relishes the memory of his days there. "For the hour of the day, for the time of his life, for this America where it is all peacefully and naturally happening, he feels an emotion at once so piercing and so buoyant it can only be described as love" (55).

In this thoroughly serious novel Roth intends no satire for such sentiments. This midwesterner of limited intellect but honestly developed emotions enjoys an intense pleasure that Roth grants is possible for a person of imagination, irrespective of region. (It is true that in addition to Roy's superior imagination he has also had more varied experiences than Lucy, at least making a brief escape from the town.) His dream of having a baby daughter is a delicious fantasy, although wholly unrelated to the pangs of childbirth and the effort of child-rearing, and is so lyrically communicated to Lucy that she is convinced to have another baby (as long as this time it is her decision). But she is not long to idealize the birth of a child. Her marriage came about because of an unwanted pregnancy, which meant the end of any fantasies for her.

In Lucy's case the forced marriage more than anything illustrates her particularly unbending and unimaginative nature. She refuses to have the abortion her father offers, preferring the unwanted marriage in which she can make Roy pay for what he has done. In this setting of the fifties with its courtship by car, that long and strenuous battle to get the girl to go "all the way," the threat of pregnancy is certainly of a magnitude not possible to the girl of the sixties with the Pill and other devices more readily available and acceptable. But the fact that Lucy is offered an abortion and refuses it begins to establish that she is more a victimizer than an innocent victim. Her desire for revenge along with the bleakness of her surroundings, to which she does not bring the imagination that enlivens her husband, work together to make her one of the super bitches of the sixties.

Lucy's problems are very much crystallized in her concept of the woman as a martyr-saint. She despises her mother's passive suffering, but her view of life rests upon the idea that men are responsible for women's misery and must be made to pay. Always with a lust for power, but with no specific course for her energies after her vague dream of college is abandoned for marriage, Lucy ironically magnifies in herself the very long-suffering quality she loathes in her mother. And her unsatisfied ambition, for want of a more spectacular focus, gradually centers into a supreme hostility for Liberty Center and its people. Her husband, who is at home there, never experiences her kind of ambition; his dreams are realizable within the realm of this small town. But the more Lucy tries to adjust to her occupation as a wife there, the more she detests it and sees herself as the martyr in a horrible system where she is fated to be a self-sacrificing domestic in a dull part of the world. Her attempts to live out this role righteously, for the sake of moral superiority if not for satisfaction (and Roth allows her no other possibilities), only increase her frustration and suggest an eventual breakdown.

In the first weeks of her marriage Lucy finds herself "trying with all her might to do what she was told" (193). She visits the in-laws "because that's what they were: she was his wife" (195). She detests everything about this pose of subservience, craving not only the subtle power of the wife who rules her husband (she has that) but a more outward form of control. Even full control over the movements of others does not satisfy; she is obsessed with changing people in ways that are impossible. As she imagines Roy to change she even believes that she might be in love with him— her creation, not the old Roy. Without even the flexibility to see that she has chosen an impossible task, she is frozen in her own hatred and frustration. The only thing left for her is to hound Roy to perform his duty, to be a father, which to her means a show of authority and responsibility having nothing to do with human warmth. She even at one time prays bitterly, *"Make him a father!"* (292).

As Lucy conceives of a rigid role for her husband as father, she also imagines an ultimately confining life for herself as wife. She must do whatever the dreary things are that a wife and a mother do, roles that she is surely to some degree forced into. From conception onward she is antagonistic toward the life growing inside her because she did not put it there. The diaphragm she wears after her child is born is much to her liking, for she now sees herself in control. Such a desire to regulate childbirth is viewed by most male writers, Roth among them, as a callous denial of what is natural and good. At the point in the novel where we learn of Lucy's birth control methods her selfishness is already so well established that her use of a contraceptive is merely given as one more vicious fact about her. Roth does not change his tone in dealing with this problem, offering no possibility that a woman might be justified in deciding not to have a child until she wants one. By the time Lucy has decided to have a second child and she makes the untimely announcement of her pregnancy, her marriage has already exploded.

Lucy is all icy letter of the law, without a drop of mercy. Her son before long senses the tyranny even her husband has not recognized and hides from her under the bathroom sink with a washrag over his face. Lucy contends that the child's withdrawal is the result of Roy's inconsistent behavior, his frequent "running off." But the only running off he does is to go to work or to make an occasional call on the parents and relatives Lucy resents, fearing that they will pull him away from her. As Roy grows more mellow, Lucy becomes more rigid. Because most of Roth's heroines do adhere to the letter of the law in marital fidelity, they can flaunt this virtue in view of the marital infidelities around them, as Lucy does when she learns of adultery in Roy's family. But while she lives out her fidelity to perfection, she does so with an incapacity for tenderness. It is by no means through restraint that someone like Lucy is sexually faithful in marriage. If a love affair were possible for her we might feel more hope for her soul. (She seems so frigid one wonders how she ever became involved with Roy in the first place.) But Lucy will never again slip from her high moral post and give up the claim to authority that it gives her.

Nowhere does Roth more effectively show the alienation and misery that come to those who opt for power instead of love than he does with Lucy. Even when she is most effective in exerting power over her husband and child she is intensely unhappy. Roy "had settled at last into the daily business, whether he liked it or not, of being a father and a husband and a man: her child had two parents to protect him, two parents each doing his job, and it was she alone who had made all this come about. This battle, too, she had fought and this battle, too, she had won, and yet it seemed that she had never in her life been miserable in the way that she was miserable now" (228).

Lucy ostensibly maintains her worthiness, protesting too much to convince us that even she continues to believe in it. Whether or not she is aware of the suffering she causes is never made clear, but if thoughts of it do occur to her she either rationalizes or represses them as effectively as she puts away the memory of her father. One wonders why she does not examine more closely the misery that persists even with her loyalty to family, hard work, and clean living habits, which if they do not bring the more spectacular victories of life do usually present quiet satisfactions. The question one wishes to ask of Lucy is, "Why doesn't your goodness bring you relief?"

At one time in her life Lucy turns to Catholicism, but not for solace or spiritual guidance, instead for the authoritarianism which her parents do not provide, the one thing she equates with parenthood. By such a standard, her parents simply do not act like parents. Lucy's attempts to adopt Catholicism reinforce her natural bent to moral severity only briefly, however. When she wants action to bring justice to her father, since Saint Teresa is no help, she immediately calls upon the law. She balks at confession, at the priests behind dark windows looking down on her. "I am their superior in every single way! People can call me all the names they want—I don't care! I have nothing to confess, because I am right and they are wrong and I will not be destroyed!" (84).

Lucy's frigid puritanism, which would appear mainly to be the product of the narrow morality of small-town midwestern thinking, is distinctly exhibited only in her case. If what she represents is an essence of place, it takes hold with none of the other citizens of Liberty Center as it does with her. Lucy's Grandfather Will, it is announced at the book's beginning, dreams only of being "civilized," which for him means a kindly, tolerant treatment of everyone, with large doses of forgiveness for the wayward son-in-law, Whitey Nelson. Neither his daughter Myra nor her husband is afflicted with a moral rigidity. Whitey feels guilty for not doing more for his wife, but not merely because it is his duty. In his weak way he loves her. Roy, a peacemaker, is as moderate as they are. His Uncle Julian, the worldiest of them all, is the spirit of goodness itself compared to Lucy's hardhearted purity. Only Willard's wife Berta is as cold and as sneering as Lucy.

Lucy uses her honesty as one of the most important signposts of her morality. In the way of many malicious people she makes it a tool of cruelty, attempting to breed hatred by using the truth to turn people against each other. In her last drama with Roy's family she renounces Julian for his adulteries in the presence of his wife and daughter. When she defends herself to the doctor who diagnoses her first pregnancy, " 'I'm not bad! . . . I'm good!' " (144), even her rationale is based on malice: " 'I hate liars and I don't lie' " (143). Her defensiveness and her later attack on one who commits adultery reflect her own guilt and self-loathing for participating in premarital sex, and forever afterward she is out to punish others for their sins as a way of expiating her own.

It takes Roy's uncle to summarize Lucy's qualities and to attempt to make Roy see them realistically. When she arrives in the middle of the night to demand her husband's return, Julian calls her " 'a little ball-breaker of a bitch . . . Saint Ball-Breaker' " (279). Only a violent occasion can convince Roy that this is true. He and Lucy spend the day with his relatives while he pleads with her to make up with them, at least for her son's sake. But Lucy remains unyielding and aloof, until later she ends their visit with deafening

screams in the car. That night, when the young son says he hates
his mother, Roy's breaking point is reached, and with the child
he goes back to Julian, the only person who can help him generate
the courage to leave Lucy. With the safety of distance Roy phones
his wife and delivers the epithets worthy of her. Referring to their
child's terror and to the odd habits that have come of it, Roy
turns the blame back on her: " 'Because of you!' she shouted.
'Not doing your job!' 'No, Lucy, because of *you!* Because of your
screaming, hateful, bossy, hateful, heartless guts! Because he
never wants to see your ugly, heartless face again, and neither do
I! Never!' " (268).

One wonders why Roy waits so long to say these things. But
even considering the provocation that leads to his denunciation,
he seems more to be mouthing his uncle's words than his own. If
Lucy had not run off as she does that night, to her death, he
would as likely fall back into his belief in her goodness as maintain
a hostility unnatural to him. On the very day before he denounces
her Roy had told Lucy how especially pretty she looked and that
she was superior to the attractive and richer Ellie. One of the
reasons he has always remained so convinced of Lucy's worthiness
is her freedom from materialism, a fatal error of judgment on
his part, for she uses her lack of wealth as she does everything
else—as a source of bitterness and as a means to power.

Lucy's father believes in her in the same way Roy does, although
she does what she can to destroy him. She is forever his dear
little girl. It is only kindness and a hope for a free life for her
that prompts him to offer her an abortion, without a word of
blame for an act that would have brought forth the rage of most
parents of her time. Perhaps punishment would earn Lucy's respect for her father, except that his life is too flawed to make his
authority count. Mr. Nelson believes in the goodness of his daughter as he believes in the goodness of his wife, who is genuinely
kind and loving. Ironically, Myra's worthiness has as unfortunate
an effect on him as Lucy's viciousness does, for it inspires violence
through the guilt it produces. His separation from his family may
be the most painful instance in the novel of the suffering which
results from the idea that women are worthier than men. Whitey's
days were always saddened by his difficulty in finding work during

the Depression, which he saw as the cause of his failure. But the image of himself as a casualty is reinforced, not counteracted, in his own home by his daughter and even by his wife. *When She Was Good* closes with his letter to Myra, to whom he has been writing from prison for years in secret so that Lucy would not find out, establishing his own sense of moral inferiority to women: "I said years ago that without you I would slide to hell in a hurry. I guess it was a prediction that came all too true" (308).

Lucy's husband might easily have become another Whitey Nelson, except that she would never have allowed him out of her sight, let alone have carried on a correspondence with a man who had abandoned his responsibilities. Her death by freezing (the body is recovered as rigid and intact as her life had been) symbolizes the inevitable result for one of her uncompromising nature. Insanity overcomes her in her final moments of terrified aloneness, and she runs from everyone out into the snow. Only her death makes it possible for Roy and her son Edward at last to be free of her domination.

In American literature Lucy Nelson ranks as one of the most monstrous bitches in a tradition made up of too many weak and bland women. She is trapped with a passion that devours, but it is a grand passion. Roth grants her near-tragic dimensions, which is in a perverse way a tribute to women, who in his fiction are superior to his men in their dramatic intensity. He never suggests that they lack intelligence or perception, as so many writers do, and he is painfully aware of their sense of limitations in a world which, as he shows it, offers few alternatives for them. Not all of his women are powerful beings, but only those who are ever truly capture his imagination and that of his heroes. Typical of the Roth position is the reaction of Roy to Lucy when he says that other girls are merely pretty, but "*her* face had character in it" (101).

And yet Roth's heroines do lack the quality that seems most important to him—genuine goodness. His capacity to produce primarily the negative as he develops his heroines' unyielding cruelty, however convincingly it is presented, not only results in a damning version of women but operates as a serious limitation to his art. If he were able to envision something of the noble in his powerful women, that which is so desired, he might create some magnificent characters. But the absence of generous qualities keeps them from eliciting our deepest sympathies. The extreme degree of their hardness at the same time makes it impossible to regard them as representative of the American woman. There is a certain clarity and obviousness in the inhumanity of Roth's women that makes them a less insidious influence than those created by the writer who projects a more likeable image but who humors his women along with affection and never allows them to think or to have real passions.

Roth never denies the masochism in his men that allies them with women who are destructive. It is directly through their selection of such women that we are led to his powerful heroines. The stress throughout Roth's work on the male concept of goodness is to some degree an attack upon a kind of idealism that ironically brings about disastrous results. But in another respect the same concept is the crucial area in dealing with Roth's vision of women, for he suggests that the "goodness" so desired in them is *altogether* a construct of the male mind. It is not unlikely that an author would place a diabolical woman at the center of his fiction for dramatic purposes. But because Roth shows his heroes specifically questing for goodness in women, and never finding it, he suggests that it is virtually impossible for it to exist there. Again and again—for Alexander Portnoy, for Gabe Wallach, for Paul Herz, for Roy Bassart—the idea of goodness is their creation (although only the reader is aware of this), something impossible actually to find in women.

If woman was at one time in literature designated as man's moral guardian, for Roth she no longer has even the possibility of containing that which is moral. There is no evidence that he wishes such a condition to be true, or that it benefits him as an artist to succumb to his obsession with women's inhumane power, which he quite honestly does, when he might fashion far more acceptable portraits of women. But instead, in his creation of heroines he projects his enormous rage and disappointment with womankind, writing with power and conviction, but as a man who rails at the world because he has never found in it a woman who is both strong and good.

three

John Updike's Love of "Dull Bovine Beauty"

John Updike the writer is an honorable man. His heroes return to their wives in the mellow atmosphere of appreciation and affection. His people do not kill or maim or intentionally cause pain. After a few rebellious starts they adjust and become at last like so many of us—comfortable. And for the woman who would be anything more than a vegetable-wife, this writer is the cunning enemy who would affectionately lull all womankind away from anything that has to do with life of the mind or self-respect or the joy of doing to a more appropriate and "natural" imbecility.

Perhaps Updike's horror of the powerful, manipulative mother turns him with an extra fondness to the docile woman who can be dominated (and slept with). Most of his women characters belong to one of these two opposing types, each deadly in its way. Some readers see in Updike's women instead a wife-whore division, but the wife and whore often resemble each other, wives acting the part of whores and whores who are considered as possible wives. The mature mother, however, exerting much the same influence as the dominant figures of Kesey and Roth, is an overpowering presence in contrast to the pliable wives and lovers. The difference for Updike's men is that they are much more successful at escaping the mother than are the inmates of the Big Nurse and the son of Mrs. Portnoy. The Oedipal problem—a mother is someone you cannot sleep with—for Updike seems to open the field to all others, a wide and delicious playground for his men. Hardly a woman here is without sexual appeal. And everything can be forgiven except frigidity.

The story "Flight" clearly distinguishes between mother, who is to be feared, and girl (or wife), who is to be embraced. When Allen Dow was eleven or twelve his mother climbed with him to the top of a hill, dug her fingers into his hair, and announced that he was going to fly away from the small town below them where everyone else would stay forever. Her genius is "to give the people closest to her mythic immensity,"[1] and her boy is to be a phoenix. When Allen takes a liking to the plump, kindly Molly Bingaman, Mrs. Dow hysterically resists this hindrance to his flight, proclaiming that to go with a little woman (she might as well have said any woman) "puts you too close to the ground" (51). Mrs. Dow's vulgar reference to "little hotpants" (55) as part of her general attempt to denigrate sexual love for Allen, however, is a failure. He now knows, after being booed at a debate and using Molly's shoulder for comfort, the marvelous possibility of burying a "humiliation in the body of a woman" (50), which is so revered by Updike's men. A woman's body may also be used for celebration. After winning a basketball game, Rabbit Angstrom makes love. When other skills are gone, the act of love is often the only means left by which to prove a victory.

The portrait of Mrs. Dow as the archetypal manipulative mother is complicated by her genuine desire for excellence, which, having no outlet in her own life, is channeled through Allen. Fortunately, since Mrs. Dow's dream is for the boy's flight, she allows Allen to escape. Giving up Molly, he admits defeat to his mother but is determined he shall never do so again. Updike's young men usually learn quite early in their lives the necessity of getting away from mother, both literally and, as best they can, emotionally. They do not generalize the fear of her into a fear of all women and find most others to be kind and comforting by comparison.

The women in "Flight" recall the account of the author's own life in "The Dogwood Tree: A Boyhood" when young John's mother forbids him to kiss his girl friend, which only increases his

1. John Updike, *Pigeon Feathers and Other Stories* (Greenwich, Conn.: Fawcett Publications, 1962), p. 47.

desire to do so. The fondness of this boy—"My love for that girl carries through all those elementary-school cloakrooms"[2]—is reflected in the creation of nearly all of Updike's male characters. What the young Allen Dow appreciates most about Molly is that she returns his love. She even comes running to him with her mother yelling at her to turn back. The Updike male is utterly vulnerable to such a woman's need for him, a dependence that is seen as unselfish and desirable. By contrast, the mother's need is always selfish. Mrs. Dow is indicted by omission as Allen reminisces that Molly "seems the one person who loved me without advantage" (54).

Updike's young mothers are not of the same ilk as their elder, more dominant counterparts. Instead of controlling their children, they neglect them. When Janice Angstrom drowns her infant daughter she does so through alcoholic clumsiness, not as a result of an attempt to manipulate, which is the core of motherhood in "Flight." Janice does not have the capacity to stand in as Harry's mother, or even to duplicate her own pettier but powerful mother. Updike does not so much suggest that mothers become more monstrous with age as that women of the past, holding more traditional values such as faith in religion and land, were stronger people. Irresponsibility and incompetence in motherhood replace the earlier ironhandedness, and while Updike shows weakness in his younger women, he is never so harsh on these gentle wives as he is on their powerful (and more interesting) mothers.

Chief among these is Mrs. Robinson in *Of the Farm*, probably Updike's most vivid woman and one of his best creations, a version of the mothers in "Flight," "Pigeon Feathers," and *Rabbit, Run*. Mrs. Robinson's verbal war with her daughter-in-law (by a second marriage) provides some of the most dramatic and realistic scenes in Updike's fiction. Joey Robinson dreads bringing his new wife to the farm, aware of the insidious power his mother is capable of exerting over both of them. Long before they get to her farmhouse Mrs. Robinson's image seems to spring out from it. Joey makes no attempt to rationalize what he considers his weakness

2. John Updike, *Assorted Prose* (Greenwich, Conn.: Fawcett Publications, 1965), p. 132.

in regard to his mother, but he complains bitterly to his wife Peggy that " 'I'm thirty-five and I've been through hell and I don't see why that old lady has to have such a hold over me. It's ridiculous. It's degrading.' "[3]

The Oedipal situation is clearly evident in the evening when Mrs. Robinson, the strap of her nightgown awry, waits while Joey takes Peggy up to her room, assuming that he will come back down to her. Later she condescendingly allows him to go to his wife's bed but equates the act with that of a dog: " 'Just give the dogs their water and take your wife to bed' " (34). The Oedipal pattern is suggested in other cases where such a mother exists, on one occasion in *The Centaur* when George Caldwell's wife remarks that it is sad how " 'they don't allow men to marry their mothers.' "[4] Angela Hanema of *Couples* half jokingly claims that her husband sleeps with women when he is really trying to murder his mother. Joey Robinson's Oedipal situation is compounded by his mother's lonely life on the farm and her neurotic and hysterical outbursts, one of them as she smashes plates in the kitchen after Joey's wife takes her place at the sink, and again on the way home from church when she screams uncontrollably.

To a degree Mrs. Robinson poses as a martyr, complaining that she is hated and let down by Joey, who left the farm and never became a poet as she had wished. But she accuses him (presumably all men) of perpetrating the erroneous idea that women like to suffer. She admits that her husband made possible the two things she wanted most, the farm and Joey, and claims that in return she granted Mr. Robinson his freedom. The fact that she assumes such a prerogative, and that she believes her husband did have his freedom (when he is so obviously shown to be trapped by the farm which was her way of life), is one instance of how Mrs. Robinson's concept of truth is merely a version of her own emotional needs.

At *Of the Farm*'s close Mrs. Robinson makes a pledge of a new freedom for her son. But it is difficult to believe she will allow

3. John Updike, *Of the Farm* (Greenwich, Conn.: Fawcett Publications, 1971), p. 38. Further page references to this edition are included in the text.

4. John Updike, *The Centaur* (Greenwich, Conn.: Fawcett Publications, 1963), p. 47.

such a freedom. On the other hand, Peggy—who enjoys possessing her husband and being possessed by him—because she is more easygoing, less distinguished by a personality, and above all because he is linked to her sexually, will be able to give him freedom. No wife in Updike's fiction *can* threaten the way a mother does. If he must, a man may replace his wife, but he has no control over his mother except in leaving her. Joey warns his mother not to poison his second marriage as she did the first, but it is unlikely that she would relinquish her power or that the couple could withstand her force if she tried to separate them.

The mother's strength is associated not only with an authoritarian family structure but with agrarian and religious values of the past, toward which Updike himself appears ambivalent. The mother's relationship to the past represents not only the literalness with which she is bound to a child's first years but the special value that tradition and nostalgia have for Updike. Mrs. Robinson is one of the last great characters before the world of Tarbox (*Couples*), in which no woman of her stature exists. As Hook pronounces in *The Poorhouse Fair*, "Women are the heroes of dead lands."[5] While land is associated with the feminine, particularly the mother, the city is associated with the father. (Updike personally claims to be a man of middles, with his allegiance to his home town of Shillington, between country and city.)

Updike questions the return to the land, so often the symbolically virtuous journey, just as he questions the character of the dominant mother, so closely associated with it. Larry Taylor's excellent study of the pastoral and anti-pastoral themes in Updike's work shows a general progression from the more nostalgic and pastoral to the soundly anti-pastoral.[6] Rabbit's flight to nature is the most obvious miscalculation of the healing power of nature, but Mrs. Robinson's mean-spirited attachment to land is another. In the story "Packed Dirt, Churchgoing, A Dying Cat, A Traded Car," it is the earth smoothed by feet that appeals to David Kern (and to Updike), a more humane soil than that of the farm.

5. John Updike, *The Poorhouse Fair* (Greenwich, Conn.: Fawcett Publications, 1958), p. 111.
6. *Pastoral and Anti-Pastoral Patterns in John Updike's Fiction* (Carbondale, Ill.: Southern Illinois University Press, 1971).

Admittedly, land as a possession is satisfying. When Joey brings his new wife and stepson to the farm, he is proudly aware of how the vast acres he owns add to his stature. In lovingly describing his wife's body, another of his possessions, he refers to her as a fine piece of land: "My wife is wide, wide-hipped and long-waisted, and, surveyed from above, gives an impression of terrain, of a wealth whose ownership imposes upon my own body a sweet strain of extension; entered, she yields a variety of landscapes . . ." (39). Land associated with feminine sexuality is glorious indeed, but women rooted to the earth may use it as a prison for their husbands, men like Mr. Robinson and George Caldwell, who must escape to the city and to the classroom. Another such prisoner of the farm is Mr. Kern of "Pigeon Feathers," who finds no soul in the soil which only reminds him of death.

The mother is frequently linked with the idea of death. When Mrs. Robinson explains to Joey's stepson that tractors are like dying people, Joey realizes she is trying to sink into him "the hook of her death" (49). As the giver of life, the mother assumes the right to destroy it, both literally and in the form of mental punishment. The association between mother and death is explicit in Updike's first novel, *The Poorhouse Fair*, in the name of the central female character, Amy Mortis. In "Pigeon Feathers" it is the authoritarian Mrs. Kern who commands that the beautiful pigeons be killed. The woman who gives life often balances it, through accident or design, with another child's death: Janice Angstrom gives birth to Nelson but accidentally kills her daughter June; Foxy Whitman (*Couples*), celebrated for her first pregnancy, terminates her second with abortion.

While mothers of an older generation are usually orthodox in religion, such as Mrs. Robinson, who would be strictly opposed to abortion, they usually lack true spirituality. Mrs. Robinson even admits she would not believe in God if she were forced to live in the city, and the discrepancy between her activities in church and her unchristian treatment of family is a further sign of the shallowness of her religious beliefs. Churchgoing, however, is not an automatic sign of hypocrisy. If a woman is responsive sexually, activity in a church may signify the addition of genuine spiritual qualities, which is the case for Foxy Whitman, the only churchgoing woman in Tarbox. By contrast, Angela Hanema, the non-churchgoer, is frigid and without spirituality. Updike is ambivalent in regard to the demise of traditional religious observances just as he is ambivalent about the value of land, seeing at the same time the beauty of traditions and the way they can become detrimental.

In his treatment of mothers Updike is on firm ground. His bitch mother represents little that is new to the type, but she is as effectively and as realistically drawn as anywhere in current fiction. Updike demonstrates with awareness and honesty not only the immense power such a woman has over her children but the mixed nature of her strength, which includes a potential that might have gone for good but instead is primarily destructive. Updike's male protagonists are as aware of the mother's potential to destroy as is the author, and for their benefit Updike presents wives who will soothe and comfort, but who are among the most dismal and hopelessly seduced beings to cross the pages of our literature. And in this case he is not entirely aware of his attitudes and of the way that they affect his fiction.

Updike makes a specific attempt to define his view of women in general in the title story of his collection *Museums and Women*. The narrator's view of his mother as "the index, inclusive and definitive of women,"[7] however, is contradicted by the woman he chooses for his wife, who does not faintly resemble his mother. The storyteller's mother, with her sense of his destiny (the true Updike mother), was the one who first brought him to the museum, pointing him in the direction of the great things of the past. The "pale creature" (8) he meets at the top of the museum stairs, on the other hand, who is to become his wife, impresses him with the very opposite of that purposefulness. In this lost soul he sees "an innocent sad blankness where I must stamp my name" (8). The museum with its valuable holdings of the past may be an apt metaphor for the mother with its emphasis on the qualities of "radiance, antiquity, mystery, and duty" (3). But what does the young woman he meets here have to do with radiance, antiquity, mystery, or even duty? What truly entrances

7. John Updike, "Museums and Women," *Museums and Women and Other Stories* (New York: Alfred A. Knopf, 1972), p. 5. Further page references to this edition are included in the text.

this visitor to the museum, however, does indeed apply only to this girl who is to become his wife: a statuette of a nude on a mattress. This figure (appropriately reclining in bed) is to him the most perfect item in the museum, a truly disturbing image of the desired woman, simply a marble object in a sexual posture.

The wives Updike creates are a sadly limited group, but their husbands like them well enough. The author has stated in an interview for the *Paris Review*[8] that he never satirizes a character (the interview was before the publication of *Bech*), and he likewise never satirizes lovemaking, that favorite preoccupation of the fabulators. And writing in the broad tradition of manners, he shows women to be an indispensable part of society. Updike's men are particularly dependent upon them, and the first thing a man does when he leaves one woman (and he seldom leaves his wife permanently) is to find another, never considering the possibility of remaining alone.

Updike's most tender reverence is reserved for women's bodies. The elegant style with which he describes female anatomy often becomes overwrought, as his descriptions do generally. But it always conveys wonder. Even in the many explicit accounts of sexual activity, some of them ludicrous and even perhaps pornographic, there is an awe for the physical aspect of women. This form of adoration is far from a true consideration of women's needs, not taking into account their feelings and the consequences to them of sexual relations, but it is a kind of naive appreciation. Rabbit Angstrom boyishly begs Ruth to let him undress her and is delighted when she allows it. A special pause of wonder is observed before the lover approaches the woman's body. If a woman represents a return to the womb, as she does most memorably when Piet Hanema of *Couples* takes milk from his lover's breast, she bears only the remotest resemblance to the man's mother, who has long since ceased to give comfort or pleasure. The womb situation is often to be found only in running from mother, as Allen Dow runs to Molly. In "Wife-wooing," woman, womb, and wife are equated: "What soul took thought and knew that

8. Charles Thomas Samuels, "The Art of Fiction XLIII: John Updike," *Paris Review*, no. 45 (Winter 1968), pp. 85–117.

adding 'wo' to man would make a woman? The difference exactly. The wide w, the receptive o. Womb."[9]

The very sight of women in the world gives a kind of grace to existence for Updike's men. A young grocery checker in "A & P" grows faint with delight as three girls in bathing suits come into the market. The loveliest girl, whose straps hang charmingly off her white shoulders, comes through his line and pays her bill with a dollar she produces from the top of her bathing suit. When the manager of the store blasphemously asks the girls to cover themselves, the checker, a martyr to their beauty, walks out on his much-needed job to protest the manager's action. A general appreciation for women is also shown, for example, by Piet Hanema, who might be speaking for all Updike men when he says he loves all the women he lies with.

Sexuality is far and away the most desirable trait in a woman, perhaps the only essential one. It is not necessarily associated with physical beauty. A woman in Updike may be remembered as pretty because of the fondness with which the love scenes are portrayed. But a close look at her features, which are usually given in detail, reveals that Ruth, for one, is marred by skin blemishes, a chunky body, and hair as multicolored as a dog's. Janice has thinning hair, tight dark skin, and a mouth that looks like a greedy slot. What endows these women with sexuality is rather an openness before men, a special and utter need for them, the lack of which makes someone like Angela Hanema, otherwise the most respected woman in Tarbox, unsatisfactory. Her husband sees her as "a lump, a barrier, a boarded door."[10] Molly Bingaman, Janice Angstrom, Ruth Leonard, Vera Hummel, Peggy Robinson, Foxy Whitman, and Joan Maple of the Maple stories are all loved for their sexuality, the homely girls as well as the pretty ones. In fact, a case can be made that homeliness of a sort that makes women soft and vulnerable is in itself an attraction for Updike's men.

Of all his images of women, the one Updike paints most ten-

9. *Pigeon Feathers and Other Stories*, p. 79.

10. John Updike, *Couples* (Greenwich, Conn.: Fawcett Publications, 1969), p. 216.

derly is the woman emerging from the tub or shower. Like Walker
Percy's Binx Bolling (*The Moviegoer*), whose eyes sting with
tears of gratitude for the beauty of his secretary's bottom as she
passes to the water cooler, the heart of a Rabbit Angstrom grows
rapturous at the sight of the steamy wife's or lover's behind. His
first nostalgic memory of Janice after he leaves her is the way she
comes from her bath, "doped and pleased with a little blue towel
lazily and unashamed her bottom bright pink with hot water the
way a woman was of two halves bending over and turning and
laughing at his expression whatever it was.[11] Vera Hummel makes
her striking first appearance in *The Centaur* as she emerges from
the high school showers to the stunned delight of George Caldwell. Harry Conant in "The Wait" rhapsodizes over his lover
Sally: "Though I live forever can I forget how I saw you step
from a tub, your body abruptly a waterfall."[12] It is not that lovemaking occurs with particular success in the shower (a favorite
motif of the sixties), but that reverence is due the pristine loveliness of a woman just out of her bath.

A desire for the natural is a first concern with Updike's men,
most noticeably with Rabbit. Without bothering about how
Ruth might feel, he insists on rubbing the makeup from her face.
This urge for the scrubbed nymph is an element of Updike's use
of the pastoral[13] as one way of idealizing women, primarily for
the wonder of their bodies. But just as Rabbit's flights into nature
to the orange groves of the south or to the hills of Mt. Judge offer
neither solace nor escape, the homage to women's "purity" is
often disastrous. When Rabbit insists on Ruth's "naturalness"
and refuses to allow her to contaminate herself with contracep-
tives, she must bear the consequences of an unwanted pregnancy.
The thought of a pastoral retreat may suggest a luscious escape,
as it does in "The Wait" when the lovers, stranded in a Washington, D.C., airport, fantasize a life together in faraway Wyoming.
But they are soon jolted back to the problems of their mundane

11. John Updike, *Rabbit, Run* (Greenwich, Conn.: Fawcett Publications, 1960),
p. 37. Further page references to this edition are included in the text.
12. John Updike, *New Yorker*, 43 (Feb. 17, 1968), 45.
13. Taylor, *Pastoral and Anti-Pastoral Patterns*, p. 2.

love affair. Updike's anti-pastoralism eventually overwhelms the
pastoral ideal.

Both as a pastoral ideal and as part of a tradition depicted by
Denis de Rougemont that love in the Western world exists only
when an obstacle is present, creating a triangular situation, Updike's characters yearn for the unattainable. In a review of *Love
in the Western World* which describes the conflict in the West
between passion and marriage, Updike agrees that "love as we
experience it *is* love for the Unattainable Lady"[14] (a statement in
which Updike characteristically assumes that his male viewpoint
is the definitive one). This lady is a form which takes on the
male lover's own spirit. For Updike, with his particular fixation
on the past, this may mean that "a woman, loved, momentarily
eases the pain of time by localizing nostalgia; the vague and ir-
recoverable objects of nostalgic longing are assimilated, under
the pressure of libidinous desire, into the details of her person."[15]
A particularly good example of the way this works is in "The
Persistence of Desire," one of Updike's finest stories. Clyde Behn,
visiting his home town, meets a former girl friend in the dentist's
office and immediately approaches her with passionate attentions,
which to her are ridiculous. The emotion that engulfs him is a
nostalgia for the youthful self he was when he first knew her, an
image now favorably tinged by time. The only value of her existence is in her connection with him. Like most Updike women
she is merely practical, not only lacking the sense of nostalgia
herself but altogether missing it in anyone else. Such women are
entirely without the nuances of feeling which enhance the Updike
hero and make him more complex than the heroine. It is Clyde's
glory to add to this woman's bareness: "Except for the interval
of himself—his splendid, perishable self—she would never see the
light."[16]

The bachelor Bech is one who, after years of deifying women,
locates the ideal in a Bulgarian poetess. For him she is quite unattainable—foreign, independent, complete—noticeably unlike

14. John Updike, "More Love in the Western World," *Assorted Prose*, p. 222.
15. Ibid., p. 223.
16. *Pigeon Feathers and Other Stories*, p. 18.

any American woman in Updike's work and his only woman, idealized or otherwise, who is given qualities, other than sexual, which are superior. It is not only distance that lends to the Bulgarian's appeal and distinction, although we realize Bech's weakness for her unattainability. She is truly an accomplished person. Apparently it would not occur to Updike to attribute any American woman with the talent and wisdom he grants to this individual. In all Bech's loves there had been an urge to rescue, to impress with his own character, but this foreign poetess needs nothing. Not even a husband. Bech admits that in America "you must be very uncharming not to marry,"[17] which is quite the way Updike portrays the American culture. Bech is a rare bachelor, one of the few single persons in Updike's fiction who is not completely alienated from society. He is not as distasteful as the women who do not marry, but his failure to do so becomes the butt of satire.

Updike's men do yearn for the unattainable, but he is finally much committed to a concept of realism and draws his characters away from their dreams into life much closer to the way it is lived in suburban America. Americans do marry often, and marriage is his topic. With full attention to its difficulties and disillusionments, Updike shows marriage to be the inevitable testing ground in contemporary life. Even the protagonist of "The Hermit" (not a typical subject for Updike) is routed from his forest retreat, after being visited there by a woman and shown the failure of his attempt to live alone. Updike's characters think so much in terms of marriage that when Rabbit spends one night with the prostitute Ruth he refers to it as their wedding night and to her as his wife.

The marriage commitment is shaky, as most people falter toward divorce, but it stands. There is good reason, other than moralistic or traditional, however, why people usually do not divorce. Updike's wives are so similar and interchangeable (unless they are frigid, and most of them are not) that divorce would serve little purpose. Bech, for whom the Bulgarian poetess is unique, admits that other women all share the trait of "narrowly missing

17. John Updike, *Bech: A Book* (Greenwich, Conn.: Fawcett Publications, 1971), p. 77. Further page references to this edition are included in the text.

an undisclosed prototype" (73). The monotonous affairs of
Couples show a general malaise which cannot be corrected by
changing partners, although out of boredom switches occur frequently on a temporary basis. Only Piet and Foxy, considered to
be the true lovers, divorce, so that they may marry each other.
But soon they will become just another couple. The same sense
of the tired exchange of partners occurs in "The Witnesses," the
story of a man who brings a second wife to visit friends who remark on her resemblance to the first wife. The only valid reason
for leaving a wife is apparently frigidity, as is the case with Angela
Hanema.

The families that stay together usually do so without the aid of
particularly dramatic events, but Updike sees them through in a
lifelike way that is based on a closer look at suburbia than many
critics of such an existence are willing to give. In an appreciative
study of American writers of the last two decades, Tony Tanner
observes that while most American novelists consider middle-
class life a "desert of unreality,"[18] Updike shows it to be more
complex than is usually admitted. He has the nerve to accept
suburban life as the place where contemporary American characters "will learn what they learn and lose what they lose."[19] It is
rare to find an American author who writes from inside the establishment and with so little reliance on acts of violence. In Updike's
fiction terrible events pass across television screens like mirages
while the bewildered souls of the sixties sit helplessly back and
watch. When asked about the infrequent use of violence in his
work, while it inundates us in the news and in literature, Updike
says his reason for showing it so rarely in his writing is that there
has been so little of it in his life.[20]

It is Updike's approach to normalcy that gives some credence to
his picture of women, even the dullest ones, whom it would be
tempting to believe are only a creation of his male chauvinism.
He appears not to be fully aware of the extent to which he de-
means the female character, and surely his heroines are not repre-

18. "A Compromised Environment (John Updike)," in *City of Words: American Fiction 1950–1970* (New York: Harper & Row, 1971), p. 273.
19. Ibid.
20. Samuels, "The Art of Fiction XLIII," p. 106.

sentative of enterprising women who contradict the theory of women's blankness. But the type he represents may be defended as one which exists in significant enough numbers to be a crucial factor in American life.

Updike gives us the dreary aspects of the housewife's existence through the lyricism of his male point of view. This stylistic quality makes the reading of Updike at times enjoyable while it soothes the reader away from the fact that from a woman's viewpoint no such lyricism in describing her life would be possible. In depicting the mundane subject with a lyrical style Updike suggests that marriage itself combines these elements in a story like "Wife-wooing," where a husband labors as any other lover might to stir his lady's desire. The *wife*, who may be as distasteful as Janice is at the beginning of *Rabbit, Run*, where marriage is a system of constraints, is not, however, essentially a distasteful concept to Updike's men. A wife is the comfort they seek. Their truest entrapment is never more to their wives than to themselves, and even a possessive wife can be a liberating force. Pastoral lyricism is thus by no means limited to praise of the unattainable lady. The speaker of "Wife-wooing" poetically relates: "I wed wide warm woman, white-thighed. Wooed and wed. Wife. A knife of a word that for all its final bite did not end the wooing. To my wonderment."[21] The seven years of marriage have brought the couple no distance, only "to the same trembling point, of beginning" (80), a statement more in praise of marriage's mysterious possibility for regeneration than an indictment of the union. Most couples in Updike's fiction continue to work for some unnameable goal which makes their lives if not extraordinary at least worth living.

Updike's lyricism in behalf of the female body and his devotion to the idea of marriage, however, depend upon an idea of the undeniably *stupid* woman. The classic statement of the Updike male regarding the Updike female (as wife, not mother) is made by Peter Caldwell (*The Centaur*), who says of Iris Osgood, "I was tired and wanted only to pillow my head on her low I.Q." (141). Iris is a future Updike wife, appealing to both boys and to men as she sits "immersed in dull bovine beauty" (31). Zimmer-

21. *Pigeon Feathers and Other Stories*, p. 79.

man, the principal of the school, fondles her arm as the class
proceeds. For Peter she is "one of those dull plain girls who was
totally unfashionable in the class and yet with whom I felt a
certain inner dance" (141). She has the sexuality first in the heart
of the Updike male, and at a young age, as will be the case later
on, her moronic niceness is the comfort men need, especially
gentle, insecure men like Peter, his father, and Rabbit Angstrom,
whose egos are so delicate that they must be insured by a superiority over women. In turning from the strong, feared mothers,
Updike's men ask little more than a safe, warm place—precisely, a
woman's body. Updike is, of course, too realistic to show marriage
as a state of easy peace, for even with relatively uncomplicated
people it is often tense and difficult. But calm is more likely to result in ennui than to erupt in violence. And the result to the Updike male who has chosen a woman who will not threaten his
limited intelligence is a boredom far beyond the normal expectations of daily existence. The dramatic clashes of will that exist
for older couples are replaced by the repetitious irritations that
plague the couples of Rabbit's generation. The younger wife is
simply too bland to be capable of an interesting confrontation,
which is one reason why marriages endure.

There is nothing subtle in Updike's qualification of his women
as "dumb." Rabbit shouts the word when he runs from Janice.
And Ruth is very little brighter, with her bad grammar and her
conventional and crude ideas. In "Giving Blood" Richard Maple
says of his wife Joan that her "stupidity I don't mind."[22] Their
marriage problems, characteristically, are sexual. A whole classroom of unintelligent girls confront George Caldwell. Judy Len-
gel, a classmate of Iris Osgood, cannot begin to understand the
questions she is asked about geology, let alone answer them. She
is as "dumb as pure white lead."[23] Caldwell tells her that after the
quiz she can forget all about it—soon she will be married with six
kids. His remark to Peter after the girl goes laments not her lack of
intelligence but the fact that "her father'll have an old maid on
his hands" (85). Peter Caldwell's girl friend Penny is lyrically

22. John Updike, *The Music School: Short Stories* (Greenwich, Conn.: Fawcett
Publications, 1967), p. 21.
23. *The Centaur*, p. 32.

referred to as "my Penny, my little dumb, worried Penny. Suddenly, thickly, I loved her" (43), the proximity of the statements suggesting a strong causal relationship between her being dumb and his loving her. In "Flight" three bright young girls are "disfigured by A's as if by acne,"[24] an equation of intelligence and ugliness. Another case of the preferred stupid woman is Joey Robinson's choice of Peggy as his second wife. His mother cleverly attacks him by pointing out how surprising it is that the boy Richard is bright, because the mother is not. She tells Joey she is ashamed that he would need a stupid woman to give him confidence. He admits that his wife is stupid but that it does not matter to him. The rejected wife was brighter but not as sensual as wife number two.

Despite the way he depicts women, Updike claims that his novels "are all about the search for useful work. So many people these days have to sell things they don't believe in, and have jobs that defy describing." A person must build his life outward from a job.[25] For Rabbit to demonstrate kitchen items or to sell used cars is pitiful, especially in view of his former glory on the basketball court. What makes Piet Hanema superior to the other residents of Tarbox (along with his virility) is an almost spiritual feeling for his work as an architect of fine traditional houses. George Caldwell, the bedraggled teacher who presumably hates his job, actually invests it with a magic that is not lost on his heathenish students. His charisma in the classroom is Updike's way of showing him to be a superior and a good man.

But if the novels are about the search for useful work, what about work for women? Updike's statement includes a sympathetic comment on the occupation of housewives whose lives show a terrible sense of emptiness. And yet not only does he fail to suggest anything better for them—he will not *allow* it. None of his women consider meaningful jobs, although they are equally if not more dissatisfied with their petty lives than their husbands are with theirs. Even if childbearing were fulfilling to women, and there is no indication in this fiction that it is, it offers nothing

24. *Pigeon Feathers and Other Stories*, p. 47.
25. Jane Howard, "Can a Nice Novelist Finish First?," *Life*, 61 (Nov. 4, 1966), 82.

for the middle and later years. And yet Updike equates childbirth
for a woman with a career for a man: in Tarbox, where everyone
has to some degree lost his soul, "the men had stopped having
careers and the women had stopped having babies."[26] In this
"post-pill paradise," the fallen state of Eden, birth control is a
form of sin. But the way Updike's women react to their children
is also a form of sin. Mothers of the past painfully dominate their
children; younger mothers neglect theirs. Sterility, however, is
disliked so intensely by the men of Tarbox that the infertile Bea
Guerin claims that men actually injure her because they cannot
impregnate her. (She becomes slightly more acceptable when she
decides to adopt a baby.) Angela is at fault for never giving her
husband a son. Reproduction is important primarily as a way of
establishing male virility, not because of any intrinsic value attributed to the child or to the woman who carries the child.

Aside from lovemaking and childbearing, there is almost nothing for Updike's women to do. Piet Hanema is appalled at the
housewife's measly chores, but it never occurs to him that any
of his lovers would be doing much during the day besides waiting
for his visit. (Presumably the men still go to work between lovemaking episodes.) The only career women Updike portrays, aside
from a pitiful secretary or two, are prostitutes, who do much the
same work as the wife or lover. Perhaps he simply cannot imagine
what a woman might want to do other than minister to a man's
needs! Bech's question to a lady friend, "What do you do?,"
which he retracts as stupid, would be an unfortunate one to ask
any of Updike's women. Bech's conclusion, which seems to be
voicing Updike's own view, is that "merely to rise each morning
and fill her skin to the brim with such loveliness was enough for
any woman to do" (161). If this statement is intended to be
humorous it is much too close to an attitude in the non-satirical
works to be identified as such.

Updike's women not only lack involving work of their own, but
they are too dull to be interested in what their husbands do,
making only the most perfunctory inquiries. In "Toward Evening" a young man in New York arrives home from work in good
spirits with an expensive present for his younger daughter. His

26. *Couples*, p. 17.

wife is irritated with the gift and with him for not answering her ritual question about his work day; but her mood is considered quite "understandable in view of her own confined existence."[27] The young wife in "Ace in the Hole" (the germ of *Rabbit, Run*) taunts her husband when he loses his job by asking what he will do next: " 'Go back to the Army? Your mother? Be a basketball pro?' "[28] A wife humiliates her husband by comparing his past achievements with the mediocrity of his present condition, understandably equating it with her own. Ace's wife ridicules the very possibility of a meaningful occupation; it does not exist for her (she has a nondescript office job), and his ambitions appear ridiculous. Suggesting that women miss out on a world of things by not being athletes, Ace laments that their daughter, who has the hands of a natural, will never be able to use them. " 'Baby, we got to have a boy' " (26). Ace (now referred to as Fred) knows he could be doing something better than parking cars for a living. It is not surprising that he is soon fired for smashing one of them.

Waiting at home is the archetypal Updike wife, Janice Springer Angstrom—vulnerable, sexual, good-natured, and stupid. She makes a striking image, this housewife of 1960, mesmerized in front of the T.V., drinking an old-fashioned and watching the Mouseketeers. Her pregnancy hardly suggests the great gift of life as she sags inertly into her chair. Both Janice and the prostitute Ruth, as Gerry Brenner points out, represent the ultimate "natural" state. They do nothing and are reduced to mere vegetables.[29] Janice's physical vegetation reflects a thorough mental vegetation. In contrast to graceful Rabbit, who has just come from shooting a perfect basket as he was able to do in high school, she is noticeably clumsy. Arriving at home, Rabbit is confronted by the absence of all grace and the presence of mere clutter, of which Janice is a part. The only light in the room comes from the T.V., which she once nearly smashed by getting tangled in the cord. His means of response to this mess is to carefully unfold his own coat and neatly hang it up.

27. John Updike, *The Same Door* (Greenwich, Conn.: Fawcett Publications, 1971), p. 56.
28. Ibid., p. 25.
29. "*Rabbit, Run*: John Updike's Criticism of 'The Return to Nature,' " *Twentieth Century Literature*, 12 (Apr. 1966), 9.

The Angstrom marriage is far from a success, but there are no dramatic, bitter battles. The couple simply drag along through years of tedious irritations. In appearance Janice is neither beautiful nor downright ugly, just small, a woman "with a tight dark skin, as if something swelling inside is straining against her littleness. . . . Her eyes dwindle in their frowning sockets and her little mouth hangs open in a dumb slot."[30] Her passivity is overwhelming. She cannot even care for her child, who has been taken, appropriately, to the more capable Mother Angstrom. Janice relies heavily on her own mother (whom she dislikes) as well, one more sign of weakness. Rabbit is in no way fond of her mother either, but a mother-in-law can never be in the class of a mother. Rabbit sees Mrs. Springer as something comic. His own mother is the one person in life whom he fears, despite others who have reason to consider him an enemy.

Rabbit's world consists of a pattern of nets and other constrictions to be escaped. When he comes home the door is locked on his domestic trap. But at the moment, at least, he is on the *outside* of that trap, enlightened enough to understand its ugliness and to attempt a retreat. Viewed from the inside, which Updike is not inclined to do, the locked door suggests much more of a trap for Janice than it does for Rabbit. She has no idea how the door got locked; it "just locked itself" (10). Only after Rabbit runs away is Janice forced to consider altering her life, and then the only possibilities are pitifully based on the simplest absolutes: she will get a divorce and be like a nun, or her husband will come back and love her. She may be too pitiful to elicit much compassion, and if she is only a caricature created to illustrate Updike's concern with the banal, she is not worth serious discussion. But Janice may be all too representative of a great many housewives sitting dully behind closed doors.

Janice first met Harry Angstrom when they both held dreary jobs in Kroll's department store, work which they and the other employees hated. Years later Rabbit's work has not improved much as he demonstrates MagiPeel Peelers in five-and-dime stores, a trifling occupation for a man, so close to the trivia of housework. We are made very aware that he must have talents for something

30. *Rabbit, Run*, pp. 10, 13.

better. Even tending Mrs. Smith's garden is an improvement. But what about Janice? Our author never allows us to *expect* her to do anything important or interesting. On the Mouseketeer show Janice is watching when Rabbit comes home, Jimmy, the big Mouseketeer, delivers this message: " 'God wants some of us to become scientists, some of us to become artists, some of us to become firemen and doctors and trapeze artists. And He gives to each of us the special talents to become these things, *provided we work to develop them*. We must *work*, boys and girls. So: Know Thyself. Learn to understand your talents, and then work to develop them. That's the way to be happy' " (12). Trite as the message sounds, the idea is not far from Updike's own stated feelings about the importance of significant work. The T.V. program presents the message effectively to children, and the Mouseketeer intrigues Rabbit, who is interested in his sales pitch. The subject of using one's talents, too, is particularly timely to Rabbit in his current struggle with his unchallenging life.

But what impact does the message have for Janice, who is the person at home watching the show? As far as we can see she has no talents (even the hot dogs she prepares are split and twisted). The vocations mentioned by the Mouseketeer are obviously those traditionally followed by men. And if she were to know herself as he suggests, what would she find? What encouragement is there for her to emerge from her stupor? Rabbit is aware of the image his company tries to present of the housewife, and he kiddingly reminds his wife of it. She is *supposed* to look tired, because she *is* a housewife. She does look tired, but not from a day's work— just from doing nothing. Rabbit seems sympathetic, but neither he nor Janice can imagine other possibilities for her. It is never suggested that *she* run away.

Janice epitomizes the trait most prominent in the Updike wife: stupidity. "There seems no escaping it: she is dumb" (14). Updike uses the word *dumb* consistently in reference to young women, although few are as dumb as poor Janice. One way of defining such stupidity is if a woman is unable to grasp the meaning of a man's jokes. Rabbit tries to tease Janice into seeing what he does with the image of the housewife by relating his work to her. When she does not laugh he considers her to be stupid. His

humor, of course, is not funny to her. She vaguely senses but does
not truly comprehend the unfortunate parallels between her
husband's work and her own life. Neither women nor men are
expected to be highly intelligent in Updike's world, but his women
lack even the merest awareness of complexity, seeing things in
simplistic absolutes as both Janice and Ruth do. Rabbit's skill has
been primarily athletic (in contrast to women's physical awkwardness), but beyond that he does imagine that there is some better
"thing" out there, a perception none of the women have.

In their stupidity the women become alike. When Ruth tells
Rabbit that Tothero's girl friend is "dumber than you can know"
(60), he says that he does know because he is married to her twin.
A wife may be unique in her association with a particular man,
but there is little else to distinguish her. The male wishes to impress his identity on the female's blankness, but she is often so
blank that little impression can be made. Rabbit dreams that
Janice is weeping for something his mother did, and "to his
horror her face begins to slide, the skin to slip slowly from the
bone, but there is no bone, just more melting stuff underneath"
(76). There is no identity to hold Janice together. He tries fu-
tilely to catch the melting stuff in his hands and form it into
something complete.

Janice, like nearly every Updike woman, is a sexual creature.
Rabbit fondly recalls how they first made love in a friend's apartment after work. They were married when she was pregnant, an
instigating factor in many Updike marriages but one having little
to do with their ultimate mediocrity. When Janice comes home
from the hospital with their second child, Rabbit is again obsessed
with making love to her. When she refuses him because it is too
soon after giving birth, he runs from her a second time. Janice,
who is not frigid, would not ordinarily have abstained from lovemaking. But this one refusal turns out to be a fatal mistake.

Like most Updike women, Janice is good-natured in her sexuality, combining qualities we rarely find linked in female characters in American literature. The undramatic virtue of geniality
can be easily passed over in light of Janice's more obvious limitations. But certainly good-naturedness such as hers is one reason
why many marriages survive as well as they do. Janice is affection-

ately forgiving when Rabbit comes to her in the hospital during the period when he is living with Ruth. In her limited way she loves him, and he always answers back, "I love *you*," somehow making it sound convincing at the moment. For her loyalty and affection Janice merits affection in return, but her meagerness of soul is incapable of inspiring great love (which is probably not possible for any of Updike's people). Rabbit, who at least envisions some kind of grandeur, laments to Tothero that the " 'little thing Janice and I had going, boy, it was really second-rate' " (90).

After Rabbit runs from Janice, the only person she can look to for help is her mother, an unfortunate choice, for the contact is always demeaning. "There was always that with Mother the feeling she was dull and plain and a disappointment, and she thought when she got a husband it would be all over, all that" (208). (Rabbit's mother also belabors Janice's incompetence, attributing her only with the skill necessary to trap a husband.) Rabbit and Janice are made primarily responsible for their baby's death, but Mrs. Springer is also partially responsible. It is immediately after she phones Janice, discovering that Rabbit has gone again and insisting on coming over immediately, that her daughter is panicked into cleaning up her house and her baby and the accident in the bathtub occurs. Mrs. Springer does not visit her daughter to help but to make fun of her because she cannot keep her husband. And Janice, already self-consciously aware of her inadequacy, tragically demonstrates it by accidentally drowning her child.

Updike rarely considers a woman's point of view. But both Janice and Ruth are shown on occasion through interior monologues, Ruth's being reminiscent of Molly Bloom's as she recalls in detail her many sexual experiences. Janice's simple mind dwells with little new insight on the crisis in her life, but there is pathos in her lonely confusion. We now begin to see the effects on her of continually being considered stupid. In her own mind she makes a sensible defense for herself which she would probably never have the confidence to announce to her husband effectively: "Here he called her dumb when he was too dumb to have any idea of how she felt" (209). Rabbit admittedly is not interested in how she feels, for the important thing, he says, is how *he* feels. Surely one reason for Janice's ineptness is the image of her that is set by others. Her consciousness of not being understood, which is shown no place outside of this one interior monologue, is as poignant as it is unexpected: "That was what made her panicky ever since she was little this thing of nobody knowing how you felt and whether nobody could know or nobody cared she had no idea" (209). Only with this rare insight into Janice do we begin to imagine the lonely horror she must feel—to be clumsy, slow, and "dumb," to be referred to constantly in such a way, and then, in a drunken daze, to bring about the death of her own child.

Rabbit, however, does have valid motivation to run from Janice. She *is* disgusting, and he is all too aware that there is something better than his limited life with her. Thus, we would expect him, in turning to another woman as he naturally does, to look for superior qualities not found in Janice. But again he opts for inferiority. Some readers see his affair with Ruth as a love match. But it is merely another sexual adventure for Rabbit, and when the involvement demands that he consider her welfare, he runs from her as he runs from everything else. Ruth is somehow sexually appealing to Rabbit, but not outstanding in any other way. She is far from beautiful, and yet her coarseness rather attracts him; she may be overweight, but he says she is "not *that* fat. Chunky, more . . . her thighs fill the front of her dress so that even standing up she has a lap. Her hair, kind of a dirty ginger color, is bundled in a roll at the back of her head" (49). From her plumpness Rabbit deduces that she is good-natured (a thought process Updike frequently employs, just as he concludes that sexual women must be stupid). The morning after his first night with Ruth he finds her homeliness pitiful, something he had not noticed the evening before. The lack of beauty never daunts the Updike lover, however. Rabbit comes back for more, drawn on by Ruth's limitations and her need for him, running toward the very things he claimed were unbearable in his marriage.

For Rabbit to prove that he is a winner he needs women like Janice and Ruth. Only their incapacity can confirm his superiority. To explain his mediocre golf game he replaces thoughts of his own inadequacy with the concept of women's stupidity: "In his head he talks to the clubs as if they're women. The irons, light and thin yet somehow treacherous in his hands, are Janice. *Come on, you dope, be calm. . . . Oh, dumb, really dumb"* (110). Like Janice, Ruth is "dumb," which is just the quality to appeal to Rabbit. When he finds her reading a book he taunts her by saying there is no need for her to read when she has him. A woman immobile is a delight to such a man; Ruth is a "perfect statue, unadorned woman, beauty's home image" (70) (the image developed in "Museums and Women"). When she speaks, however, the image is spoiled as her crude expressions spill forth. When Tothero, Rabbit's former coach, claims that he develops his athletes' three tools—head, body, and heart—she quickly adds, "the crotch" (54). When Ruth is not immobile, like Janice she is uncoordinated—an awkward bowler, a bloated and a lazy swimmer—while Rabbit continues to regard himself as the graceful athlete. His concepts are lyrical and ideal in contrast to the practical, dull thoughts that enter the heads of his women. Life for them holds no quest of higher things, no sense of the meaningful ambiguities which make Rabbit a more interesting character than they have the possibility of being.

For Updike to consider the "dreams" of his women characters is something of a parody, although he claims that he never satirizes. When Rabbit reminisces about his glory as a basketball star, which he frequently refers to in his conversation with Ruth, she admits to her dream of wanting to be a great cook. This accomplishment would presumably distinguish her from the inadequate Janice, whose lamb chops are greasy. But in fact Ruth has become a good eater, not a good cook. Her culinary skill is given a test only in the preparation of hot dogs, which she can indeed cook without splitting them open as Janice does. When Rabbit first asks Ruth, "What do you do?," that question terrible to so many women, she answers the familiar "Nothing." She can hardly reply that she is a prostitute, although the lowly state of whore, as Ruth later points out, it not really unlike that of other women. Rabbit is aware of this and declines to use the word *prostitute* in reference to Ruth unless it is used for every woman who is not married. Categorizing all unmarried women this way, however, which is meant to elevate Ruth, only results in denigrating all

unmarried women. Married women, if not referred to as prostitutes, are often treated as such. When Rabbit attempts to make
love to his wife after she has had her baby, demanding that she
"roll over," she points out to him that he treats her like a prostitute.

Janice appears as a hopelessly limited being throughout *Rabbit,
Run*, but ten years later in *Rabbit Redux* her life is surprisingly on
the upswing. As if to be fair (Updike does not support a double
standard of morality), it is her turn for a love affair, and she finds
Charlie Stavros while working part-time at her father's car lot. In
the last ten years her smallness has hardened into a leaner, better
figure, and she has discovered the joy of sex, the one thing a person
is made for, which she feels Rabbit locked up for her through the
years. As she becomes more active physically, if not mentally,
Rabbit grows fatter, slower, and more conservative politically. His
response to women has not basically changed, but he is tiring.
He admits that "all this fucking . . . just makes me too sad."[31]
Rabbit Redux ends with Rabbit and Janice in a motel room,
falling asleep without making love, either as a weary resignation
to their unexciting marriage or with a new emphasis for Updike on
the platonic. (His attitudes elsewhere make it difficult to believe
the latter.) In either case, the Angstrom marriage is more solid
than ever as Janice proves to be Harry's true mate.

Even though a dramatic change has apparently taken place
in Janice, the effects are demonstrated primarily when she is not
with her husband. Her adventures do little to change his former
concept of her. A new vitality results from her love affair, which
splits them apart for a time, but Janice's dowdy familiarity predominates as the affair dies and she comes back to Harry. Changed
as he might be by living with Jill and Skeeter, a teenage girl and
her Negro friend, he has not changed about "dumb" Janice. He
is surprised by her affair, amazed that she could appeal to anyone
but him: " 'Who'd have that mutt?' " (9), a comment not necessarily meant to be nasty but uttered as a mere statement of
fact. And yet it is assumed that all the women involved with Harry
love him and want him. He is not joking when he remarks of
Janice, " 'At her age, are you supposed to have a good time?' "

31. John Updike, *Rabbit Redux* (New York: Alfred A. Knopf, 1971), pp. 397–
98. Further references to this edition are included in the text.

(58). Harry's conviction that another man could not be deeply
interested in Janice is borne out as Updike sees to it that Stavros
tires of Janice. When she returns to Harry, still charming as she
emerges from the shower, we are reminded that this is the familiar,
clumsy Janice as she cuts herself several times while shaving her
legs in the bathtub.

Updike's attempt to give Janice a new image, while retaining
her basic stupidity, is unsuccessful. He is unable to allow her the
capacity or even the good luck for any significant changes. Her
way of expressing a new sense of self is artificial and trite: " 'It's
the year nineteen sixty-nine and there's no reason for two mature
people to smother each other to death simply out of inertia. I'm
searching for a valid identity and I suggest you do the same' "
(104). Rabbit recognizes that any ideas she might have picked up
all come from her new lover. The attempt to be witty or topical
only reveals her lack of intelligence in a clearer light. Stavros
comes to recognize Janice's inadequacy, but at least, as she relates
to Harry, " 'he never told me how dumb I am, every hour on the
hour like you do' " (75). This quality so predominates in Harry's
thoughts of her that when he learns of her love affair his first
reaction is not one of shock or hurt but a repetition of the familiar
adjective: "You dumb bitch." When he and Stavros later discuss
the situation which Harry has passively accepted, he says, " 'So
now you've tried her in all positions and want to ship her back.
Poor old Jan. So dumb' " (181). This is not the outburst of bitterness or a ploy to get Stavros to give her up, but merely his
customary remark. One of the rare compliments he directs to
Janice, given while he makes love to Jill, poorly, is in combination
with the insulting epithet: " 'My poor dumb mutt of a wife throws
a better piece of ass backwards than you can manage frontwards' "
(170). Stupidity in a woman is as ever linked with her sexuality
in the mind of the Updike male.

Stavros is affected by Janice's stupidity when he has some kind
of attack and calls on her to get his pills. The bathroom door
sticks (the clumsy Janice); she cannot find the light cord (the
incompetent Janice); and then it takes time for her eyes to become
accustomed to the dark (the slow Janice). Finally, when she brings
the wrong pills Charlie tells himself, "Harry is right. She is stupid"

(387). In her panic she is genuinely concerned about him, but her good will never makes the dramatic impact that is made by her incapacity. As Charlie writhes on the bed, she "very stupidly lets the faucet water run to get cold" (386). Janice, in desperation, recalls Harry's telling her she has the touch of death. Her only instinct, which proves to be the right one, is to press herself against Charlie, as if in the act of love. His spasm passes, and she feels that the mark of death on her has been lifted. Her warmth and sexuality in this case outweigh the stigma of her stupidity.

Janice's sexual coming of age is her salvation. Rabbit once left her because she would not make love, and she will not commit such an error again. She is redeemed from the greatest sin (which she only committed once)—failure in bed. Harry does want her back, which is obvious to everyone who knows him. Now the score has been evened, which seems the real motivation on Updike's part for Janice's affair. While she genuinely needs rejuvenation, the Janice of *Rabbit, Run* is not capable of seeking it. Only Rabbit has the nerve to run. But if anything is to happen to her it must be a sexual affair, for this is the only valid experience Updike can imagine for a woman. And being the utterly dependent woman she is, Janice places her whole sense of identity with Stavros just as she once did with Rabbit. Updike's men never become so involved with particular women, nor do their quests end with them. His heroes continue to seek something higher in work, athletics, or a vague spirituality. In a sense they go through women to find their higher selves, while a person like Janice finds what she values in Harry or Stavros specifically.

Janice's lover soon tires of her, and she returns from her affair mellowed but not buoyed up. More dependent on Harry than ever, she now knows that no one else will have her. The return to him comes about with none of the style she was beginning to show when she left. Once again she is dowdy Janice, properly humbled and inept. If *Rabbit Redux* is indicative, Updike's wife of the future will be as bound in her limitations as ever. Janice is again the wife of *Rabbit, Run*:

> Janice gets out of the driver's seat and stands beside the car looking lumpy and stubborn in a charcoal-gray loden coat he remembers from winters past. He had forgotten how short she

is, how the dark hair has thinned back from the tight forehead, with that oily shine that puts little bumps along the hairline. She has abandoned the madonna hairdo, wears her hair parted way over on one side, unflatteringly. But her mouth seems less tight; her lips have lost the crimp in the corners and seem much readier to laugh, with less to lose, than before. His instinct, crazy, is to reach out and pet her—do something, like tickle behind her ear, that you would do to a dog; but they do nothing [392].

Janice as the family pet—mindless, dependent, cuddly—is exactly what Harry wants. He announces to her that in his affections she ranks third in the family, after their son Nelson and after his own mother. When Janice and Harry meet again after their separation, her suggestion that they go to a motel gives her the shabby sense of a pickup, not the acceptability of a wife. At the Safe Haven Motel Harry signs up for the room while she waits in the car like "some dubious modern product extravagantly wrapped, in a metal package rich with waste space." When he motions for her to show the suitcase to the desk clerk and she does not understand, he exclaims in the familiar way, " 'God, she's dumb!' " (401).

The strength of *Rabbit Redux* is the natural way it links with the Angstroms of ten years earlier, not by illustrating sweeping developments of character but by showing how people continue in their habits. It is expected that Janice will return to her husband and that he will desire her for the same reasons he always has, which are emphasized now by time and familiarity. Approaching middle age and disillusioned by their quests, the Angstroms accept what is comfortable. Janice's love affair may have awakened her to a degree, but it only reinforces Harry's custom of condescending to his inferior.

It is quite credible that Harry would live out his life with a Janice, but his liaison with Jill, the eighteen-year-old waif who lives with him for a time, is a less believable and more doomed combination. As a younger man, Harry had the Updike tenderness for all women, especially for those who were not beautiful but who were easygoing and sexual. He is now unable to be warm to someone like Jill, a new kind of girl in a new age. He sees her as being all dried up sexually, and while he continues to make love to her, their lovemaking is a dismal experience. With her, the wonder he previously felt for women is gone. Because of their age difference he at first appears as the protective father, but her apparent sophistication and wildly foreign way of life harden him to the possibilities of being close to her. He is anything but protective. Her form of dependence is not the open vulnerability he is used to, and her toughness makes him impotent.

When Jill first comes home with Harry they bathe together, at her request. The sight of the woman in her bath, a favorite of Updike men, in Jill's case fails to create the usual awed response. Even after bathing she never seems quite clean enough, not being plump and pink like the others but lean and hard and gray. Harry notes with disappointment, as she does, that he is not sexually aroused with her, a failure which is not merely the result of fatigue. His characteristic virility is evident during the same period with the less attractive, alcoholic, and vulnerable Peggy Fosnacht, a neighbor and friend of Janice. There is nothing to do but kiss that woman and then make love to her, which Harry does with his customary skill and pleasure, coming partially from the thought of what he is giving to her. She is the blank check, like most women, "blank until you fuck her" (310), a concept he attributes to Skeeter but which is a version of his own. Jill lacks a kind of animal succulence that brings out what chivalry Harry is capable of. She is sadly aware of her failure to arouse men—Harry is not the first. From the moment he notes his impotence with her he shows a marked coolness to Jill which he has never before demonstrated, even to the most vulgar or simple woman.

We are led to believe that Harry's coolness to Jill is a result of an attitude toward her wealth. He is angry at this "rich bitch" for "calling his living room tacky" (142), and he notes with scorn that the money spent for her Porsche, now in disrepair, could support a whole family of less extravagant people. But such materialism has never been an obsession with Rabbit, to whom the clutter and banality, not precisely the poverty, of his middle-class life are the focus of *Rabbit, Run*. He can hardly fault Jill for not working to support herself: the Updike male does not ask that of his women. But it is rather a fear of new qualities in Jill, nonexistent in his other women, that disturbs Harry. She knows a world of drugs, freedom, and ideas, all incomprehensible to him.

Because she makes love with any man who wants her, he assumes she can have no feeling for him. Like his other lovers, she desires and needs him, but she is so unlike them that he does not admit to her kind of need. Only his son Nelson is aware of it. Nelson's camaraderie with Jill is another thing that threatens Harry. These young people are more mature than he is and make a conscious attempt to educate themselves, a process quite foreign to Harry. He is on sure ground as he watches young boys play basketball, but he has no sense of these new mental games. He is thus hostile to this new kind of woman who suggests them, "wombing" Jill, as she says, as if to violate her hardness.

Jill pleads with Harry to protect her from the drugs Skeeter attempts to force upon her. Even though she may consider Harry old-fashioned, only he can save her from the doom of her own time, in particular the addiction she has suffered from before. There is something to rely on in Harry which Janice also appreciates over the years as she watches him work at a tedious job to support her and Nelson. In growing older Harry has hardened into an unpleasant conservatism, but it is this kind of a bias that strengthens his loyalty to his father and his responsibility for his wife and child. This common man cannot match the dramatic sense of Skeeter's diabolism, but he does, with some honor, what a man can do in a bizarre world of moon landings, drugs, and a Vietnam war: he provides for his family and stays with them (until Janice leaves him). Jill, however, is too new and strange to be included in Harry's loyalties. She realizes after futile trying that she can never be anything in his "real life" (192).

When Jill first becomes a part of Harry's household she is distinguished as a superior woman by being a good cook, her "filet of sole, lemony, light, simmered in sunshine" (171). With mock pastoral lyricism Updike evokes an aura around such items as the coffee she brews, which is "black nectar compared to the watery tar Janice used to serve" (172). But even Jill's excellent cookery fails as Harry's coolness toward her intensifies: the girl who is thin and hard and sexless now serves rubbery lamb chops and charred chicken livers with frozen insides (an unfortunately prophetic image for her).

However else he might consider her, Harry can never say that

Jill is stupid. Her intellectuality may not be deep, but she does think and make an attempt to be educated, something new to the Updike heroine. Seeing the low educational level of the Angstrom household, she decides to cultivate Nelson. Harry is invited to join Jill and her eager pupil in lengthy discussions of God, beauty, and religion. Harry never complains of these learning sessions, but they are strange and threatening to him. On one occasion he loses an erection with Jill when "all her talk, her wild wanting it, have scared him down to nothing" (201).

Since Harry considers a woman only in terms of her sexuality, he suspects that Jill must be Nelson's instructor in sex (with no real basis for this assumption). His resentment of her makes him fascinated with Skeeter's schemes to destroy her. At this point something sinister occurs in Updike's writing: he allows his bias in behalf of the stupid-sexual woman to intrude to the point of forcing a violent death (and violence is not usually his subject) upon this intelligent girl whom he dislikes and cannot deal with. In creating a new type of woman and brutally disposing of her Updike seems unaware of what he does, not only in terms of artistic distortion but as a revelation of his determination to preserve a bovine image of women. In doing so, his character Harry, in regard to Jill, must become callous to the point of a cruelty that is not in character for him, even in his most destructive acts. He is so taken by Skeeter's rituals that he joins with him in abusing Jill. At Skeeter's request Harry reads from *The Life and Times of Frederick Douglass* the section about Esther, a beautiful slave girl who is whipped by a master who is " 'cruelly deliberate, and protracted the torture as one who was delighted with the agony of his victim' " (278). After the reading Skeeter grabs Jill by the throat and rips her white (mock-virginal) dress while Harry watches, his instinct "not to rescue her but to shield Nelson" (279), who moans that she will be killed. Harry disagrees, suggesting that anyway she probably likes what Skeeter does to her.

Either Harry imagines that women love to suffer, or he is glad to see this particular girl suffer, which is more likely the case. Charles Thomas Samuels perceptively questions why Harry would watch the humiliation of the white woman so willingly. He suggests that perhaps Harry hates Jill for being upper-class with the

same intensity that Skeeter resents whites.[32] Samuels is quite right
in questioning the motivation for Harry's odd behavior, which
even Skeeter cannot understand. But there is little in either of the
Rabbit novels to indicate such an intense concern with the upper
class. The real preoccupation is with being a successful lover.
Thus Jill, who talks too much and thinks too much, is a failure as
a lover, and it is this which Harry truly resents, not her wealth.

Harry's characteristic passivity is partially responsible for his
failure to help Jill. He is passive regarding Janice's love affair, the
loss of his job, and his son's antagonism toward him. But there
is a difference in his failure to act in regard to Jill which reflects
a genuine satisfaction with her misfortune. What should be a
truly frightening event—his house burning with Jill inside—is a
serene occasion. We would not necessarily expect Harry to dash
into the flames to save Jill. But his placidity shows something
newly disturbing about him. There is no horror as she burns to
death (and we know how capable he is of panic) in what is a
rare scene of violence for Updike. As Jill dies, Harry talks quietly
to his son, not as a man stunned or sickened, but as an extraordi-
narily callous person who would stand by and let a fellow being
die. Nelson reflects the terror his father should feel, and after
accusing him of letting Jill die, he runs into the burning house to
save her himself. He knows she must be inside, as we all do, but
Harry says vaguely, " 'She must have gotten out. . . . She's safe and
far away' " (320, 323).

If shock were the reason for Harry's calm, then we might
expect him to be horrified later on when he realizes the manner
in which Jill has died. But his sorrow for the loss of his wife, his
job, and his home includes hardly a notice of Jill. The question of
whether he might have saved her aside, there is no *feeling* for her
death. Harry makes a peculiar analogy of his part in Jill's death
with Janice's accidental killing of their daughter June: "Her trip
drowns babies; his burns girls" (395). If he considers himself
guilty, then he also considers Janice guilty of June's death. But if
he sees the baby's death simply as a terrible accident, which he
is by now inclined to do, then by his analogy he takes no responsibility for letting Jill die. But the cases are not the same. One

32. "Updike on the Present," *New Republic*, 165 (Nov. 20, 1971), 30.

significant difference between the two incidents is the impact on the persons involved: for Janice, the baby's death is a tragedy of the first order, both because her child dies and because she causes the accident. She will suffer a lifetime for it. On the other hand, Harry is hardly affected by Jill's death, which he might have prevented. It is no accident that he so calmly watches the house burn with her inside.

The construction of *Rabbit Redux* is deeply flawed in that Updike uses unlike incidents, June's death and Jill's death, to provide an apparent symmetry of plot as a way of balancing out the Angstrom marriage. But what is far more disturbing is that Updike allows his bias in favor of stupid women to determine that a thinking woman must be killed off. Jill is also one of the few women in Updike who falls outside the sacred category of wife, and in this world of couples, extra women must be disposed of one way or another. In *Rabbit Redux* Janice is restored to her marriage; Ruth is now married with children, the wife she was always considered to be; Jill is dead, hauled away in a rubber bag; and Rabbit's sister Mim, a visitor from the West Coast, which might for its foreignness be the Ivory Coast, is only allowed to pass through town.

Mim was always the exotic member of the Angstrom family, adding a barbaric note even in high school when she wore earrings that made her look like a gypsy or an Arab. She arrives from California as if from another planet, her life jangling to a foreign tune, "her eyes, which are inhuman, Egyptian, drenched in peacock purple and blue" (352). Mim is Updike's career girl, with the only career he can imagine for a woman, prostitution. Mim knows things. She understands about Rabbit and Janice and others in Mt. Judge and helpfully goes to bed with Charlie Stavros to precipitate Janice's return to her husband. Harry is affectionate with his sister, an affection which in Updike's frame of reference can only be demonstrated by the male's erotic attraction to the female. As Harry embraces Mim he wants to feel all the men who have already held her.

But there is something hopeless about Mim which puts her beyond the pale of society, related, no doubt, to her type of prostitution (like Jill's cold promiscuity), a tougher version than Ruth's vulnerable whoring and one entailing an involvement in worldly experience which in Updike's society is not acceptable for a woman. When she becomes in any way competent and self-supportive, a woman must be dehumanized. (Obviously the issue is not merely prostitution, because Updike approves of certain kinds of prostitutes.) Mim says people in California build hard shells around themselves, almost as the sun bakes them brown; she is paid for what she gives, "because anything free has a rattlesnake under it" (359). As he does with the creation of Jill, Updike equates Mim's intelligence with the absence of the sexuality which makes a woman desirable as a wife and a bona fide member of society. A woman cannot be both intelligent and sexually desirable; thus Mim is dehumanized, to an even greater extent than are the sexual automatons of Tarbox, who are at least wives. Her smile and laugh appear as "electronic images" (352) created by a coded tape fed into her head. Her only purpose for existence is to be used by men with failed careers and broken marriages, who, like her, are merely waste products of society.

Only a few other single girls drift through Updike's stories, one an odd-looking and pitiful girl of twenty-nine, Penelope Vogel of "Eros Rampant," whom Richard Maple believes only a Negro could make love to now. (Maple never makes clear the nature of his own involvement with Penelope, which we can only surmise to be sexual, given Updike's outlook on men's singular attraction to women.) If she is sexual enough the single girl, such as Rebecca Cune in "Snowing in Greenwich Village" (Cune equals cunt, according to the Hamiltons' study[33]), is a natural threat to other marriages, as are all divorcées, the few of them that exist. Divorce appears to change the nature of the wife automatically from her good-natured open desirability into a mean, threatening quality. While one's undesirable traits may surface with the strain of divorce, such a condition is highly exaggerated by Updike, who knows that someone like Angela Hanema becomes immediately and thoroughly distasteful when she divorces. She is now a threatening being who will not be allowed to remain in her separate

33. Alice and Kenneth Hamilton, *The Elements of John Updike* (New York: William B. Eerdmans, 1970), p. 56.

condition. Like the single woman (always a version of prostitute), she must become a wife or be disposed of.

The new, more strident and independent woman is clearly a threat to the Updike male. Such an attitude is explicit in the story "Marching through Boston," written with a humor that not often enough surfaces in Updike's fiction. The problem of the male ego is faced directly as a wife takes up an interest in life outside the home. The Maples are now entering middle age, after love affairs for both, contemplated divorce, and a transfusion to liven their marriage ("Giving Blood"). Joan Maple's burgeoning interest in the civil rights movement suggests a genuine concern which was never true, for example, when Janice Angstrom took her part-time job. But in both cases the venture outside the home is a threat to the marriage.

Joan Maple, in glowing health, her voice melodious as she makes her business calls (her husband even thinks her posture has improved), is having the fun of doing something well. Richard Maple is pointed out as the husband of the woman who makes such good speeches. She persuades him to march with her in Boston, which as we would expect turns out to be as miserable an experience for him as it is an exhilarating one for her. His whole body resists the intrusion of his wife's outside life, and he starts the day with a fever (a man who has weathered her love affairs in good health). After the march he goes to his sickbed, raving at the foolishness of the speeches, while Joan, who cannot soothe him, gaily makes calls from the downstairs phone. This story explicitly announces that signs of intelligence, independence, or strength in a woman are considered threatening to a man. But while Updike is aware of such an attitude in this case, which he treats lightly, he seems oblivious to its pernicious effects in *Rabbit Redux.*

In the story "Home" a young father returning to America after living in London sees his mother waiting on the dock with the "face of a woman whose country has never quite settled what to do with its women."[34] Updike has expressed a concern with correcting this problem as it occurs in our literature: "American

34. *Pigeon Feathers and Other Stories*, p. 108.

fiction is notoriously thin on women, and I *have* attempted a number of portraits of women, and we may have reached that point of civilization, or decadence, where we can look at women."[35] The "we" for Updike, which can mean only the male point of view, betrays the impossibility of his being able to look at a broad spectrum of women or to deal in much detail with their feelings. But the fact that he so seldom attempts to show the woman's point of view does not necessarily negate his portraits of those women who have allowed themselves to be formed by the concepts of men.

As a progression from the manipulating mothers of the past, Updike accepts only the bovine wives who comfortably merge with his failing heroes. It is here that he apparently wishes the development of women to end. The current wave of feminism is very much related to the stagnant conditions he portrays, but Updike offers a backlash effect as he denigrates new kinds of women. Under the guise of tolerant acceptance, his fiction insidiously goes about making female mediocrity and inertia seem inevitable, even lovable. And he consistently reasserts the worn dichotomy that a woman is sexual and stupid (human) or that she is frigid and intelligent (inhuman). Only the woman as a comfortable blank is to be desired and accepted by individual men and by society. Women who do not fit this standard are not really human and must be rubbed out of the world.

35. Samuels, "The Art of Fiction XLIII," p. 101.

four

The Terrified Women
of Joyce Carol Oates

The overwhelming fact in the lives of Joyce Carol Oates's best characters is economic: "The greatest realities are physical and economic; all the subtleties of life come afterward. Intellectuals have forgotten, or else they never understood, how difficult it is to make one's way up from a low economic level, to assert one's will in a great crude way. It's so difficult. You have to go through it. You have to be poor."[1] Oates's sympathies are so obviously with these poor that her treatment of women characters is frequently divided more clearly along the lines of poverty and affluence than as some writers make a division, between the types of the bitch mother and the dull wife. The women of the middle and upper classes, particularly as they are satirized, seldom come to life as her lower-class women do. Among the latter are those who somewhat obtusely survive better than anyone else, such as Loretta Botsford of *them*, and the more passive and intelligent sufferers like her daughter Maureen Wendall, Oates's most excellent creation and one of the most interesting women in the literature of the sixties.

In their efforts at economic survival, Oates's male characters traditionally pursue more varied methods, both legitimate and illegitimate, than her women do. Men enter the life of the streets and are in closer touch with the world's goods, even if they are not to possess them. Women, in their more limited spheres, are resigned to improving their financial status rather by attachment

1. Quoted in Alfred Kazin, "Oates," *Harper's*, 243 (Aug. 1971), 81.

to men. Clara Walpole (*A Garden of Earthly Delights*) raises herself to a life on her own farm through her manipulation of the wealthy Revere. The toughness of women like Clara is not found, perhaps because it is not demanded, in, for instance, Updike's young women, who are adequately provided for. His middle-class wives are not forced to claw their way to financial security. The sense of power (which usually breaks down) in Oates's lower-class women, developed as the men disappear or destroy themselves through some form of violence, is both frightening and refreshing after the many accounts of sterile middle-class women whose leisure allows them to become bored neurotics.

Clara Walpole is bitterly determined to escape the doom of her mother's life—a woman first shown to us as she is trapped in her third pregnancy, traveling as a migrant worker. The facts of Mrs. Walpole's life flow together in a blur. She never understands or controls. "The women had no opinion; opinions belonged to men."[2] Clara flees such a situation to offer herself shamelessly to Lowry, the most immediately available man of any appeal; she literally walks into his room and turns her life over to him. Such a response has nothing to do with love, of course, but is the way a man and a woman painfully, irrevocably collide and become bound by sexual and other destructive forces. Clara gladly leaves her father, but she soon wishes he would find her and kill Lowry. (And such a fantasy in one of these stories is not to be taken lightly.) She eventually escapes Lowry, but only for a time, as she sets herself up with Revere's wealth.

Clara, afraid at first of being crushed like her mother, when she has her own child and property, is terrified of losing them. Underlying the calm that prevails as she works in her garden is the dread of Lowry's return, which is in some way a threat to everything established in her new life. Harboring her hatred of him, Clara carefully cultivates their delicate son Swan, a sensitive, nervous child. Since violence is bound to be the outcome of inward tensions, considering that few things remain abstract for Oates, we await an explosion in Swan's future.

2. Joyce Carol Oates, *A Garden of Earthly Delights* (Greenwich, Conn.: Fawcett Publications, 1966), p. 14. Further page references to this edition are included in the text.

Clara's garden is not the Eden it appears to be but the literal sign of economic gain, just as Revere represents concrete wealth and power, not romantic attachment. The idea of marrying for money is a pragmatic law of life neither Clara nor Oates would call into question. Clara's icy materialism and her eventual insanity are not the result of a wrong choice regarding Revere but merely deterministic responses to negative conditions. If her very secularized garden is to remind us that Eden is no more, it is a version of the author's own expiation of the supernatural which she says was worked out of her system in her first novel, With Shuddering Fall. Even when people do obey "God's commands," she states, they are not rewarded. Living in this world is "a sufficiently intricate hopeless problem itself without bringing in another world, bringing in an extra dimension."[3]

When Lowry demonically appears to break the surface peace of Clara's pastoral life, her panic is handled with the great skill the author has developed for such scenes. Against her will Clara is once again drawn to her lover, who shatters the careful surface of the life she has so painstakingly built:

> She stared miserably at the floor. Everything was draining out of her, all her strength, all the hatred that had kept Lowry close to her for so long. It struck her that she had fed on this hatred and that it had kept her going, given her life. Now that he was here and standing before her, she could not remember why she had hated him.
>
> "You bastard," she whispered. "Coming back here like this— You—"
>
> "Let me make you quiet," Lowry said.
>
> She looked up at his smile, which was exactly like the smile she remembered [242].

Determined that Swan shall have more control over his life than she has had, Clara tries to keep him from a knowledge of Lowry; when he comes, the boy is shunted out of the way, but he feels the degree of his mother's anxiety. Beneath her attempt to control is the greater sense of things crumbling. Even the land they own

3. Linda Kuehl, "An Interview with Joyce Carol Oates," Commonweal, 91 (Dec. 5, 1969), 309.

offers no security. Clara's tenuous hold on her realities is reflected in her son, whose tension erupts first in an accidental shooting of his stepbrother, and finally in the shooting of his stepfather and himself. Clara is last seen in a nursing home dwindling in a passive state of insanity, the feminine alternative to the explosive response of Swan.

Under the surface of the toughest of Oates's people, like those of Barth, Pynchon, Purdy, and others, is a desperate emptiness. Both men and women face a void; but men are typically much more active in attempting to fill that void than are women, who are more likely simply to collide with men's violence in their sexual encounters. While sexual activity provides the raucous action of the fabulators, and for a writer like Updike remains the best and often the only communication between men and women, for Oates it is more a hard fact of existence, like others which women must frequently deal with sheerly as matters of economic expediency. A woman will inevitably be used by men. Whether or not she can profit financially from the experience is the crucial matter. It is true that serious female writers seldom write explicitly of sex, but it is not mere reticence that is responsible for the swift, non-erotic scenes of lovemaking for Oates. Women most often offer themselves to men as business transactions, and the sooner the matter is done with the better. The sexual act is not necessarily repulsive, but frequently women feel nothing, simply allowing their bodies to be used for pay. In this Oates understands prostitution as do none of her contemporaries for its basically economic aspects. Her coldly pragmatic view of it makes Updike's treatment of Ruth, for example, seem absurdly romantic.

For some women, more often those of the middle class, sexual experience is painful. In a fascinating story, "Unmailed, Unwritten Letters," a woman's thoughts to her parents, her husband, her lover, and her lover's daughter, who sends bitter notices in the mail, she claims that the second time a woman falls in love "the sensation is terrifying, bitter, violent." At the age of thirty she would say good-by to love and to the act of love. "A woman in the act of love feels no joy but only terror, a parody of labor, giving birth. Torture. Heartbeat racing at 160, 180 beats a minute, where is joy in this, what is this deception, this joke. Isn't the body itself a joke?"[4]

Some women are necessarily conscious of their bodies as their only equipment in an ultimately concrete world, and they pay careful but grudging attention to the care of skin, hair, and figure, as they must to attract men. But since beauty often brings on the abuse of men, women frequently make themselves hideously fat, or ugly with misshapen clothes. The body is a liability, after all, always out of control, the center of pain and the source of excretions that proliferate in Oates's work: vomit, blood, diseased tissue, menstrual blood, and the newborn child itself, the most terrible excretion of all.

There are a great many fat people in Oates's fiction, fat often as a result of efforts to fill up the empty self. (Since the author's sympathies are primarily with the poor, she makes abundance particularly gross.) Richard Everett, the boy murderer of his mother in *Expensive People*, at the telling of his story is a 250-pound eighteen-year-old, planning suicide by eating until his stomach bursts. Parents endlessly stuff their children with treats. The second section of *Wonderland* is an orgy of eating, with the monstrous Dr. Pedersen guiding his family into one gargantuan meal after another as they grow into helpless giants. Fat girls balloon perversely fatter, often merely to spite men. Dr. Pedersen's daughter Hilda arrives at dinner in burlap to rankle her expensively dressed father. The scene where he coerces her into a dress shop and hovers in the lobby to pass judgment on the clothes she models is unforgettable. How splendidly Oates understands such things as the misery of tugging on a tight dress in one of those stuffy chambers of a clothing store, pestered by a clerk who is bound to enter at any moment to pull at the zipper and remark that the ill-fitting garment looks fine. Hilda is sure that the dress she must tug on will rip. Her father sees her in it and bellows out "No!" to his blimp-like daughter, who trots back to try again.

The male characters of the family are as fat as the females but never so disgusting, and never does their ugliness represent such a

4. Joyce Carol Oates, *The Wheel of Love* (Greenwich, Conn.: Fawcett Publications, 1972), pp. 57, 63–64.

vilification of self. Dr. Pedersen's unfortunate and very fat wife is found prostrate in her bathroom by the innocent Jesse, their adopted son (the protagonist of the novel), who is also an enormous blob of fat. She convinces Jesse to help her escape her monster husband, and the two of them perform a fantastic scene of eating in a neighboring town—one giant meal after another. (He consumes an entire Chinese dinner with his hands while waiting outside her hotel room.) Mrs. Pedersen refuses to answer the calls of her husband, but she is quite incapable of creating a life apart from him. Perhaps the most pathetic fat person of all, she is given a gruesome sympathy reserved for physically grotesque women, which surpasses any pity we might feel for the desperate Jesse, distraught as he is with his more profound problems. He goes on to a thinner more varied life, if not a satisfying one, while the Pedersen women remain trapped in their fat.

Both beautiful and unbeautiful women masochistically attempt to make themselves repulsive to men. Since so much distress comes with sexual involvement, it is preferable to discourage men by being ugly. In a story entitled "Normal Love" a woman of forty desires but fears the attentions of her husband of many years. "Why am I not at peace, being forty years old?" she asks herself; "a woman wants to rake her body with her nails, streaming blood, she wants to gash her face so that no man need look at it."[5] She wants to be safe, and to be safe a woman must be beyond sex. Her sex draws her back into life, and with that comes a frightening loss of control, which is the case for the beautiful widow in "What Is the Connection between Men and Women?" After her husband dies her life is as blank as the white china in the shop where she works, but she feels that no calamity can touch her. Then another man comes along and draws her from deathlike boredom to that only other alternative for a woman, a threatening connection with a man. Some women obliterate their beauty but at the same time plunge self-destructively into such a connection. In "Pastoral Blood" a very pretty young girl named Grace, a week before she is to be married, suddenly proceeds to make love to strangers. Repulsed by the kind of femininity she has represented,

5. Joyce Carol Oates, *Marriages and Infidelities* (New York: Vanguard Press, 1972), p. 275.

she ritualistically replaces her pink flowered dress with a black blouse and a black striped skirt, attire representative of a lower-class promiscuity. Thwarting "the work of centuries, civilizations, to bring forth such a product. . . . Pretty girl!,"[6] she drives out of town to her new fate.

The most original and stunning account of a woman's masochistic delight in making herself gross to men is the unforgettable "At the Seminary." An obviously neurotic family of three—father, mother, and fat, fat daughter—visit the son at the seminary. Sally resents the emphasis placed on her brother's pious life, with its denial of the physical, and the seriousness with which his minor problems are discussed. Her problems are the crucial ones. She hates smug mothers, disapproves of children, in short is digusted by life. "Her mother had wanted her to be pretty, she thought, and deliberately she was not pretty."[7] She revels in her obesity and is charmed at the seminary to detect the start of her menstrual period. Before the shocked but gracious priest, and her family, she crosses the room slamming her feet loudly to the floor, giggling all the while as the menstrual blood dribbles horribly down her legs and into her shoes before the gaze of the incredulous men. She triumphs with the excuse, "I never asked God to make me a woman!"[8]

Women's mortifying effects to their bodies, committed in spite against the importance placed upon appearance or as a direct design against their specific antagonists, are also a way of reacting to the genuine fear of assault. A combination of these motives in a particularly paranoid form appears in "Stalking," in which a heavy-set girl of thirteen fantasizes that she is being followed by an "Adversary." Gretchen, who like other fat girls flaunts her ugliness in defiance of the commercialized standard of beauty, also uses it as a defense against her imagined pursuer. There are hints that she could be a handsome girl, but out of disgust and fear she makes herself dowdy and sexless. As an attack upon methods of

6. Joyce Carol Oates, *By the North Gate* (Greenwich, Conn.: Fawcett Publications, 1963), p. 77.

7. Joyce Carol Oates, *Upon the Sweeping Flood and Other Stories* (Greenwich, Conn.: Fawcett Publications, 1966), p. 99.

8. Ibid., p. 106.

beautification, she smears lipstick (which she has stolen from a drugstore) on the mirror in the ladies' room of a department store, shoves a towel in the toilet, and flushes. But rather than try to actually destroy her adversary, she fantasizes his death by envisioning pools of blood in his front hallway.

Women's fear of violent action is usually accompanied by a fascination with it. If given the choice between duplicating their mothers' trapped lives at home or joining men in their wild destruction, most make the second choice. Such is the story of Mae in "What Death with Love Should Have to Do," a paradigm of the novel *With Shuddering Fall*. The image of a woman clinging to a man's back as he roars along on his motorcycle is an appropriate picture of her parasitic and dangerous relationship to him. Male power is enhanced by man's use of the machine, and a woman cleaves to these mysterious forces. But as Jules Wendall of *them* points out, women know nothing about machines. And this deficiency increases their sense of powerlessness in a power-driven world. Mae's wild ride on the motorcycle brings about a miscarriage, and as the bleeding begins (Oates's penchant for blood) she pleads for her lover to stop. Riding along in the wind he cannot hear her. When they finally do stop, she vomits (another familiar Oates touch). Despite these destructive effects, Mae chooses the male world of energy and action, seeing herself only as the "anonymous hard-faced girl surrounded by men."[9] She dies from the miscarriage.

Mae's counterpart in *With Shuddering Fall*, Karen Hertz, also wills her life from a drab existence to a dangerous one, with similar results. Karen is drawn to her father's brute power and is similarly attracted to Shar and his race cars. Like many of Oates's women, she at first mistakenly imagines that men in all their activity have a control over their lives that she does not have. But Shar is badly out of control with his cars, causing collisions both on and off the racetrack. Oates (who learned about cars from *Hot Rod Magazine*) makes excellent use here of the destructive potential of man's favorite machine, both as a literal element in her naturalistic detail and as an image to illustrate sexual and emotional collisions.

9. Ibid., pp. 193–94.

Karen enters Shar's life as she once intentionally dashed in front of a speeding car and was almost killed. The destructive and the sexual are perfectly united, the lovers even referring to each other as killers. Despairing her lack of control over love and its devastation, Karen twists her face into ugly patterns before the mirror to fend off her lover and love. But she suffers the usual pregnancy, which results in a miscarriage that almost kills her, and her dealings with Shar bring on the expected insanity. Back at her own home she is presumably at peace, but such a possibility seems unlikely. Both Karen and Shar suffer the effects of violence, but with a difference: Shar at least has more to do with how his life will end. As Karen says, " 'His death was no accident: only his life is.' "[10] Her only choice is for the violent over the sedentary. After that decision, she is a victim.

Despite the frequency of violence in the writing of Joyce Carol Oates, and she often treats it brilliantly, its truth borne out to us by newspaper accounts every day, she is even better at showing the quiet terror that so often lies under the surface of normal things, *the apprehension of violence*. On an ordinary afternoon a suburban housewife drives into a parking lot of a major department store and imagines a man there to be following her: "My heart begins to pound absurdly, I know there is no danger and yet my muscles stiffen as if in expectation of danger, the very shape of my skeleton tensing as if to receive a blow. . . . The elevator comes. The door opens. I step inside, the man steps quickly inside, for a moment I feel a sense of panic, as if inside me a door is opening suddenly upon nothing, upon blackness."[11] Nothing happens. But the chill evoked in this everyday setting is astonishing. Many of Oates's best scenes, like this one, reveal women's solitary, haunting fears, especially of men. In this the author is at least as effective with her more affluent women as she is with her poor ones.

"Where Are You Going, Where Have You Been?" is probably the most powerful example of fear in a normal setting. Connie, a fifteen-year-old, is ever so typical a teenager of the fifties—arguing

10. Joyce Carol Oates, *With Shuddering Fall* (New York: Fawcett World Library, 1964), p. 191.
11. "Normal Love," *Marriages and Infidelities*, p. 261.

with her mother about not wanting to clean her room, using junky hair spray, considering her older, unmarried sister a social disaster. To her friends she complains about her mother, but her irritations are not unusual for a teenage girl. Such are the normalcies of a life drawn without a flaw and with just the right touches of sleaziness. One dull Sunday afternoon, with her parents off to a barbeque at an aunt's house, Connie spends the day drying her hair in the sun and daydreaming of love. A gold-tinted jalopy pulls up in the drive and out comes Arnold Friend, who wants her to go for a ride. A thousand Sunday afternoons in a thousand small towns are like this one. After a long, half-bored, half-flirtatious conversation, a girl finally gives in and goes for the ride, which usually results in more suggestion than action.

In her boredom Connie is mildly curious as to the stranger she has seen only once before, but she dawdles about going for a ride with him. She has things to do. Things. He laughs, and they jostle for position casually for a good length of the story until something frightening begins to happen, slowly, quietly, with very little surface indication. Mr. Friend lets Connie know that he wants more than a Sunday drive and will not stop until he gets it. The subtle strain of paranoia most women feel about the possibilities of sexual attack turns chillingly into a real threat for Connie. Her flippant, easy approach freezes in her as she dares to realize the threat, which Friend refers to in such a proper way: " 'It's real nice and you couldn't ask for nobody better than me, or more polite. I always keep my word. I'll tell you how it is, I'm always nice at first, the first time.' "[12] Under the impact of fear the familiar kitchen is no longer familiar to Connie, and the screen door that a moment ago was such a homey, teasing barrier for her becomes a startlingly flimsy protection from what Mr. Friend now represents. His promise not to come in the house after her is more disturbing than a blunt demand might be, for we know he will enter when he is ready. The screen door is slight, he observes; locking it will never keep him out if he cares to come in. Friend's language is commonplace, filled with words Connie's mother might have said a few hours before—" 'Now, you be a good girl' " (43)—more frightening than any obscenity could be. Eventually,

12. *The Wheel of Love*, p. 40.

with the stiffness terror puts into this once-cocky girl, Connie watches herself push open the screen door and go out to Arnold Friend, into a sunlit afternoon and a landscape she can no longer recognize. The story exhibits no violence. But it is more terrifying than those that do, with a fear that transforms familiar objects and the landscape in a way that suggests that they will never be quite normal again. A short passage of time is immense. Such treatment of the anticipation of violence is Oates's great strength, not the account of actual violence, which is often anticlimactic.

Women's fear of men is seldom dramatized through scenes of rape and mutilation. When such acts occur the information comes by way of the news or through gossip. The distance of these events in comparison with other acts of violence—there are several closeups of murder—is in keeping with the emphasis on the *fear* perpetrated by the thought of rape and its accompanying brutality, rather than on the acts themselves. What woman has not at some time imagined rape, especially when the news announces that it has been committed a block from her home? After reading of a rape-murder in her neighborhood, a woman cannot pass a familiar doorway without being afraid. Most women never will be attacked, but there is no way they can insure their safety against a threat that is not limited to any particular social or economic class, age group, or location. Oates never allows us to forget the sheer amount of violence in America. If we never encounter it directly ourselves, we will probably know someone who does. The fact that some form of brutality occurs on our streets every few minutes is the kind of knowledge that rules the minds of Oates's people.

The affluent housewife who is freed of the economic burdens and other pressures of poverty is even more likely to be obsessed by quiet terrors than is her poorer counterpart. Oates's later stories frequently turn to the fears of the suburban woman, and in dealing with this subject she is much more effective than she is in satirizing suburbia's emptiness, also coming closer to her own experience in the treatment of anxiety than in scenes of brutality. *The Wheel of Love* volume of stories, which does not contain as much violence as the earlier collections (although the most recent novels deal with her usual dosage of blood), is particularly effective. In one of the rare interviews with Oates, a clue to her own fearful perceptions is very revealing. She is sitting in her back yard, which leads to a lake; the water is calm, the day is mild, and "far out on the sunny river a small blue boat is rocking gently with two boys in it. She says softly, 'I don't like to see them out there. These boats turn over very easily and you can't get them upright again. If that happened, I'm not sure what I could do.' "[13] This is exactly the sense of disturbance that she portrays so powerfully in her quiet women of refinement, who feel incapable of dealing with dangerous action or even strong emotions.

One such account is "What Is the Connection between Men and Women?," in which a man simply glances at a woman in a supermarket and the terror of lust is upon her. Back in her comfortable apartment she sits alone and tense, jarred by the ringing of the phone. She waits. When the man comes to her door at five o'clock in the morning, after they have both been awake all night, she answers his knock, slides back the bolt, and "everything comes open, comes apart."[14] A man's arrival is characteristically treated as a fearful but inevitable happening, bringing the disintegration that leads to life and to madness. This effect is found in "6:27" in dealing with the return of a woman's ex-husband. She is a hairdresser, nervously edging through her day in anticipation of the fearful moment he will enter the shop. He calls her and then hangs up, but never appears in the story, which ends at 6:25 with Glenda and her unwanted son in the supermarket. We never know what happens at 6:27.

Just as effectively as Oates shows the fear of the strange or the estranged man, she captures the anxieties of a woman regarding the familiar and apparently trusted man. In "Normal Love" Mrs. York respects and "loves" her husband, who is never cruel but who does preserve a disturbing silence. The trappings of normal life in a contemporary American suburb give what should be a comfortable surface—the neighborhood supermarket with its tinseled tree for Christmas, the family meals prepared with care, and the sound of the telephone. But alone in her quiet home Mrs.

13. Walter Clemons, "Joyce Carol Oates at Home," *New York Times Book Review*, Sept. 28, 1969, p. 48.
14. *The Wheel of Love*, p. 383.

York cannot place herself and jumps nervously whenever the phone rings. She misses her children, who are at school, but the thought of their return is threatening. "Do they want to damage me, my flesh? No. Does my husband want to damage me? No."[15] And at the hairdresser's the chatter drifts casually to the topic of thalidomide babies. The regular schedule Mrs. York and her family keep shows no deviations that would be disturbing. Her husband, a doctor, has a drink every night at five, and they eat dinner punctually at six. Although she considers herself a blessed woman, loving the very knives and forks that feed her family, alternating with her pleasure in these signs of "normal" love she envisions herself retching over the bathroom sink.

It is common enough to show the calm distances in the modern marriage, often its sheer vacancy. But in the specific quality of fear felt in these vacancies Oates gives us something peculiarly her own. It is the predominant feeling her married women have. Unlike most of Oates's contemporaries, she has little to say of sex in marriage, making it conspicuous by its absence. Perhaps her women repress thoughts of sex. Either they fear sexual experience or their emotions are not deeply touched by it any more than the act of prostitution affects women who are forced into it for their livelihood. Women seem to make love in their sleep. Mrs. York remembers being pregnant but not how she came to her condition. But far from being at peace, she is disturbed when her husband even looks at her.

The texture of this normal life is interrupted when Dr. York finds a girl's purse in the vacant lot by their home. The owner is later discovered as only a torso floating in the river. The fact of the girl's murder is related to Mrs. York by a friend at a party; the victim was apparently murdered by the lover she had spent the previous night with in a motel. Such an event is naturally a piece of gossip, and it is necessarily related to Mrs. York because her husband discovered the girl's purse. But there is a foreboding connection between Mrs. York's feelings of dread and the brutalizing of the girl, which is nothing so specific as anxiety for her life, since it is her kindly husband she fears. And he would never harm her. Would he? Mrs. York's awareness of what a woman's physical

15. *Marriages and Infidelities*, p. 264.

appeal can lead to—the girl's murder—is related to her desire to gash her face, as an escape. She is too refined and controlled, however, to do anything like this. Oates's later stories increasingly deal with the tensions of people who are locked in without the release of violence, with an emphasis on the strangeness and anxiety in their seemingly amiable relationships. The bizarre murder in "Normal Love" is kept at a distance (although not too far distant) and is used not as a direct threat to the suburban woman but as a focal point for her anxiety.

The story "Puzzle" poses the question of what brings people together in marriage, and then what holds them together, the queerest puzzle of all. The connection between men and women in these stories is especially disturbing, for there is no suggestion of a happiness to mitigate the fear involved in the bond. There are no lighthearted, joyful, or even sensuous experiences. But a dangerous association is preferred to the alternative of separation, which results in lifelessness for the woman.

There is no actual violence in "Puzzle," only the memory of the death of the couple's child that occurred years before, which is made crucial to their present relationship. The young boy was drowned in a drainage ditch. His mother, who has no other children, is understandably awkward and upset whenever she meets children on the street. The memory of the lost child provokes hostility between the couple, but at the same time it connects them. Like the murdered girl in "Normal Love," the death of the boy serves as a focal point for the inherent tension of the marriage. Meanwhile, the woman is afraid of her husband and at times wishes he were dead. One evening as they arrive home late she plans to announce that she is leaving him. Oates is expert at making real the dread of these people as they enter their own seemingly safe home. The husband goes to the refrigerator, his wife waits nervously, and then he surprises her by saying it was his own carelessness that was responsible for the accident that took their boy's life. This sudden vulnerability is apparently the clue to the puzzle that keeps this couple together. She is now unable to leave him. They embrace, and she admits (as so many of Oates's characters feel) that she understands nothing outside of the present moment.

The children that inevitably result from even the briefest encounters with men are as unfortunate as the connections that bring them about. The mother, or ex-mother as she calls herself in "Puzzle," who laments the loss of her child, would probably be pained by his existence if he were alive. Childbirth is another of the violent disasters that make women bitter and afraid; it is bloody and painful, very often fatal. Women seldom commit the murders that fill Oates's fiction, but when they do become violent they are most likely to vent themselves against their children, perhaps because only in this connection are they physically superior to their antagonists.

One of the few times a woman commits murder is in an early story, "Swamps." An animal-like, pregnant girl wandering in the swamps, scorned by the townspeople, is finally taken in by an old man who cares for her. After giving birth to her child she drowns it, leaving it head down in a basin in the man's cabin. It is no surprise that this girl admittedly hates women; having a child is the ugly punishment of being female. Deserted by the father of the child, she is left to care for the baby that issues from her like a foreign object and to confront the scorn of the community, in this most familiar plight of woman. With no compunction she murders the child, an act Oates does not repeat (although in some cases fathers murder their children). But if mothers do not kill their children, few of them have any helpful maternal concern for them.

Motherhood is a sinister concept in the literature of this period from almost any point of view, particularly when the mother takes overwhelming control. Oates's best characters are not her manipulating mothers, however. Natashya Everett, whom she satirizes in *Expensive People*, the mother Richard Everett kills for warping him into a monster, is supposedly everything the American woman wants to be; and the result is a great nothing. Clara Walpole, who for a time manipulates her son, is so shattered by her own fears that the boy is soon quite out of her control. From the lower-class woman's point of view, children, like sex, are simply another of the tangible and incomprehensible facts of life to be reckoned with as part of the economic burden. Fathers see children in much the same way. (The maniacal father of Jesse Harte in

Wonderland slays everyone in his family except Jesse, who escapes, after a long period during which he is unemployed.)

As much as these women resent motherhood, however, few of them seem aware of any methods of birth control. Having a child is a dreaded inevitability. When Jules Wendall comes to his mother's place after her divorce from her second husband and sees another man at the table, he automatically expects another baby. (Mrs. Wendall is at the time taking care of one unwanted infant, the undesired result of her most recent marriage.) A child is often a threat to the sanity or to the lives of his parents. Oates has stated that her stories do not usually deal with the Oedipal theme because the fathers are not strong enough, but there is often a clear hint of it as one source of the violence—obviously so with Richard Everett's murder of his mother. Mothers may desire to kill their children, but they are usually too passive to take such decisive action.

Certainly one reason why mothers (young or middle-aged) are usually not shown to be manipulators is that from their point of view, and we see this through a female writer, they who feel incapable of ruling their own lives do not feel able to rule the lives of others. Mothers are afraid of their children as they watch them grow into separate beings whose nature they can never understand or control. The mother of two sons in "Extraordinary Popular Delusions" and Mrs. York in "Normal Love" believe that their children are not even aware of them. The motherly duties they perform mean nothing. Conscientious housewives often feel alien and trapped in their own homes, unable to understand why. They cannot make any sensible connection between the unasked-for attraction to the men they marry, the sexual act, which is usually treated as a dim memory, the children that result, their duties as housewives, and the strangers who are their husbands. Clara Walpole vividly recalls two facts about her mother's life: one night a man had climbed on top of her, and months later she died of it.

The dread of motherhood combines a woman's fears of men, among other things for causing pregnancy, and of children, both beyond her understanding and control. Like most male writers, Oates accepts the traditional roles of women. But where the male point of view suggests that motherhood should be a positive experience, Oates shows it only to be an awful one, as it brings to a climax the lifelong fears and hostilities her women have experienced. Their tensions erupt in some of the ugliest acts in her fiction.

A story simply called "The Children" consists of another of those smooth surfaces with a sinister underlying current which Oates creates so effectively. As graduate students Ronald and Ginny marry, and she relinquishes her career with relief. Surprised to enjoy her move to the suburbs, she mingles with other wives, talking and acting as they do. The daughter born to her seems a perfect child, and for a time the mother's life passes in a comfortable blur as she considers herself in control. The concentration on others is a relief, for she may now define her life through the activities of her family. But as the beautiful, willful daughter grows, Ginny becomes increasingly frightened of her. A son is born, and young Rachel pokes at him to irritate her mother, telling her how the neighbors say she is a bad parent. The quiet afternoons in the suburbs gradually take on a nightmarish quality, and without understanding why, Ginny is terrified. Rachel keeps foreboding secrets from her, and at last the clash comes. Ginny beats her child wildly with a spoon, which is bloody by the time her husband comes home and takes it from her, as she screams at him, " 'Oh, *you* don't know! What do *you* know about it? What the hell do *you* know?' "[16] "The Children" ranks with "Where Are You Going, Where Have You Been?" and "Normal Love" as one more superb account of the quiet terror women experience under "normal" circumstances.

In "The Children" hysteria breaks out early in the life of the young mother who beats her daughter, but the pattern is usually more prolonged and subtle, showing a gradual disintegration. Oates's works are everywhere informed by a fear of entropy—of things vanishing, wearing down, being torn away. Maureen Wendall is obsessed with the idea: "What would happen if everything broke into pieces? . . . How could you get hold of something that wouldn't end? Marriages ended. Love ended. Money could be stolen, found out and taken, Furlong himself might find it, or

16. Ibid., p. 236.

it might disappear by itself, like that secretary's notebook. Such things happened. Objects disappeared, slipped through cracks, devoured, kicked aside, knocked under the bed or into the trash, lost. Nothing lasted for long."[17]

In "The Dead" an intelligent and successful young woman writer is shown in the fatal process of disintegration. In great demand as a speaker after the success of one of her novels, Ilena visits college campuses, satisfying the crowds who apparently see nothing strange in her condition, although she is heavily drugged. The story begins with the directions on a bottle of pills: *"Useful in acute and chronic depression, where accompanied by anxiety,"*[18] an accurate diagnosis of Ilena's general condition. She is frightened all the time. But the doctor claims she is normal. When her husband is in the hospital she does not visit him once, "being hard of heart, like stone, and terrified of seeing him again. She feared his mother too."[19] Her fears of sleep with its nightmares of Kennedy's assassination are one of the more obvious reminders of how the catastrophes of our times figure in our neuroses.

Ilena, one of the few professional and creative women to exist in this period of literature, is in even worse mental condition than most other women. Her novels are created out of her misery, and unlike the heavy physical work that keeps some women too occupied to go insane, her activity and awareness only feed the tensions that lead to insanity. She speaks fluently and intelligently, in the meantime fingering the pills in her pocket. Her teaching is either sluggish or hysterical, the two familiar sides of the same madness. Ilena is further split by taking a lover while she is married. But hers is not a problem of divided passion; she is simply exhausted by repeating the motions required of her body without the invigoration of true sexuality. She cannot live with two men. She cannot live with one. Oates has admitted her affinity with this intellectual type of person; and it is these people, she says, who are most given to violence, whether through the aggressive physical demonstrations of men or the insane and sui-

17. Joyce Carol Oates, *them* (Greenwich, Conn.: Fawcett Publications, 1969), p. 197. Further page references to this edition are included in the text.
18. *Marriages and Infidelities*, p. 453.
19. Ibid., p. 457.

cidal leanings of women. On the verge of suicide, Ilena gives an
indifferent consent to marry again as a pattern of least resistance.
In her madness the faces of men blend together, the only one
standing out that of a student who died from an overdose of hero-
in. In her disintegration she imagines herself on a bed crammed
with men merging into each other, becoming protoplasm. The
snow falls as in Joyce's "The Dead," but it does not bring the
peace of death for Ilena.

Since women never offer themselves to men for pleasure, of
which they seem incapable, it is surprising in "The Sacred Marriage" to find a beautiful, gracious lady, widow of a famous poet,
who immediately and happily goes to bed with the young instructor who visits her home to study her husband's papers—surprising,
until we learn the real reason for her generous sexuality. After
two weeks of cosy cohabitation with Howard Dean, his allotted
time, Emilia greets a second scholar who has come for his turn
with the precious papers and, it now becomes apparent, her bed
that accompanies the project. Such easy lovemaking is indeed
too good to be true. Dean discovers the answer in the author's
papers, a short story of a famous novelist about to die who marries
a beautiful woman so that she might pass on his divinity by taking
a multitude of lovers. Thus Emilia is merely an agent. The male as
the creator and the female who lives only through him form a
version of the pattern found among less sophisticated Oatesian
people for whom a man's relation to a woman is based on his
physical and economic attributes rather than on creative achievements. In either case, women must have men to fill up their
blankness. Men may be as dependent upon women to fill sexual
and some emotional needs, but other things are also important
to them: action, machinery, or, in this case, art. The best chance
for a woman's healthy survival is for her not to resist her blankness but to succumb to it as Emilia does, or to develop the simple
and fatalistic resilience of Loretta Botsford, mother of Maureen
Wendall.

Most of the ideas important to women in Oates's fiction are
brought together in Maureen. The frame for *them* is the claim
that Maureen was one of the author's students, who wrote to her
years after flunking her composition course, still disturbed by the

discussions of form in literature and life which to her had nothing to do with the mess life really is. Oates states that she was so affected by the girl's story that she took it down in detail and presented it as a "work of history in fictional form," which she says is "the only kind of fiction that is real."[20] The author's obvious affinity to this character is surely responsible in part for the novel's success. Maureen's anxieties, her anguish for having no fixed identity (which women seldom recognize in such an acute way), and the context of poverty are the materials that Oates works with best. Poverty and violence are not necessarily the sources of women's terror—Ilena's madness follows no such obstacles, and the quiet hysteria of Mrs. York, residing comfortably in the suburbs, is as acute as Maureen's. But her story powerfully combines fear of actual physical danger with anxiety for the subtle and the unknown. She is afraid of everything. "Asleep or awake I am afraid, and how can you live that way, always afraid? I am afraid of men out on the street if I see them or don't see them, I am afraid of cars hitting me, of people laughing at me, I am afraid of losing my purse, of throwing up in a store, of screaming out loud in the library and being kicked out and never allowed back" (310).

Typically of Oates's novels, *them* opens with an announcement of violence: the teenage Loretta Botsford brings her young lover to her bed and is awakened the next morning by the sound of her brother shooting him in the head. Loretta's youth is over. She who the day before gazed frivolously at her own reflection and was pleased with its resemblance to a Hollywood image now dashes wildly into the street, half dresssed, looking for the gun she realizes is necessary for survival in her neighborhood. The panic so clearly motivated in this early scene suggests a story that will keep us tied to the tangibles. The action is horrible, but we know exactly the source of Loretta's fears. In pragmatically closing her dreamy past as she takes up a gun to protect herself after her lover's death, Loretta proves to be one of the more fortunate women. She assumes no guilt, accepts events as inevitable, and then she acts.

Loretta lacks the deeper sensitivity that would allow her to see

20. "Author's Note" to *them*, p. 5.

more, and fear more, as her daughter Maureen does. Loretta is, in fact, glad to be without a unique identity, the very thing her daughter desires: "She liked the fact that there were so many Lorettas, that she'd seen two girls in one week with a sailor outfit like her own, and a hundred girls with curly hair flung back over their shoulders!" (21). This ability to be a blank on which a familiar copy might be impressed, whatever is popular at the time, keeps her from the great loneliness that is to plague Maureen as it plagues most people who are as self-consciously unusual as she.

In *them* men are outsiders either because they are at work or because they have left dreary domesticity for the excitement and profit they hope for in the random life of the city. Mama Wendall, the despised mother of Loretta's first husband, the policeman Howard Wendall, is a power-hungry old woman trying to head the matriarchy at home. She can control Maureen, who is easily affected by authority. But the younger sister Betty, a tough wench, has no qualms about shoving the old lady out the back door and kicking her down the steps. The strongest woman rules, not the oldest. Men may have control when they are at home, but since they are usually absent, women make up the lasting center of this life. Even the favored Jules is gradually lost to his family as the action centers on the women who remain at home.

Loretta is happier between husbands when she is working, gossipping, and going to movies, free for a time of pregnancy, than she is with a husband. Her addiction to Hollywood ideals brings her back to dreams of romantic love, but her marriages have no resemblance to such dreams. Children come as part of the unromantic reality, but she likes them, nevertheless, and they like her, perhaps because she is too fatalistic to believe she can manipulate them. What has she to do with the creation and control of the mysterious Maureen? Loretta is often thoughtless with her daughter, rousing the girl from sleep in order to use her bed to escape a fight with her husband. And Maureen is forced to take care of her violent stepfather Furlong, a contact which leads to a murderous attack on her. But Loretta is no bitch mother whose determination is to mold her children's identity. She leaves Maureen with the burden of housework but allows her to do it her own way. This mother is so vulnerable that the daughter is never given an illusion of perfection, which is often the weapon of a manipulating mother. Maureen is baffled because her mother does not love her more, but she pities her and fears the consequences of her haphazard life.

Loretta escapes with a few beers every afternoon and the fellowship of women like herself. Maureen has no such escape—her solitary hours in the library only lead to disturbing thoughts. Loretta has never had either the inclination or the capacity for such contemplation. Her fantasies, and they are rather ordinary ones, make up only a small part of her life. Even as a teenager in the spell of Hollywood she worked six days a week in a laundry before emerging for one Saturday night as a star. Such a proportion of pleasure to drudgery is an accurate estimation of what her experiences are to be, but for her the general heaviness of life only increases the pleasure of its few satisfactions. Oates, who has been accused of eliminating the possibilities of life's delights, has not made existence completely dismal for Loretta. She gets a crude enjoyment from unloading the groceries as if they were special prizes for her children. Such delight is not meant to romanticize the economic and spiritual poverty of the Wendalls but to show the person who will thrive best in such a condition.

Maureen, Loretta's second-born after her favorite child Jules, is a strangely diligent daughter. She cleans up after the others, and her half of the bedroom is noticeably the neat half. But her silence and withdrawal from the rest of the family make them suspicious of her and reluctant to accept her as one of them. Sometimes she reveals a hatred of her confinement and occasionally of her entire family, but much stronger than rebellion is her desire to fit in somewhere and to be safe. Maureen is angry and hard without being a fighter. Above all, she desires form and control. Not wishing to destroy, she is forced to live in the midst of destructive forces.

One of the most memorable things about Maureen is the lustful way she hoards her money between the pages of a book of poetry. We might ask why this cautious and intelligent girl never puts her money in the bank, for it is painfully obvious that it will be discovered or stolen if she leaves it in her room. But the actual touch of money is important to her. The one greatest pleasure in her life is to be alone with her bills, which are so sacred to her that she will not even count them and reduce them to a mere numerical value. Her possibilities of escape to a job and a place of her own are so remote that the money in her hand is all she can believe in.

Maureen makes this money through prostitution. An unnamed man picks her up after school each day, and they go to a motel where she passively allows him to make love to her (while all she thinks of is the payment she is about to receive). Like Oates's other women, she is without sexual response. She never asks her client, who remains dim to us because she has no interest in him, about his work or his family. While prostitution is often shown as a sordid, perverted, or even an erotic experience for a woman, here it is simply a means to an end, not desirable, not terrible, not even memorable. It is simply *the* way for a woman to get money, which is almost always the property of men. Maureen's family keep up a pretense to a strong taboo against any loose dealings between men and women, and Mrs. Wendall appears to be shocked that her daughter could be anything but a "nice" girl. But she did her time as a prostitute quite as easily as Maureen does, when she first came to Detroit as the penniless mother of three children.

Sexual experience under such circumstances is a relatively unimportant event in a girl's life, except as it brings money. Maureen's lack of feeling is the most striking thing about her activities as a prostitute. The sex act is swiftly passed over, apparently making little impression on the woman. No foreplay here. The act of sex often merely announces that a child will be born, accompanied by none of the explicit detail that marks a discussion of it in most contemporary fiction. And to the women of *them*, burdened with the practical, the idea of love is as remote as other elements in the lives of the rich, who are considered to possess it as one of their luxuries. Only Jules has a romantic notion of love, which he dramatically lives out in his affair with Nadine Green (who later tries to kill him). Maureen does not even understand the fantasies of romantic love. To her teacher she addresses the pathetic question, " 'But how do you fall in love?' " (315).

While Maureen may not fantasize about love or sexual pleasure, the thought of sexual assault with its threat of mutilation and murder is an unspoken but primary source of fear, as it is elsewhere in Oates's fiction. While Maureen's inner life is shown in quite extensive detail with little attention to rape, this may be because it is too nightmarish a thought to bring to the surface often. Only in one of her few moments of relative safety—she is under the hair dryer between her mother and a friend who comfortably gossip—does she dare openly consider things that ordinarily frighten her: "A girl dragged into a car not two blocks away and raped and pushed out the door, ending up half dead, and the girl was someone Maureen knew" (143). She is not obsessed with an irrational fear. She simply knows what can happen and is understandably afraid.

When Maureen's stepfather discovers her money (and knows immediately how she got it), he almost kills her. The attack puts her in a comatose condition that lasts thirteen months, a period in which all she does is grow fat, one of the Oatesian woman's bizarre responses to her disgust with men and with her life in general. Maureen's long lapse from sanity pushes the traditional passivity of the woman to an extreme: she simply lies in bed and becomes a very large vegetable. Unlike Jules, who lashes out in his frustration, Maureen, the "good girl," turns her miseries in upon herself, giving up the struggle and assimilating death in her catatonic condition.

Maureen's life is guided by a fear that operates much as it does for the Kafka character who considers himself a guilty stranger. (During one period of her life, Oates says she felt she *was* Kafka.) In those lofty edifices which call forth Maureen's respect, such as the library, she is particularly intimidated and afraid. She always feels herself in the wrong in the presence of authority. When the librarian blames her for the torn page in her library book, proving it could not have been ripped when the book was checked out, Maureen believes her. She borrows a quarter from Jules to pay for the damaged book, without telling him why, acting as desperate as one who has committed a severe crime. She does well at school until she loses the notebook of class records when she is the homeroom secretary. Oates says that this is the worst thing that ever happens to Maureen. Her responsibility is more important to her than any she is ever to have, and such a failure is stunning. The nun in charge of the class sternly advises her to keep looking for the notebook, but the search along city streets is hopeless. This is one of those horribly conclusive experiences it is possible to have when you are young that have the power of suggesting the way things will always be, an event more profound to Maureen than even the murder of Loretta's lover is to her.

But if Maureen is merely paranoid, the reader is far too convinced of the real destructive potential in her life to consider her so. At home her stepfather lustfully approaches her and finally beats her. Where can she be safe? One of the visitors to her home is her Uncle Brock, Loretta's brother who murdered her lover several years before. Maureen's fears arise from contact with such tangible evidence of violence, and her statements often have the flat, unemotional, but uncontroversial quality of fact. Her fear is cold, certain, and pervasive, but it seldom breaks into the hysteria that would threaten herself or others, for she also operates under a pressure to control herself and to achieve, which is usually the curse of the more affluent child. Maureen's particular misfortune is to suffer both the threats of actual violence and the anxieties for real and imagined harm to come from the forces of authority lurking everywhere.

The most likeable one of them is Jules, whose freedom of movement and capacity for romanticizing his love affairs is a pleasant contrast to Maureen's sense of entrapment. Jules is every bit as desperate as Maureen, and he comes to lead a more disastrous life than hers. But his is at least enlivened by greater energy and choice. A comparison of this brother and sister make the particular fears and responses of a woman more noticeable. The differences between them could be merely the quirks of two personalities, but too much arises from their roles as man and woman to ignore.

Jules was always a daring child, frightened of nothing and soon known as the troublemaker who set the barn on fire when he first learned to strike a match. His grandmother predicts that he will die in the electric chair, a prediction to be repeated precisely by others throughout his life. When we last see Jules he has killed a policeman. But he manages to remain lovable all along, adored by the mother and sister he continues to care for and send money to whenever he can. He becomes a thief in behalf of his girl friend Nadine, taking a car so they can escape together. Each night from their motel rooms across the country he steals supper for her as conscientiously as another man might bring home his paycheck. Nadine remains an icy, sadistic, although fairly unconvincing character, a stimulant for Jules's crime, spurred on by his wildness but scornful of his talk of love.

Jules goes far out to Texas, while Maureen remains ensconced in her room. She pleads for a chance to go to work, but the excuse is that she is needed at home. A job is as remote to her as are other desirable, untouchable prizes somewhere outside. Surely this is one reason why she hoards her money, while Jules is generous with his. One of his companions observes that women " 'don't understand where money comes from or what it means or how a man can be worth money though he hasn't any at the moment' " (224). Women know only that men have the money, and that is where they must get it. Jules appreciates this same principle to the extent that he feels it his duty to somehow provide things for Nadine and his mother. To capture a special girl like Nadine Green he believes he needs a million.

Maureen goes back to school a few years after her recovery from Furlong's beating, and the following months of inactivity, a thinner and more determined person. Her schooling does not open her to experience, however, but serves as a means of new protection. She now attends carefully to the face and figure that will capture the appropriate man, someone she thinks will make life safe by giving her a house and children. Her gentle, married instructor, father of three children, will do. Maureen's success in taking this man from his wife is not entirely credible, but she is correct in seeing him as a person so worried by one failure in marriage that he would not have the nerve to leave a second wife. The deliberate act of taking another woman's husband is carried out in much the same amoral way as is Maureen's earlier act of prostitution. It is incongruous but believable that this girl's conscience, which could be blown out of proportion by the slightest infringement of the rules as a child (e.g., her experience in the library), could be blotted out this way later on. Her pragmatic plan of survival succeeds, but with a totally narrowing effect.

Perhaps taking a married man is Maureen's only way of by-passing the romantic stages between men and women that she never believed in or understood anyway and getting on to the tangible results of husband and house which are her goal. In a letter to her teacher (presumably Joyce Carol Oates) she admits that she could not divulge the plan of taking another woman's husband to a married woman, who would obviously not want someone to steal her husband, although she suspects that her teacher might not mind taking someone else's husband if the story were pretty enough. But she needs someone to know of her greatest success. And yet as we last see her nervously closing the door on her brother Jules after a brief, whispered conversation with him, the person she had cared for more than anyone else, we know that her life is closing. She may have mastered certain surface elements of her life by obtaining a husband and some financial security, but in turning away her brother she shows how numbed she is to any truly lifegiving responses.

Oates is deadly accurate with Maureen and others like her whose dread she makes vivid. Her women treated only satirically are not as successful. The Nada of *Expensive People* is never quite present (as her son and husband discover). The too obvious allusion to nothingness and the catalogs of products that make up her life may document the malaise of the expensive people, but they do not give us a real woman. And Maureen Wendall is that. The fears of poverty with its accompanying physical violence, as well as the quiet terror created by the powers that rule, are impressively true. And no one is better at showing the female consciousness aware of the possibilities of rape than Joyce Carol Oates. She is a master at depicting women's anxieties of many sorts, and she makes a striking contribution to our understanding of contemporary America as seen by women. Here is an author to read if one dares to know the particular fear there is in being a woman—here and now—even when the surface of life may appear as familiar and safe as a supermarket on a sunny day.

five

Sylvia Plath's Defiance: *The Bell Jar*

In Sylvia Plath's story "The Fifteen-Dollar Eagle," a weathered tattoo artist imaginatively embellishes his customers with colorful images from his own fantasies and from theirs: for one woman, a huge butterfly on the upper legs which appears to flutter every time she moves; for another, the complete scene of Calvary projected on her back. Carmey's wild tales of tattooing are halted when his own Wife appears, a large fleshy woman who hates tattoos. She will oblige none of his artistry on her, remaining "death-lily-white and totally bare—the body of a woman immune as a nun to the eagle's anger, the desire of the rose."[1] Like this resistant woman, and the persona of most of Plath's poetry, Esther Greenwood of *The Bell Jar* spitefully defies the role of *tabula rasa* for the projection of men's images of their dreams and of themselves. Not that this alone is the subject of her scorn, for she is repelled by life generally. But while we may never fully understand her reasons for attempting suicide (there is little self-analysis), her disgust of life is shown expressly in terms of being a woman.

No woman in American literature is quite so thoroughly repulsed by what women are as is Esther Greenwood. She is an unusually ambitious girl, successful in every apparent way with fifteen years of straight A's behind her, who has now won a contest to work for *Ladies' Day* fashion magazine in New York for one

1. *Sewanee Review*, 68 (Fall 1960), 618.

month in the summer. (Sylvia Plath won the award to work for *Mademoiselle* in 1953.) But what could be a thrilling experience is a deadening one, like all others in her adult life. The summer concludes with several suicide attempts, all made the more terrible to the reader by the fact of Plath's own suicide in 1963, one month after publication of *The Bell Jar*.

Like Joyce Carol Oates, Sylvia Plath is obsessed with images of blood. Both women see things disintegrating in a world filled with signs of death, where women find no hint of the romantic in their lives and are disgusted by their bodies. But one great difference between the two writers is the intimidation Oates's women feel in relation to outside forces in contrast with the disdain of Esther Greenwood, who projects much more of her own will, self-destructive as it is. If she cannot control what society expects of her, she does dramatically register her disgust for how she is supposed to live and how she is to look, which is perhaps the most overwhelming fact of herself a woman must cope with.

While she is not unattractive, Esther never considers herself a beauty and is overwhelmed by the world of fashion among the clientele of *Ladies' Day*. Like them she buys glossy patent leather shoes from Bloomingdale's, symbolic of the surfacy nature of style. She is at the same time repulsed and envious of girls who are bored by too many love affairs and who spend their days painting their fingernails and keeping up Bermuda tans. The Amazon Hotel, where only girls stay, is presumed by their mothers to keep them safely away from men, announcing an attitude held throughout *The Bell Jar* that men are polluters. Female conversation disgusts Esther, but she is sickeningly drawn to it. She is in awe of the glittery Doreen, who dwells on such trivia as the way she and her friends at college make pocketbook covers of the same material as their clothes so that each outfit matches. Esther confesses that "this kind of detail impressed me. It suggested a whole life of marvelous, elaborate decadence that attracted me like a magnet."[2] Aware of her intrigue with what appalls her, Esther increasingly loathes herself, realizing the great extent to which her image of herself is based on the objects of fashion. A gift for

2. Sylvia Plath, *The Bell Jar* (New York: Bantam Books, 1972), p. 4. Further page references to this edition are included in the text.

each girl when she arrives in New York is a makeup kit, created exactly for a person of such-and-such a color, the first essential item in establishing her new life. Each girl is photographed carrying a prop to indicate her identity: an ear of corn for one who looks forward to being a farmer's wife, a gold-embroidered sari for another who plans on being a social worker in India. Before Esther leaves New York she mocks a suicide by abandoning her props, the fashionable clothes that have identified her, letting each item float down over the city from the top of her hotel as a way of renouncing the standards of fashion and also of obliterating herself. The climax of Esther's encounter with New York's world of fashion, dramatically proving it to be insidious, comes when a luncheon sponsored by *Ladies' Day* results in the ptomaine poisoning of all the girls who attend.

After her distressing stay in New York, Esther returns to Massachusetts, where she attempts suicide in a way that is particularly gross in terms of its physical distortions. She is found slumped in a crevice in her basement after a dosage of sleeping pills, her face puffed out of shape and badly discolored. The nurse at the hospital has been instructed not to allow her a mirror to see the ugliness, but Esther finds one and takes a look:

> You couldn't tell whether the person in the picture was a man or a woman, because their hair was shaved off and sprouted in bristly chicken-feather tufts all over their head. One side of the person's face was purple, and bulged out in a shapeless way, shading to green along the edges, and then to a sallow yellow. The person's mouth was pale brown, with a rose-colored sore at either corner.
>
> The most startling thing about the face was its supernatural conglomeration of bright colors.
>
> I smiled.
>
> The mouth in the mirror cracked into a grin [142–43].

This is the same grim satisfaction Oates's characters take in becoming hideously fat or in distorting their faces to blot out the beauty that is their mark of identity and the initiating factor in their painful involvements with men. Esther's attempt to destroy herself is linked specifically with the destruction of her beauty, not merely in the sense that all death is decay, but that by obliterating herself as an object of sexual appeal she can attack the role expected of her as a woman.

The preoccupation with appearance has everything to do with woman as a commodity for man. In her poem "The Applicant" Plath poses the prospective bride as an applicant before the buyer bridegroom and his family. She is scrutinized carefully for possible physical imperfections: "Do you wear / A glass eye . . . / Rubber breasts or a rubber crotch, / Stitches to show something's missing?" Her useful hand becomes a metaphor for the bride's identity as a whole, the bride who is an "it." If "it" does all you tell it, the poet continues sarcastically, "Will you marry it?" At the husband's death, "it" is guaranteed to "dissolve of sorrow,"[3] having nothing left of self when the husband is gone.

Esther's loathing of men equals her loathing of women, but she is not obsessed by them and their ways. She is that rare woman who can (once she learns how) truly and devastatingly dismiss men, reducing them to objects for discard. In a brilliant tour de force of the usual male seduction of the virgin, Esther, determined to rid herself of her virginity, which weighs "like a millstone" (186) around her neck, seduces a young professor she picks up on the steps of the Widener Library. Naive but spiteful, she passively requires him to take all the action. He carries her to the bed, where she lazily waits for the event to take place. "I lay, rapt and naked, on Irwin's rough blanket, waiting for the miraculous change to make itself felt. . . . But all I felt was a sharp, startlingly bad pain" (187). If Esther ever had any romantic notions about sexual experience or men, they are permanently dispelled at this cynical stage in her life. In the next few weeks she pesters the bewildered professor to pay off her hospital bill but refuses ever to see him again. Her callousness throughout this brief affair constitutes a thoroughly amoral deflowering of the virgin. The effect of seduction on her is sheerly physical, as she hemorrhages. Otherwise she feels nothing. The same absence of sympathetic emotions is evident in Esther's defiance of Buddy Willard's offer of marriage. The idea of marrying him is so ridiculous her only impulse is to laugh.

But while she is in New York Esther is caught in the old game

3. Sylvia Plath, *Ariel* (New York: Harper & Row, 1966), p. 4.

of trying to be attractive and desirable to men, a need repulsive to her which battles with her impulse to refuse them callously. (Such conflicts between her scorn of conventional attitudes about women and her bondage to them are found throughout the novel.) No idea is more central to the concept of the American girl found here than that of her passion for popularity, which figures above all other considerations, certainly above her value as a good student. In college when Esther is discovered to have a date to the Yale prom she is suddenly thrust into the limelight, something no quantity of good grades is capable of doing. In New York the proof of popularity is established by success with strangers. The first test case is a man in cowboy boots who strolls up to Esther and Doreen, dressed in their best and waiting in the back seat of a taxi. Esther senses that he has come for Doreen, and once this choice is made, putting her at the center of attention, Esther feels herself "melting into the shadows like the negative of a person I'd never seen before in my life" (8). Although there is nothing in this unknown man that she likes or admires, he has the power, by ignoring her, to reduce her self-esteem to nothing. Later in the man's apartment, as he and Doreen grow increasingly intimate, Esther is conscious of herself "shrinking to a small black dot" (14). A further rejection comes from Constantin, the interpreter at the United Nations whom she selects to be her first lover, but who disappointingly makes no attempt to seduce her. From this experience she concludes that she is not only unattractive but intellectually dull: "I thought if only I had a keen, shapely bone structure to my face or could discuss politics shrewdly or was a famous writer Constantin might find me interesting enough to sleep with" (67). Esther looks on at her own adventures with disdain but is unable to free herself of her attitudes, which are expressed with wry honesty and self-loathing.

Esther's revenge on the world for making sexual appeal so important is her rejection and scorn of Buddy Willard, the boy she adores from afar for several years before he finally proposes to her. At first he is a savior, rescuing her from the ordeal of a different blind date each Saturday night and the drab status of bookworm. But getting to know him better she discovers the

flaws she always finds in men at close quarters. The ultimate putdown of this ultra-eligible male hero results when, as a gesture
of his male pride in a move to both shock and condescend to
her, he offers to let her see him in the nude. She has never before
seen a man, and he intends this to be one of her great adventures.
Esther recalls (with Plath's sarcastic relish of cliché) that her
mother and grandmother always said "what a fine, clean boy
Buddy Willard was, coming from such a fine, clean family, and
how everybody at church thought he was a model person" (55).
If he is so clean and fine, she imagines, it must surely be fine to
see his clean body. But there is no awe or shock in her response,
just the same dulled reaction she has for everything else, which
is the perfect putdown: "Then he just stood there in front of me
and I kept staring at him. The only thing I could think of was
turkey neck and turkey gizzards and I felt very depressed" (55).
In the words of Robert Scholes, "she takes masculine pride in
flesh and reduces it to the level of giblets."[4]

Esther sees Buddy as foolish rather than unfortunate for being
hospitalized with the tuberculosis he contracts from his work in
the hospital. She is relieved to learn that he will be kept out of
her way and especially charmed that the good health he was so
proud of is gone. Having gained a lot of weight in the sanatorium,
Buddy is more ridiculous than ever. At this point he proposes,
giving Esther the opportunity to become Mrs. Buddy Willard,
which she would have swooned over a few years before. But it
now seems hardly worth her trouble even to explain why she
could not consider marrying him. He says she is crazy, believing
quite sincerely that any girl would be insane to refuse such an
offer. She too, to some degree, considers herself a fool for violating the college girl's dream of marrying a handsome medical
student, source of wealth and status. But if Buddy and his offer
represent a sane choice, she will gladly be considered insane.
Horrified at the thought of his mother, who braids fine rugs
from her husband's old suits to make kitchen mats that go dull
in a few days, Esther knows that what Buddy "secretly wanted
when the wedding service ended was for her to flatten out underneath his feet like Mrs. Willard's kitchen mat" (69). She not

4. *New York Times Book Review*, Apr. 11, 1971, p. 7.

only despises humiliating service, but she hates "the idea of serving men in any way" (62).

Esther's first big disillusionment with Buddy comes when she finds out that he is not a virgin (she is), an instance revealing her competitiveness and the determination to have as much as men have. She claims bitterly that Buddy is a hypocrite for pretending sexual innocence (which he has never done in any specific way), but the real reason for her anger is that he is one experience ahead of her. She decides she must be seduced in order to catch up. The pursuit of such an experience is entirely sexless, and yet the idea of it as an overwhelming issue remains, not so from any feeling of her own but because of the social import of the event. It is so significant to her at the age of nineteen that "instead of the world being divided up into Catholics and Protestants or Republicans and Democrats or white men and black men or even men and women, I saw the world divided into people who had slept with somebody and people who hadn't" (66).

Purity is a great issue of Esther's time, leaving her at the age of nineteen, arriving in New York as a prize-winning scholar, incredibly naive. Vague information about birth control has filtered to her, but the most emphatic propaganda comes from such tracts as "In Defense of Chastity" from the *Reader's Digest*, admonishing the young girl, "better be safe than sorry" (66). It occurs to Esther that although the article is written by a woman it does not consider the feelings of the girl, an omission reflecting the puritanical notion that sexual pleasure is for men only. Far from representing a hedonistic urge, however, Esther's quest for sexual experience resembles her quest for death, significantly resulting in the blood flow that could have been fatal.

The deflowering of Esther is a bitingly funny scene, reducing the bewildered victim Irwin to the moronic as he fetches towels for his bleeding stranger. After one evening with him she is ready for purity again, vainly craving chastity now that she is convinced of men's worthlessness. Esther is unique among women for being able to ridicule sex, belittle the male, and then turn from men altogether, something Oates's women are incapable of doing. For none of them is there any expectation of pleasure to come from men. But Esther escapes the painful dependency that most women suffer.

The poem "Fever 103°" similarly illustrates an attitude of female superiority and the desire to be purified of men:

> I am too pure for you or anyone.
> Your body
> Hurts me as the world hurts God.
>
> . . . .
>
> I
>
> Am a pure acetylene
> Virgin
> Attended by roses.[5]

The speaker in her superiority, not only to men but to all staining aspects of life, would transcend the soiled earth through her own beauty and finally through death. Esther attempts to purify herself by withdrawal from all activity and emergence into the hot baths she takes at the Amazon Hotel (usually after disturbing encounters with men). The bath, while it purifies, allows a deathlike descent into the boiling water. "The water needs to be very hot, so hot you can barely stand putting your foot in it. Then you lower yourself, inch by inch, till the water's up to your neck. . . . I never feel so much myself as when I'm in a hot bath. . . . The longer I lay there in the clear hot water the purer I felt" (16–17).

Esther sees men very much in types, as predators and as fools. There is little reflection on the death of her father in *The Bell Jar*, which might have changed this view, although she does visit his grave. Plath admittedly uses a persona with an Electra complex in her poetry, but that is not the case here. Mr. Greenwood's death is not shown to have had the profound effect on Esther that Mr. Plath's death had on Sylvia. Even though Esther loathes most women, they are much more individualized and important to her than men are. Many of the women she knows are grotesques, awful images of what she could become if she were to marry and remain in a small town as her mother has done. Very few are admirable. But only women have the possibility of helping

5. *Ariel*, p. 54.

her—from the wealthy female novelist, Philomena Guinea, who provides Esther's scholarship, to the female psychiatrist who is responsible for helping her recover from a nervous breakdown.

Esther's mother is a model of the mundane, exhibiting well-meaning but plodding tendencies that are reflected in the lethargy of her daughter. Always faithfully attending to her child, in and out of the hospital, she offers platitudinous encouragement in place of realistic appraisal of her daughter's condition. According to Esther, she never tells her what to do and reasons with her like one intelligent being with another—just the thing to infuriate Esther, to whom reasoning is as meaningless as other formulas. If this mother represents the perpetuation of life, then her child rebels by wishing to end it. After the suicide attempt, Esther must face her mother's sorrowful expression and pathetic questions: "She was sure the doctors thought she had done something wrong because they asked her a lot of questions about my toilet training, and I had been perfectly trained at a very early age and given her no trouble whatsoever" (166). Mrs. Greenwood's belief that a cure "for thinking too much about yourself" is to help somebody "worse off than you" (132) has no relevance to Esther, who for a short time makes a fumbling attempt at charity work in a hospital, with no resultant enlightenment. Like all clichés in *The Bell Jar*, the mother's conventionality is irrelevant and stupid. ⌐ Mother.

But if her own mother cannot help her, Esther seeks a surrogate mother. The worst possible choice she could make would be Mrs. Willard, her potential mother-in-law, whom she hates for her subservience in her home as well as for the way she exemplifies the petty strictures of society. As Esther strolls with a sailor in downtown Boston, boldly letting his arm linger around her waist, she imagines Mrs. Willard to be watching her and instinctively pulls away from the man. The girls Esther meets in New York are, with their shallow sorrows, to which Esther becomes cold-bloodedly indifferent, no more suitable substitutes for mother. When Doreen comes in late after drinking and shakes Esther out of sleep, she feels no compunction at leaving the inebriated girl lying in a pool of vomit in the hall and returning as naturally to bed. "I made a decision about Doreen that night. I decided

I would watch her and listen to what she said, but deep down I would have nothing at all to do with her" (19). After the fatal luncheon where the girls are food poisoned, it is during a technicolor movie of boys playing football and girls going to the powder room to say catty things that Esther becomes nauseous, signifying her revulsion against the way the fashion world and the collegiate world exemplify women.

Esther does respect her supervisor at *Ladies' Day*, Jay Cee, a woman the girls immediately label by appearance "ugly as sin" (4). Perhaps it is because she is homely that Esther likes the woman, who, true to the type, appears capable because she cannot be beautiful. Sensitive to something disturbed in her bright young apprentice, Jay Cee calls Esther in to discuss her future. But Esther, in no condition to will her life at the moment, only wishes she had had "a mother like Jay Cee. Then I'd know what to do" (42). The scarcity of female models she can look to is clearly a factor in Esther's limited view of her own life.

When Esther first seeks psychiatric help, the doctor is not the somber and perceptive man she had expected, but rather a handsome and jovial fellow with a photo of his happy family beaming up from the desk. The image is repulsive. What can he say to her? Can he tell her why everything seems so silly because people all die in the end? After shock treatments, which cause a major trauma for Esther, she at last meets a friend, Doctor Nolan, a female psychiatrist who wisely promises her she will not be required to see any more visitors. This woman becomes almost directly a replacement of Esther's mother: in a corner of the hospital room are a dozen long-stemmed roses from Mrs. Greenwood for her daughter's birthday—now stuffed in a trash can. What Esther appreciates in Doctor Nolan is not her training but her natural understanding. Surprisingly affectionate for one in her professional position, she hugs Esther before accompanying her to shock therapy, which she promises will not be traumatic as it was the first time. Esther, the frightened child, pleads with her to be there when the treatments are over. On one occasion she asks Doctor Nolan, " 'What does a woman see in a woman that she can't see in a man?' " The answer is " 'Tenderness.' . . . That shut me up" (179). Characteristics most often attributed to women such as gentleness, and particularly intuition, are the qualities Esther values most. At one point she holds Buddy Willard's scientific mind in awe, but she soon comes to regard him as a fool when she detects his lack of understanding. Only in Constantin does she find the quality she says no American man could have—intuition. She feels that he would not mind a little thing like her being taller than he is. But Esther's real affections are reserved for Doctor Nolan, who proves more worthy than anyone else to be mother and friend.

Sylvia Plath creates antagonism for the mom in *The Bell Jar*, but Mrs. Greenwood is not a clever manipulator. She is only a dowdy and disgusting image of what Esther is determined not to become. Mrs. Greenwood's niceness and her industry to support the family after her husband's death, at a seemingly dull job of teaching shorthand, are repellent to her highly ambitious daughter. Ahead of her time, Esther blasphemes the mystique that a girl must be beautiful, get married, raise children, and do dull work. What Robert Lowell says of Sylvia Plath in his Foreword to *Ariel* is true of Esther: she is feminine, "though almost everything we customarily think of as feminine is turned on its head."[6]

Esther's refusal to marry the eligible medical student is a kind of suicidal act in itself. She sees marriage as the plot of men for the subjection of women, especially talented women: "I also remembered Buddy Willard saying in a sinister, knowing way that after I had children I would feel differently, I wouldn't want to write poems any more. So I began to think maybe it was true that when you were married and had children it was like being brainwashed, and afterward you went about numb as a slave in some private, totalitarian state" (69). Even with a man like Constantin, who is not disgusting personally to Esther, she imagines the thought of marriage to him as a process of cooking bacon and eggs for breakfast and then another big meal at night, followed by washing up the dirty plates, to the point of exhaustion. "This seemed a dreary and wasted life for a girl with fifteen years of straight A's, but I knew that's what marriage was like" (68).

Sylvia Plath tells us nothing new in such a formulation of a

6. Ibid., Foreword, p. ix.

housewife's existence, which in the last decade has become commonplace. But the bitter, dry tone of *The Bell Jar*, with its ultimate defiance, carries a conviction of its own. It is unlikely that Plath's actual experience of marriage and motherhood is responsible for the view of marriage projected by Esther Greenwood (Plath's best poetry was written after her children were born), but through her we see an *expectation* of what life is like for a housewife in the America where she grows up, a life of mundane stupidity. Plath relates that it was not until she attended Cambridge that a beautiful woman supervisor became her "salvation" for proving, for the first time, that "a woman no longer had to sacrifice all claims to femininity and family to be a scholar!"[7]

Esther has no one to give her such advice and cannot imagine what the course of her life is to be. "I saw the years of my life spaced along a road in the form of telephone poles, threaded together by wires . . . and try as I would, I couldn't see a single pole beyond the nineteenth" (101). This feeling of purposelessness, which can be directly related to her suicidal tendencies, is far more than the discouragement of the moment. What suggestions were there as she grew up of a meaningful life apart from the common route, marriage American style?

If she does nothing, Esther will be stuck at home with her mother, whom she has vowed never to stay with for more than one week. At home she views the worst of possibilities. Probably the most devastating portrait of marriage and motherhood is that of her neighbor Dodo Conway:

> A woman not five feet tall, with a grotesque, protruding stomach, was wheeling an old black baby carriage down the street. Two or three small children of various sizes, all pale, with smudgy faces and bare smudgy knees, wobbled along in the shadow of her skirts.
>
> A serene, almost religious smile lit up the woman's face. Her head tilted happily back, like a sparrow egg perched on a duck egg, she smiled into the sun.
>
> I knew the woman well [95].

7. Lois Ames, "Notes toward a Biography," in *The Art of Sylvia Plath: A Symposium*, ed. Charles Newman (Bloomington: Indiana University Press, 1970), p. 165.

After this sight Esther crawls back into bed, pulls the sheet over her face (we are never far from the image of death), and buries her head under the pillow. Deadened by this sample of womanhood as well as by her mother's obtuse existence, she feels she has "nothing to look forward to" (96). On another occasion, while looking for her father's grave, she contemplates the dreary life she might have by marrying someone like the prison guard who gives her directions to the grave: "I was thinking that if I'd had the sense to go on living in that old town I might just have met this prison guard in school and married him and had a parcel of kids by now. It would be nice, living by the sea with piles of little kids and pigs and chickens, wearing what my grandmother called wash dresses, and sitting about in some kitchen with bright linoleum and fat arms, drinking pots of coffee" (123). This heavily sarcastic portrait is followed by her question, " 'How do you get into that prison?' " (123), meaning, of course, the prison where the guard works, but having unmistakable proximity to the preceding picture of marriage. One of the most disgusting analyses of women's relationship to men is given by Mrs. Willard, who says that a man is an arrow, and the woman is "the place the arrow shoots off from" (58). Esther naturally wants to be the arrow.

Plath's work is filled with images of babies, in one case an explicit description of childbirth, which is a relatively rare subject in literature. And such images are usually disgusting. The poem "Lesbos" shows a child lying face down like an "unstrung puppet,"[8] implicating the mother as a manipulator; she imagines her child to be schizophrenic, mad at the age of two and likely to cut her throat at ten, an obvious projection of the mother's own dismal state. But lamenting her morning among "a stink of fat and baby crap,"[9] helpless to improve her own life, she sees that she cannot help the child and resents him for crying out. Like this mother, Esther is plagued by obsessions that lead to such a concentration on her own bleakness that she has little to offer anyone else, certainly not a demanding child.

Sylvia Plath relates that as a child, when her mother was in

8. *Ariel*, p. 30.
9. Ibid., p. 31.

the hospital for the delivery of a younger brother, she "hated babies."[10] She felt that the new child would make her a bystander, no longer everyone's favorite. For Esther Greenwood babies are associated with someone like Dodo Conway, whom "everybody loved" and whose swelling family "was the talk of the neighborhood. . . . nobody but Dodo was on the verge of a seventh" (96). She is clearly not envious of this woman in the sense that she wants several children of her own, then or ever, but there is a certain jealous touch in the admission that everyone loves Dodo, which makes sense especially after reading Plath's account of her childhood resentment of the birth of her brother. Esther is an ambitious girl, the golden girl, always winning the prizes that climax in her award of a month at *Ladies' Day*. When she returns to her home in a small town where the neighborhood values are conceived in terms of an advantageous marriage, and the number of children produced is the sign of achievement, she is naturally scornful of the simple animality of the accomplishment. But she may also resent the fact that praise is no longer coming her way. She declares she will write a novel, that will show them, but momentarily she realizes her lack of experience—no affair, no baby, no closeup view of death. Even the women who are having babies, as repellent as they are to Esther, represent an experience she has not had. If for no other reason than this she envies them, just as she resents Buddy Willard for having sexual experience before she does (although when her own initiation comes it means nothing more to her than an accomplishment).

The most crucial experience having to do with childbirth in *The Bell Jar*, one which emphatically alienates Esther from Buddy Willard, occurs on her visit to his medical school. He is proudly at home there, dressed in white, playing the part of tour guide of the hospital. They are to watch a woman give birth, but what could be an awesome event for Esther is, as usual, a disgusting one. Before directing her to the delivery room Buddy shows her the big glass bottles "full of babies that had died before they were born." One is curled up the size of a frog, another smiling a "piggy smile" (51). Thus, before a baby is associated with life on this occasion, it is associated with death. The scien-

10. "Ocean 1212-W," *The Art of Sylvia Plath*, p. 268.

tific atmosphere of the hospital pervades the relationship of Esther and Buddy, making it more sterile than ever. But if he fails with her, he very competently dissects a lung.

The prospective mother is rolled into the delivery room reduced to the status of a thing, a "big white lump" (52) lifted onto an "awful torture table" (53) with its stirrups and strange wires and tubes. With her face covered, all that is visible of the woman is an "enormous spider-fat stomach and two little ugly spindly legs" (53). In giving birth she makes unhuman noises that to Esther can only be signs of pain, despite what she is told of a drug given the woman to kill the pain. The delivery room at this time of birth takes on the quality of a battleground dividing woman from man: he is in control of medication and instruments, apparently performing a violation of the woman, who lies helpless like an ugly animal. Even the drug to keep her from pain seems to Esther "just like the sort of a drug a man would invent. Here was a woman in terrible pain, obviously feeling every bit of it or she wouldn't groan like that, and she would go straight home and start another baby, because the drug would make her forget how bad the pain had been, when all the time, in some secret part of her, that long, blind, doorless and windowless corridor of pain was waiting to open up and shut her in again" (53).

Nothing about a woman in labor is linked to creation. It would be necessary actually to see the baby "come out of you yourself" to make "sure it was yours" figures Esther (54), to realize the connection, and even that would be momentary. The newborn child, streaked with blood and blue as a plum, is like a foreign object that violates the mother's body, just as men have abused her. On some occasions Plath uses the baby as an image of purity, in one case when Esther emerges from her bath as "pure and sweet as a new baby" (17). But the actual child being born is clearly not an image of anything either pure or sweet.

Not only do children represent a violation of a woman's body, as well as the manifestation of a vulgar life-style such as that of Dodo Conway, but the baby as the embodiment of new life is antithetical to the overriding appeal of death in The Bell Jar. Such an appeal is examined by A. Alvarez in his excellent work on

suicide (with a chapter on Plath), which concludes that while
he has learned very little about the motivation for suicide he is
convinced that the urge to self-destruction is a long-standing
temptation, having all the appeal of other obsessive drives. What
the child feels when he childishly blurts out "I wish I were dead"
becomes a tantalizingly real possibility later on.[11] Esther regularly
reverts to this desire, which becomes a real possibility for her
when she is in the community that loves and honors Dodo Conway, mother of seven, making the attempt to destroy life a form
of rebellion against the crude breeding of life that Dodo represents. This is not, of course, to suggest that Esther would kill
herself merely out of spite, but that she has enough resentment
of small-town mores to perform her grossest attempt at suicide
in the place which most persuasively suggests such an act to her
and where her deed will make the greatest impact.

In reacting against life forces, one of the most important being
children, Esther in her suicidal tendencies and in nearly everything else she does is extremely passive. Turning against the life
she sees prescribed for women, boring and inactive as it appears,
she ironically, in her own way, exemplifies the worst of that passivity. Her movement toward death requires that all human ties
which might draw her into emotional life be broken, thus allowing
her the state of complete inactivity, the state of a thing. As Mar-
jorie Perloff points out in an article on the poetry, Plath shows
a preference for things, which she animates, over live beings,
which she relegates to the level of things.[12] In the poem "Tulips"
the flowers that have been brought into the hospital room disturb
its cold serenity just as human emotions might disturb the patient who wishes for the cold state of death. The patient learns
peacefulness, considering herself nobody after giving up her name,
her clothes, and her history. Left without such credentials, she
enjoys the peace of being an object: "They have propped my head
between the pillow and the sheet-cuff. . . . My body is a pebble to
them, they tend it as water / Tends to the pebbles it must run

11. *The Savage God: A Study of Suicide* (New York: Random House, 1971),
p. 268.

12. "Angst and Animism in the Poetry of Sylvia Plath," *Journal of Modern
Literature*, 1, no. 1 (1970), 57.

over, smoothing them gently."[13] The faces of her husband and child from the family photo catch onto her skin like "little smiling hooks." Her quest for death being also a quest for purity, she feels she has been swabbed clean of these associations. The state of clean passivity gives her a freedom that increases as she approaches death. The red tulips are too much of life—they breathe "like an awful baby."[14]

In the midst of New York's activity and opportunity Esther enters a numbing depression, as though selection and will are unknown to her, having excelled only in the structured situation of the classroom. "I felt like a racehorse in a world without racetracks or a champion college footballer suddenly confronted by Wall Street and a business suit" (62). She is a figure bumped from one hotel to another, incapable of steering herself. In her hotel room she flattens out on the bed trying to think of people who have her phone number and who might call, never considering the possibility of making the calls herself. Rather than attend a fashion show she wants only to stay in bed all day or to lie on the grass in Central Park. Esther considers herself "dealt" to the woman-hater Marco as his blind date, who informs her that it makes no difference if she cannot dance since it takes only one person to dance anyway. All she must do is be on the dance floor with him. Esther has always waited for men to fall in love with her; there is no thought of affection for any of them. Her most decisive action is the project to unload her virginity, but even in this she merely reclines on the bed and lets it happen.

The situation of the college girl whose self-esteem hinges on a phone call might not merit our attention here if it were not that this stance remains basic in the woman. The passivity that operates in Esther's view of herself as a girl continues in her means of attempting suicide and in the desire for the ultimate passivity in death. Even the fact that she must take some kind of action to accomplish her death is distressing to her, doubly so because of her sense of incapacity. On one occasion she tries bleeding herself with a razor in a warm bath, on the advice of an ancient Roman, but she cannot tolerate the sight of blood. On the calm day of a

13. *Ariel*, p. 10.
14. Ibid., p. 11.

beach party she tries to drown, diving down several times but popping back into the sunlight from the force of the sea. She asks her timid date Cal how he would try killing himself, and when he tells her he would use a gun she figures "it was just like a man to do it with a gun. A fat chance I had of laying my hands on a gun. And even if I did, I wouldn't have a clue as to what part of me to shoot at" (127). Ineffective as Cal appears to Esther, she grants that as a male he has more nerve, more know-how, and better circumstances than hers for committing a decisive act. Her attempt at hanging is another failure, and she despairs at her inability to make a good knot. Her most nearly successful suicide attempt is carried out with sleeping pills, the easiest and most passive of the methods, offering a transition through sleep to death, an extension of her earlier retreats into sleep.

In Plath's poetry the urge to die is often given dignity and artistic significance as it is made a kind of awful quest for purity. But there is no grandeur associated with Esther Greenwood's death wish. The tone throughout *The Bell Jar* is grimly humorous, with little pathos developed for the heroine, who is clumsy, un-heroic, we could even say shoddy, in her attempts to die. In this coldly realistic and truly ugly version of the suicidal, Plath dispels any romantic notions of the subject we might have had. And such a treatment appropriately reflects Esther's spiteful and unimagina-tive way of dealing with her own talents: if the world is so heed-less of her abilities that the best it can offer her is a job in the fashion industry, she who is one of society's best female products will commit the ultimate offense by stuffing her body into a crevice and leaving it there to die. We cannot admire her method of attack. But neither can we dismiss her as merely one individu-ally neurotic woman who cannot deal with her problems. The issue of Esther's response to her situation aside, the problem she inherits is a thoroughly dismal view of the expectations for a woman in this country, a view which is not uncommon. The waste of her gifts and her life, even though it is not portrayed tragically, is a crucial loss. It brutally raises the question that must be put to Americans: What is a woman to do with her life if she does not follow the conventional pattern of wife and mother? Is there no other valid existence for her?

Charles Newman says that *The Bell Jar* gives us "one of the few sympathetic portraits . . . of a girl who refuses to be simply an *event* in anyone's life." [15] It does indeed do this, and it is time such a story was told. Plath presents one of the most unusual and disturbing accounts of a woman ever recorded in American fiction. But no one seems to know where such a story can go or quite what to do with the woman who does not choose to join her life to the lives of others. There is no tradition of women characters dealing with dilemmas that do not revolve around the men or children in their lives. Esther's unconventional pattern can only close off life for her. In her refusal to be like other women she finds no alternative and is trapped in "the bell jar, blank and stopped as a dead baby" (193). The awful irony is that in avoiding one blankness, which for her is a hideously empty view of everything female, Esther takes on another, more terrible and complete. Her brilliance and accomplishments have no power to lead her to a place in the world. Instead, they drive her out of it.

15. "Candor Is the Only Wile," *The Art of Sylvia Plath*, p. 35.

Conclusion

Women in current American fiction need help. Not that life is made triumphant for our heroes—but at least they make a variety of wild attempts, in literature that is often amazingly energetic. And yet idleness, more than any single element, makes for women characters who are freakish nonentities, and something powerful is keeping that line of development in place. Women are static, blank, and on occasion hysterical. They are expected to stay at home to live out their long, unproductive lives.

I am asked, "Do you think women in the novel reflect what American women are really like?" and if so, "What should they do?" Anyone who has lived for long with literary characters, as I have, is in danger of accepting their ways as the truth of a time and place. And when that time is the near present, it is intriguing to try to match characters of fiction with actual contemporaries. But whatever images our fiction presents, there is surely that in American life which does not foster greatness in women. Few come to prominence for their own achievements, as evidenced by polls devised to determine the most admired women in this country which yield the usual list of powerful men's wives, with perhaps an occasional entertainer thrown in. From this we need not conclude that American women accomplish nothing of merit; but we can see, at best, that their achievements are not well publicized. I recently asked a group of students studying women in literature just who the women in American life might be that girls could look to as models. After a couple of presidents' wives were named there was an awkward pause, and then one of the few young men in the class came out with the most desperate and one of the saddest answers I have ever heard, "Helen Keller."

My purpose here, of course, is not to make a conclusion about the nature of American women, which I am not qualified to do, but to show how I find them in our fiction. As for what might improve women's lives, both actual and fictional, I would suggest more action. While the literature of our age does not offer a rational or a heroic vision, neither is it nihlistic. Characters live out their lives, which can be made more or less interesting even when they are not guided by grand designs. The female character might be released from her bland status if she were granted more choices, such options as we increasingly hear of now thanks to the current feminist movement, which is bound to stretch women's views of themselves. I say, set women in motion. Stain them with the issues of their times.

Fiction of the sixties is antagonistic toward new attitudes regarding birth control and abortion, which in this decade have had such a liberating effect on women's lives. Writers of fiction have yet to deal with the concept of population control as a moral act. But whatever an author's views on such matters, the threat of unwanted pregnancy, which has had so much to do with establishing sexual mores for women, can never in the future be looked upon as quite the crucial factor it was in the past. The theme of sexual freedom is, as we would expect, a predominant aspect of the literature of the sixties, of particular importance in the creation of female characters. And how a woman considers her own sexuality has much to do with concepts of humor, motherhood, and madness, the other issues which figure most importantly in determining her character during this time.

Authors of the decade agree that sexual freedom for both men and women, which for many people may have blasted reverence between the sexes away for good, is surely here to stay. As lamentable as the emptiness of most interaction is, no major author suggests a return to a double standard of sexual morality. This is rather an amazing advance if we consider how much our notion of the heroine of the past depends upon her sexual status, which is usually either that of virgin, wife, or whore. Sexual activity may involve humiliation or brutality, but in most cases it has become more casual, lighthearted, even comic. At least for men.

The humorlessness of women is particularly noticeable in the works of Barth, Kesey, and Updike, where the humor of men is pitted directly against it. The female failure to develop a sense of humor is usually equated with a lack of intelligence or perhaps with sexual stinginess. Still, a woman's "promiscuity" has a way of denigrating her or making her laughable. And she is influenced not to use birth control devices, mostly because they make the sex act less natural and exciting for her partner. If pregnancy results it will, as ever, be her problem—but it is no longer a tragic situation, just a messy irritation. While the heroine of the sixties often initiates sexual activity, with her husband and with others, she seldom enjoys it. Barth and Pynchon satirically show that only in lesbian connections do women truly enjoy themselves. The women writers considered here indicate that sexual experience is either painful for women or else they feel nothing, performing as if in their sleep. They never anticipate or fantasize sexual pleasure. All they expect is the burden of pregnancy and motherhood.

Perhaps these concerns make it impossible for women to smile at sex, while a new wave of hilarity over the subject has hit their male companions. Spokesmen for the women's liberation movement in America have suffered from the same lack of humor as have these literary figures. Contrast the limitations inherent in the sobriety of Kate Millett, whose intelligent but heavy approach is humorless, with the possibilities for persuasion in the brilliant wit of her British counterpart, Germaine Greer. Humor is so essential to much fiction of the sixties that the sober woman is damned as never before. Many a schlemiel survives and is lovable solely because of his ability to laugh at his meager condition. Plath's heroine is one of the few with any sense of humor, and while it gives a deliciously vicious edge to her story, it does not mellow or endear her to us. In their failure to laugh, women do not reflect an awareness of anything sobering and profound. They merely become distasteful.

Of all the themes in current literature concerned with women, motherhood raises the most perplexing problems and will probably continue to do so for some time. Just as the furor over the

abortion issue continues, various passionate reactions to motherhood arrive at no consensus. But if the fiction does not sanction
any form of birth control, either for moral or for practical reasons,
it is nevertheless adamant as to the abuses of motherhood. Purdy,
Kesey, and Roth portray the most vicious bitch mothers, but
Updike's moms are almost as awful, even with some redeeming
traditional values. Plath's mother figure, while more innocuous
than the super bitches, tiresomely offends by attempting to force
unwanted values on her daughter.

From a woman's point of view motherhood is also ugly and
destructive, but the mother is more victim than victimizer. Far
from being in control of her family, which is the way they may
see it, she is haunted by the children she never chose to have.
Childbirth is a disaster brought on by men, a violation to a woman's body and a way of manipulating her life. But in spite of such
views, female writers along with male show the inhumanity or
impossibility of thwarting the process of birth, with a censure
that hardly distinguishes between natural sterility, birth control,
abortion, desertion of a child, the accidental killing of a child,
or—employment for women.

A conservative attitude toward childbirth is at least understandable in terms of the artist's traditional defense of the creative
forces of life. But where under heaven does the idea come from
in our literature that it is immoral for women to work? It is absurd to consider a woman at work as either moral or immoral,
per se. A job is the obvious opportunity for developing oneself
as well as for paying bills, as essential a need for most people as
affection, food, or breath. There are those rare people, women
and men, who are fully satisfied to stay at home. But I speak of
the many more I have known who are not fulfilled there; and it
should be as much in the course of a woman's life to seek her
vocation as it is for a man. Yes, such a thought is by now a feminist cliché. But why is it that women's natural need for many
kinds of development has not worked its way into our literature?
Is it only because writers of the sixties lag behind the general
culture in their awareness, or do they see a truth that will outlive
current "fads" about women?

The bias in our literature which envisions women only in the home is by no means limited to the idea that mothers with small children should remain there, although that may be its source. Are men simply afraid for women to have professional status and the power that goes with it? Are women too afraid or too lazy to achieve it? (Few are handicapped with Janice Angstrom's stupidity.) And yet no major author of the sixties, to my knowledge, male or female, gives us heroines whose jobs have any meaning for them, in the few cases where they work at all. Most women stay at home hating their existence and becoming more neurotic, without even considering careers. No one factor has more to do with their lack of character, their blankness, than this restriction. Surely a job is no panacea; it adds new problems. But it would give women something to do and make them more interesting. The housewife in fiction is a trapped being who wanders around her house trying to figure out what trivia to attend to next; after a day of idleness she may turn shrieking to a psychiatrist or brutalize her family, as Roth's heroines are prone to do. Updike's housewives are the most pitiful sloths of all, and apparently he intends to keep them that way. The suburban wives of Joyce Carol Oates are no better off as they nervously pace in their quiet homes, even more distraught than the poorer women with more to do. The account of the talented, achieving girl should tell us something different about women and work: Plath's Esther Greenwood is given a coveted position with a fashion magazine. But this sophisticated form of perpetuating women as beauty objects is as foreign to her as the two job options she grew up to expect: typing or waitress work.

Somewhere in the beginnings of thought about women earning their own money is the idea of prostitution, which was for a long time one of the few ways women could make a living. In the wild literature of the sixties prostitution remains as *the* career of a woman. (Unfortunately, there are no call girls who get rich from the profession.) Perhaps somehow in the odd workings of the mind prostitution is associated with *all* work for which women are paid. Far better that a woman should be forced to wheedle money from her husband than to earn it by any means. When a heroine does take a job she usually works only part-time, as a diversion from her dull and pointless life. In performing her job she is incompetent because she has no training and no concept of what meaningful work can be. Or else the job is so simple that it calls for no skill at all. (At least the dwarfed hero who is trapped in a dull job seems to have made more of a choice than these women who work part-time.) The author of fiction is hardly to be blamed for the fact that few American women achieve a high degree of professional success. But why should such a situation be casually accepted and reinforced by the same writers who so vividly depict the housewife's hell?

It is often difficult to distinguish between those who portray an attitude and those who approve and perpetuate it. None of the authors here except Kesey show a woman involved in full-time work, an omission which surely makes for an incomplete portrait of American women. But in some cases the reason that working women are not depicted may be that writers are not intimately acquainted with professional women or because their sympathies lie with the housewife, not because of a bias that women should not work. This seems particularly true of Roth, who gives such a powerful portrayal of a housewife's misery that to believe he would perpetuate it would be to consider him inhumane. His fiction may show him to be angry, but I do not believe he is cruel.

It is gentle Updike who most devastatingly perpetuates the idea of woman as blankness. I question how well he understands his own attitudes, for while he pities his hopeless housewives he protects them with family loyalty, with a kind of romanticism, and with affection. It is all too credible that Rabbit would run from the uninspiring Janice. But what is much more disturbing is that ten years later when she strays from home, on the verge of improvement, he wants her back in the original dowdy condition. I take Updike's statement that he has tried to portray women to mean that he has made an attempt at full characterization, but the result shows only women who are overcome by the singular trait of stupidity. And a perfect image of a woman is a recumbent, marble statue in a museum!

Updike fools us by genuinely liking women so much. His fondness is pleasing at times, as it is in the case of his chivalrous grocery checker in "A & P." But such affection of Updike and men like him surely has something to do with women's blankness, in fiction or otherwise: men like Updike love them this way, and they understandably want to be loved. And if a woman is incompetent enough, the weakest man may be comforted. How else can we explain Rabbit's desire for Janice? His appreciation for her inadequacies is, of course, a horribly stifling influence, as it would be for anyone. Updike's writing would not be so disturbing if it revealed merely the fantasies of one man. But I believe he portrays a truth regarding the essential nature of the bond between the sexes that pertains not only to the vapid women in fiction but to the actual ones who resemble them. He deals with one of the powerful reasons why women remain so pale: the fear of being alone.

Most heroines of the sixties have no concept of fulfillment outside marriage. But even those who do may consider a serious career or other genuine involvement (only sexual interests are made credible) threatening to their connection with men. And indeed, many heroes of the period are so weak that they might not hold up under the apparent threat of careers for their wives. This is one reason for the myth that calls for the woman as a necessary blankness, which is willed by both men and women to ensure their connection—not a happy connection, but the something that always seems better than nothing. The woman of current fiction is not much enlightened by sexual freedom; she is not effectual as a mother; she develops no skills or talents. And the absurd humor of it all never penetrates her undeveloped mind. No wonder she is miserable, verging on madness. But she is not alone.

The rare woman of brilliance has no place here. She is an aberration in a world with no sane use of her abilities, no heroics for girls, no men to match her, and no purpose for her existence.

This is a terrible myth. An old one. May the future prove it a lie.

Bibliography
of Works Consulted

GENERAL

Aldridge, John. *Time to Murder and Create: The Contemporary Novel in Crisis*. New York: David McKay, 1966.

Balakian, Nona, and Charles Simmons, eds. *The Creative Present*. Garden City, N.Y.: Doubleday, 1963.

Baumbach, Jonathan. *The Landscape of Nightmare: Studies in the Contemporary American Novel*. New York: New York University Press, 1965.

Beauvoir, Simone de. *The Second Sex* (1949), trans. and ed. H. M. Parshley. New York: Alfred A. Knopf, 1953.

Bergonzi, Bernard. *The Situation of the Novel*. Pittsburgh: University of Pittsburgh Press, 1971.

Carlson, Constance Hedin. "Heroines in Certain American Novels," Diss., Brown University, 1971.

Chesler, Phyllis. *Women and Madness*. Garden City, N.Y.: Doubleday, 1972.

Ellmann, Mary. *Thinking about Women*. New York: Harcourt, Brace & World, 1968.

Fiedler, Leslie A. *Love and Death in the American Novel* (1960). New York: Dell, 1966.

———. *The Return of the Vanishing American*. New York: Stein and Day, 1968.

———. *Waiting for the End*. New York: Stein and Day, 1964.

French, Michael R. "The American Novel in the Sixties," *Midwest Quarterly*, 9 (July 1968), 365–79.

Friedan, Betty. *The Feminine Mystique* (1963). New York: Dell, 1964.

Friedman, Bruce Jay. "Those Clowns of Conscience," *Book Week,* July 18, 1965, pp. 2, 7.

Galloway, David G. "Clown and Saint: The Hero in Current American Fiction," *Critique,* 7 (Spring–Summer 1965), 46–65.

Gilman, Richard. *The Confusion of Realms.* New York: Vintage Books, 1970.

Glicksberg, Charles I. *The Sexual Revolution in Modern American Literature.* The Hague: Martinus Nijhoff, 1971.

Gold, Herbert. "Fiction of the Sixties," *The Atlantic,* 206 (Sept. 1960), 53–56.

Greer, Germaine. *The Female Eunuch.* New York: McGraw-Hill, 1970.

Harris, Charles B. *Contemporary American Novelists of the Absurd.* New Haven: College and University Press, 1971.

Hassan, Ihab. "The Existential Novel," *Massachusetts Review,* 3 (Summer 1962), 795–97.

———. *Radical Innocence: Studies in the Contemporary American Novel.* Princeton: Princeton University Press, 1961.

Hicks, Granville, ed. *The Living Novel: A Symposium.* New York: Macmillan, 1957.

Hoerchner, Susan Jane. " 'I Have to Keep the Two Things Separate': Polarity in Women in the Contemporary American Novel." Diss., Emory University, 1973.

Howe, Irving. *Decline of the New.* New York: Harcourt, Brace & World, 1963.

Jefchak, Andrew T. "Marital and Familial Relationships in the Post–World War II American Novel." Diss., Michigan State University, 1970.

Jung, Carl. "Psychological Aspects of the Mother Archetype," in *The Basic Writings of C. G. Jung,* ed. Violet Staub de Laszlo. New York: Modern Library, 1959.

Karl, Frederick R. "Picaresque and the American Experience," *Yale Review,* 57 (Winter 1968), 196–212.

Kazin, Alfred. *Contemporaries.* Boston: Little, Brown, 1962.

Klein, Marcus. *After Alienation: American Novels in Mid-Century* (1962). New York: World, 1964.

Kostelanetz, Richard. "The Point Is That Life Doesn't Have Any Point," *New York Times Book Review,* June 6, 1965, pp. 3, 28.

Levine, Paul. "The Intemperate Zone: The Climate of Contemporary American Fiction," *Massachusetts Review*, 8 (Summer 1967), 505–23.

Lewis, R. W. B. "Days of Wrath and Laughter," in *Trials of the Word: Essays in American Literature and the Humanistic Tradition*. New Haven: Yale University Press, 1965.

Malin, Irving. *New American Gothic*. Carbondale: Southern Illinois University Press, 1962.

May, John R. *Toward a New Earth: Apocalypse in the American Novel*. Notre Dame: University of Notre Dame Press, 1972.

Miller, Norman. "The Self-Conscious Narrator-Protagonist in American Fiction since World War II." Diss., University of Wisconsin, 1972.

Millett, Kate. *Sexual Politics*. Garden City, N.Y.: Doubleday, 1970.

Morgan, Robin, ed. *Sisterhood Is Powerful: An Anthology of Writings from the Women's Liberation Movement*. New York: Vintage Books, 1970.

O'Faolain, Sean. *The Vanishing Hero: Studies in Novelists of the Twenties*. Boston: Little, Brown, 1956.

Olderman, Raymond Michael. *Beyond the Waste Land: A Study of the American Novel in the Nineteen-Sixties*. New Haven: Yale University Press, 1972.

Poirier, Richard. "A Literature of Law and Order," *Partisan Review*, 36, no. 2 (1969), 189–204.

Rice, Joseph Allen. "Flash of Darkness: Black Humor in the Contemporary American Novel." Diss., Florida State University, 1967.

Rogers, Katherine M. *The Troublesome Helpmate: A History of Misogyny in Literature*. Seattle: University of Washington Press, 1966.

Sarraute, Nathalie. *The Age of Suspicion: Essays on the Novel* (1956), trans. Maria Jolas. New York: George Braziller, 1963.

Schulz, Max F. *Black Humor Fiction of the Sixties: A Pluralistic Definition of Man and His World*. Athens: Ohio University Press, 1973.

Simmons, Lydia. "Existentialism in the Modern American Novel, 1945–1967." Diss., New York University, 1970.

Solotaroff, Theodore. *The Red Hot Vacuum*. New York: Atheneum, 1970.

Southern, Terry. "New Trends and Old Hats," *The Nation*, 191 (Nov. 19, 1960), 380–83.

Waldmeir, Joseph J., ed. *Recent American Fiction: Some Critical Views*. Boston: Houghton Mifflin, 1963.

Weinberg, Helen. *The New Novel in America: The Kafkan Mode in Contemporary Fiction*. Ithaca, N.Y.: Cornell University Press, 1970.

Williams, Raymond. "Realism and the Contemporary Novel," *Partisan Review*, 26 (Spring 1959), 200–213.

WORKS BY JOHN BARTH

"Autobiography: A Self-Recorded Fiction," *New American Review*, 2 (1968), 72–75.

The End of the Road (1958). New York: Bantam Books, 1969.

The Floating Opera (1956). New York: Avon Books, 1965.

"A Gift of Books," *Holiday*, 40 (Dec. 1966), 171–72, 174, 177.

Giles Goat-Boy (1966). New York: Fawcett World Library, 1967.

"Landscape: The Eastern Shore," *Kenyon Review*, 22 (Winter 1960), 104–10.

"The Literature of Exhaustion," *The Atlantic*, 220 (Aug. 1967), 29–34.

Lost in the Funhouse (1963–68). New York: Grosset & Dunlap, 1969.

"Muse, Spare Me," *Book Week*, Sept. 26, 1965, pp. 28–29.

"My Two Muses," *Johns Hopkins Magazine*, 12 (Apr. 1961), 9–13.

"The Remobilization of Jacob Horner," *Esquire*, 50 (July 1958), 55–59.

The Sot-Weed Factor (1960). New York: Grosset & Dunlap, 1966.

"A Tribute to John Hawkes," *Harvard Advocate*, 104 (Oct. 1970), 11.

"A Tribute to Vladimir Nabokov," in *Nabokov: Criticism, Reminiscences, Translations and Tributes*, ed. Alfred Appel, Jr., and Charles Newman. Evanston: Northwestern University Press, 1970.

WORKS ABOUT JOHN BARTH

Appel, Alfred, Jr. "The Art of Artifice," *The Nation*, 207 (Oct. 28, 1968), 441–42.

Beagle, Peter S. "John Barth: Long Reach, Near Miss," *Holiday*, 40 (Sept. 1966), 131–32, 134–35.

Bean, John C. "John Barth and Festive Comedy: A Failure of Imagination in *The Sot-Weed Factor*," *Xavier University Studies*, 10, no. 1 (1971), 3–15.

Bellamy, Joe David. "Exclusive Interview with John Barth," 1972 *Writer's Yearbook*, 43 (1972), 70–72.

Bienstock, Beverly Gray, "Lingering on the Autognostic Verge: John Barth, *Lost in the Funhouse*," *Modern Fiction Studies*, 19 (Spring 1973), 69–78.

Bluestone, George. "John Wain and John Barth: The Angry and the Accurate," *Massachusetts Review*, 1 (Spring 1960), 582–89.

Bradbury, John M. "Absurd Insurrection: The Barth-Percy Affair," *South Atlantic Quarterly*, 68, no. 3 (1969), 319–29.

Brooks, Peter. "John Barth," *Encounter*, 28 (June 1967), 71–75.

Bryer, Jackson. "John Barth," *Bibliography*, *Critique*, 6 (Fall 1963), 86–89.

Burgess, Anthony. "Caliban Messiah," *The Spectator*, Mar. 31, 1967, pp. 69–70.

Byrd, Scott. "*Giles Goat-Boy* Visited," *Critique*, 9, no. 1 (1967), 108–12.

Davenport, Guy. "Like Nothing Nameable," *New York Times Book Review*, Oct. 20, 1968, pp. 4, 63.

Davis, Douglas M. "The End Is a Beginning for Barth's '*Funhouse*,'" *National Observer*, Sept. 16, 1968, p. 19.

Decker, Sharon David. "Passionate Virtuosity: The Fiction of John Barth." Diss., University of Virginia, 1972.

Dientsfrey, Harris. "Blended Especially for a Heady Smoke," *Book Week*, Mar. 15, 1964, p. 18.

Dippie, Brian W. "'His Visage Wild; His Form Exotick': Indian Themes and Cultural Guilt in John Barth's *The Sot-Weed Factor*,'" *American Quarterly*, 21 (Spring 1969), 113–21.

Diser, Philip E. "The Historical Ebenezer Cooke," *Critique*, 10, no. 3 (1968), 48–59.

Donoghue, Denis. "Grand Old Opry," *New York Review of Books*, 7 (Aug. 18, 1966), 25–26.

Enck, John. "John Barth: An Interview," *Wisconsin Studies in Contemporary Literature*, 6 (Winter–Spring 1965), 3–14.

Featherstone, Joseph. "John Barth as Jonathan Swift," *New Republic*, 155 (Sept. 3, 1966), 17–18.

Fiedler, Leslie A. "John Barth: An Eccentric Genius," *New Leader*, 44 (Feb. 13, 1961), 22–24.

Fuller, Edmund. "The Joke Is on Mankind," *New York Times Book Review*, Aug. 21, 1960, p. 4.

Garis, Robert. "What Happened to John Barth?" *Commentary*, 42 (Oct. 1966), 89–95.

Gresham, James Thomas. "John Barth as Menippean Satirist." Diss., Michigan State University, 1972.

Gross, Beverly. "The Anti-Novels of John Barth," *Chicago Review*, 20 (Nov. 1958), 95–109.

Hauck, Richard Boyd. "These Fruitful Odysseys: John Barth," in *A Cheerful Nihilism: Confidence and 'The Absurd' in American Humorous Fiction*. Bloomington: Indiana University Press, 1971.

Hicks, Granville. "Crowned with the Shame of Men," *Saturday Review*, 44 (Aug. 6, 1966), 21–23.

————. "Doubt without Skepticism," *Saturday Review*, 48 (July 3, 1965), 23–24.

————. "The Up-to-Date Looking Glass," *Saturday Review*, 51 (Sept. 28, 1968), 31–32.

Hinden, Michael. "*Lost in the Funhouse*: Barth's Use of the Recent Past," *Twentieth Century Literature*, 19 (Jan. 1973), 107–18.

Hirsch, David. "John Barth's Freedom Road," *Mediterranean Review*, 2 (Spring 1966), 38–47.

Holder, Alan. " 'What Marvelous Plot . . . Was Afoot?': History in Barth's *The Sot-Weed Factor*," *American Quarterly*, 20 (Fall 1968), 596–604.

Hyman, Stanley Edgar. "The American Adam," *New Leader*, 47 (Mar. 2, 1964), 20–21.

————. "John Barth's First Novel," *New Leader*, 48 (Apr. 12, 1965), 20–21.

Janoff, Bruce Lee. "Beyond Satire: Black Humor in the Novels of John Barth and Joseph Heller." Diss., Ohio University, 1972.

"John Barth: Goat-Boy's Father," *Playboy*, 14 (March 1967), 142.

"John Barth Papers," *Quarterly Journal of the Library of Congress*, 26 (Oct. 1969), 243, 247–49, 262.

Johnstone, Douglas Blake. "Myth and Psychology in the Novels of John Barth." Diss., University of Oregon, 1973.

Joseph, Gerhard. *John Barth*. (Pamphlets on American Writers ser.) Minneapolis: University of Minnesota Press, 1970.

Kerner, David. "Psychodrama in Eden," *Chicago Review*, 13 (Winter–Spring 1969), 59–67.

Kiely, Benedict. "Ripeness Was Not All: John Barth's *Giles Goat-Boy*," *Hollins Critic*, 3 (Dec. 1966), 1–12.

Klein, Marcus. "Gods and Goats," *The Reporter*, 35 (Sept. 22, 1966), 60–62.

Knapp, Edgar H. "Found in the Barthhouse: Novelist as Savior," *Modern Fiction Studies*, 14 (Winter 1968–69), 446–51.

Kyle, Carol A. "The Unity of Anatomy: The Structure of Barth's *Lost in the Funhouse*," *Critique*, 13, no. 3 (1972), 31–43.

Lask, Thomas. "Art Is Artifice in Barth Reading," *New York Times*, Nov. 21, 1967, p. 52.

Le Clair, Thomas. "John Barth's *The Floating Opera*: Death and the Craft of Fiction," *Texas Studies in Literature and Language*, 14 (Winter 1973), 711–30.

Lee, L. L. "Some Uses of *Finnegans Wake* in John Barth's *The Sot-Weed*," *James Joyce Quarterly*, 5 (Winter 1968), 177–78.

Levenson, M. Michael. "The Short Fiction of John Barth, Donald Barthelme, and Robert Coover," *Harvard Advocate*, 105 (Fall 1971), 26–28.

"The Logical and the Lost," *Esquire*, 50 (July 1958), 16.

Loughman, Celeste Marie. "Mirrors and Masks in the Novels of John Barth." Diss., University of Massachusetts, 1971.

Majdiak, Daniel. "Barth and the Representation of Life," *Criticism*, 12 (Winter 1970), 51–67.

Malin, Irving. *Commonweal*, 85 (Dec. 2, 1966), 270.

Mandel, Seigfried. "Gaudy Showboat," *New York Times Book Review*, Aug. 26, 1956, p. 27.

McColm, Pearlmarie. "The Revised New Syllabus and the Unrevised Old," *Denver Quarterly*, 1 (Autumn 1966), 136–41.

McDonald, James L. "Barth's Syllabus: The Frame of *Giles Goat-Boy*," *Critique*, 13, no. 3 (1972), 5–10.

Meras, Phyllis. "John Barth: A Truffle No Longer," *New York Times Book Review*, Aug. 7, 1966, p. 22.

———. Interview, "John Barth's Formula for Fiction," *Chicago Tribune*, Aug. 7, 1966, p. 3.

Mercer, Peter. "The Rhetoric of *Giles Goat-Boy*," *Novel*, 4 (Winter 1971), 147–58.

Miller, Russell H. "*The Sot-Weed Factor*: A Contemporary Mock-Epic," *Critique*, 8 (Winter 1965), 88–100.

Morrell, David Bernard. "John Barth: An Introduction." Diss., Pennsylvania State University, 1970.

Morse, J. Mitchell. "Fiction Chronicle," *Hudson Review*, 19 (Autumn 1966), 507–14.

Murphy, Richard W. "In Print: John Barth," *Horizon*, 5 (Jan. 1963), 36–37.

Noland, Richard W. "John Barth and the Novel of Comic Nihilism," *Wisconsin Studies in Contemporary Literature*, 7 (Autumn 1966), 239–57.

Plater, William Marmaduke. "Metamorphosis: An Examination of Communication and Community in Barth, Beckett and Pynchon." Diss., University of Illinois, 1973.

Poirier, Richard. "The Politics of Self-Parody," *Partisan Review*, 35 (Summer 1968), 339–53.

Prince, Alan. "An Interview with John Barth," *Prism* (Spring 1968), pp. 42–62.

Richardson, Jack. "Amusement and Revelation," *New Republic*, 159 (Nov. 23, 1968), 30, 34–35.

Rodrigues, Eusebio. "The Living Sakhyan in Barth's *Giles Goat-Boy*," *Notes on Contemporary Literature*, 2 (Sept. 1972), 7–8.

Rogers, Thomas. "John Barth: A Profile," *Book Week*, Aug. 7, 1966, p. 6.

Rovit, Earl. "The Novel as Parody: John Barth," *Critique*, 6 (Fall 1963), 77–85.

Samuels, Charles Thomas. "John Barth: A Buoyant Denial of Relevance," *Commonweal*, 85 (Oct. 21, 1966), 80–81.

Schickel, Richard. "*The Floating Opera*," *Critique*, 6 (Fall 1963), 53–67.

Scholes, Robert. "Disciple of Scheherazade," *New York Times Book Review*, May 8, 1966, pp. 5, 22.

———. *The Fabulators*. New York: Oxford University Press, 1967.

———. " 'George Is My Name,' " *New York Times Book Review*, Aug. 7, 1966, pp. 1, 22.

Scofield, James Davis. "Absurd Man and the Esthetics of the Absurd: The Fiction of John Barth." Diss., Kent State University, 1973.

Shenker, Israel. "Complicated Simple Things," *New York Times Book Review*, Sept. 24, 1972, pp. 35–38.

Sherman, Marilyn R. " 'Point of View' and the Creative Process in the Novels of John Barth." Diss., University of Florida, 1973.

Slethaug, Gordon E. "Barth's Refutation of the Idea of Progress," *Critique*, 13, no. 3 (1972), 11–29.

Smith, Herbert F. "Barth's Endless Road," *Critique*, 6 (Fall 1963), 68–76.

Storms, Charles Gilbert, III. "Satire in the Fiction of John Barth."
    Diss., Rutgers University, 1974.
Stubbs, John C. "John Barth as a Novelist of Ideas," Critique, 8
    (Winter 1966), 101–16
Sutcliffe, Denham. "Worth a Guilty Conscience," Kenyon Review,
    23 (Winter 1961), 181–84.
Tanner, Stephen L. "John Barth's Hamlet," Southwest Review, 56
    (Autumn 1971), 347–54.
Tanner, Tony, "The Hoax That Joke Bilked," Partisan Review, 34
    (Winter 1967), 102–9.
———. "What Is the Case? (John Barth)," in City of Words:
    American Fiction 1950–1970. New York. Harper & Row, 1971.
Tatham, Campbell. "The Giles Goat Monomyth: Some Remarks on the
    Structure of Giles Goat-Boy," Genre, 3 (Dec. 1970), 364–75
———. "John Barth and the Aesthetics of Artifice," Contemporary
    Literature, 12 (Winter 1971), 61–73.
Tilton, John W. "Giles Goat-Boy: An Interpretation," Bucknell Re-
    view, 18, no. 1 (1970), 92–119.
Trachtenberg, Alan, "Barth and Hawkes. Two Fabulists," Critique,
    6 (Fall 1963), 4–18.
Urbanski, Kenneth John. "The Forming Artifice in John Barth's Fic
    tions." Diss., University of Kansas, 1973.
Weixlmann, Joseph. "Counter-Type and Anti-Myth: Black and In-
    dian Characters in the Fiction of John Barth," Diss., Kansas State
    University, 1973.
———. "John Barth: A Bibliography," Critique, 13, no. 3 (1972),
    45–55.
Young, Philip. "The Mother of Us All: Pocahontas Reconsidered,"
    Kenyon Review, 24 (Summer 1962), 391–415.

WORKS BY THOMAS PYNCHON

The Crying of Lot 49 (1966). New York: Bantam Books, 1967.
"Entropy," Kenyon Review, 22 (Spring 1960), 277–92.
"A Journey into the Mind of Watts," New York Times Magazine,
    June 12, 1966, pp. 34–35, 78, 80–82, 84.
"Low-lands," New World Writing, 16 (1960), 85–108.
"Mortality and Mercy in Vienna," Epoch, 9 (Spring 1959), 195–213.
"The Secret Integration," Saturday Evening Post, 237 (Dec. 19, 1964),
    36–37, 39, 42–44, 46–49, 51.

"Under the Rose," *Noble Savage*, 3 (1961), 223–51.
V. (1963). New York: Bantam Books, 1968.

WORKS ABOUT THOMAS PYNCHON

Abernethy, Peter L. "Entropy in Pynchon's *The Crying of Lot 49*," *Critique*, 14, no. 2 (1973), 18–33.

Alter, Robert. "The Apocalyptic Temper," *Commentary*, 41 (June 1966), 61–66.

Balliett, Whitney. "Wha," *New Yorker*, 39 (June 15, 1963), 113–14, 117.

Buckeye, Robert. "The Anatomy of the Psychic Novel," *Critique*, 9, no. 2 (1967), 33–45.

Burrows, Miles. "Paranoid Quests," *New Statesman*, 73 (Apr. 14, 1967), 513–14.

Donadio, Stephen. "America, America," *Partisan Review*, 33 (Summer 1966), 448–52.

"Faulkner Novel Award Given," *New York Times*, Feb. 3, 1964, p. 25.

Feldman, Irving. "Keeping Cool," *Commentary*, 36 (Sept. 1963), 258–60.

Gold, Arthur R. "Like a Yo-Yo, Spinning through a Dehumanized Age," *New York Herald Tribune Books*, Apr. 21, 1963, p. 3.

———. "A Mad Dash after an Unholy Grail," *Book Week*, Apr. 24, 1966, p. 5.

Golden, Robert E. "Mass Man and Modernism: Violence in Pynchon's *V.*," *Critique*, 14, no. 2 (1973), 5–17.

Hall, James. "The New Pleasures of the Imagination," *Virginia Quarterly Review*, 46 (Autumn 1970), 596–612.

Handlin, Oscar. "Reader's Choice," *The Atlantic*, 217 (May 1966), 127–28.

Hausdorff, Don. "Thomas Pynchon's Multiple Absurdities," *Wisconsin Studies in Contemporary Literature*, 7 (Autumn 1966), 258–69.

Henkle, Roger B. "Pynchon's Tapestries on the Western Wall," *Modern Fiction Studies*, 17 (Summer 1971), 207–20.

Hicks, Granville. "A Plot against the Post Office," *Saturday Review*, 49 (Apr. 30, 1966), 27–28.

Hoffman, Frederick J. "The Questing Comedian: Thomas Pynchon's *V.*," *Critique*, 6 (Winter 1964), 174–77.

Hunt, John W. "Comic Escape and Anti-Vision: The Novels of Joseph Heller and Thomas Pynchon," in *Adversity and Grace:*

Studies in Recent American Literature, ed. Nathan A. Scott, Jr.
Chicago: University of Chicago Press, 1968.

Hyman, Stanley Edgar. "The Futility Corner," *Saturday Review,* 46
(Mar. 23, 1963), 44.

————. "The Goddess and the Schlemihl," *Standards: A Chronicle
of Books for Our Time.* New York: Horizon Press, 1966.

Kirby, David K. "Two Modern Versions of the Quest," *Southern
Humanities Review,* 5 (Fall 1971), 387–95.

Koch, Stephen. "Imagination in the Abstract," *Antioch Review,* 24
(Summer 1964), 253–63.

Kolodny, Annette, and Daniel James Peters. "Pynchon's *The Crying
of Lot 49:* The Novel as Subversive Experience," *Modern Fiction
Studies,* 19 (Spring 1973), 79–87.

Larner, Jeremy. "The New Schemihl," *Partisan Review,* 30 (Summer
1963), 273–76.

Lehan, Richard. "The American Novel—a Survey of 1966," *Wisconsin Studies in Contemporary Literature,* 8 (Summer 1967), 437–49.

————. "Man and His Fictions: Ellison, Pynchon, Heller, and Barth,"
in *A Dangerous Crossing: French Literary Existentialism and the
Modern American Novel.* Carbondale: Southern Illinois University
Press, 1973.

Lehmann-Haupt, Christopher. "End-of-the-World Machine," *New
York Times,* June 3, 1966, p. 37.

Lhamon, W. T., Jr. "The Most Irresponsible Bastard," *New Republic,*
168 (Apr. 14, 1973), 24–28.

Mangel, Anne. "Maxwell's Demon, Entropy, Information: *The Crying
of Lot 49,*" *Tri-Quarterly,* 20 (Winter 1971), 194–208.

Meixner, John A. "The All-Purpose Quest," *Kenyon Review,* 25
(Autumn 1963), 729–35.

Mizener, Arthur. "The New Romance," *Southern Review,* 8 (Jan.
1972), 106–17.

Morse, J. Mitchell. "Fiction Chronicle," *Hudson Review,* 19 (Autumn
1966), 507–14.

Nichols, Lewis. "Author," *New York Times Book Review,* Apr. 28,
1963, p. 8.

Plimpton, George. "Mata Hari with a Clockwork Eye, Alligators in
the Sewer," *New York Times Book Review,* Apr. 21, 1963, p. 5.

Poirier, Richard. "Embattled Underground," *New York Times Book
Review,* May 1, 1966, pp. 5, 42–43.

Robinson, David Edgar. "Unaccommodated Man: The Estranged

World in Contemporary Fiction." Diss., Duke University, 1971.

Rose, Remington. "At Home with Oedipa Maas," *New Republic*, 154 (May 14, 1966), 39–40.

Shattuck, Roger. "Fiction a la Mode," *New York Review of Books*, 6 (June 23, 1966), 22–24.

Shorris, Earl. "The Worldly Palimpsest of Thomas Pynchon," *Harper's*, 246 (June 1973), 78–80, 83.

Sklar, Robert. "The New Novel, USA, Thomas Pynchon," *The Nation*, 205 (Sept. 25, 1967), 277–80.

Slade, Joseph W. *Thomas Pynchon*. New York: Warner Paperback Library, 1974.

Tanner, Tony. "Caries and Cabals (Thomas Pynchon)," in *City of Words: American Fiction 1950–1970*. New York: Harper & Row, 1971.

Thorburn, David. "A Dissent on Pynchon," *Commentary*, 56 (Sept. 1973), 68–70.

Trachtenberg, Stanley. "Beyond Initiation: Some Recent Novels," *Yale Review*, 56 (Autumn 1966), 131–38.

Wazeka, Robert Thomas. "The Solitary Escape in Recent American Literature." Diss., University of Colorado, 1972.

Weixlmann, Joseph. "Thomas Pynchon: A Bibliography," *Critique*, 14, no. 2 (1973), 34–43.

Wensberg, Erik. *Commonweal*, 84 (July 8, 1966), 446–48.

Young, James Dean. "The Enigma Variations of Thomas Pynchon," *Critique*, 10, no. 1 (1967), 69–77.

WORKS BY JAMES PURDY

Cabot Wright Begins. New York: Avon Books, 1964.

Children Is All. New York: New Directions, 1962.

Color of Darkness (1957). New York: Bantam Books, 1970.

Eustace Chisholm and the Works (1967). New York: Bantam Books, 1970.

Jeremy's Version (1970). New York: Bantam Books, 1971.

Malcolm. New York: Farrar, Straus & Cudahy, 1959.

The Nephew. New York: Avon Books, 1960.

WORKS ABOUT JAMES PURDY

Algren, Nelson. "It's a Gay and Dreary Life," *The Critic*, 26 (Aug.–Sept. 1967), 67–68.

Bailey, Anthony. "The Possessed," *Commonweal*, 67 (Jan. 1958), 415.

Baldanza, Frank. "James Purdy on the Corruption of Innocents," *Contemporary Literature*, 15 (Summer 1974), 315–30.

————. "Playing House for Keeps with James Purdy," *Contemporary Literature*, 11 (Autumn 1970), 488–510.

Bittner, William. "The State of the Story," *The Nation*, 186 (Jan. 11, 1958), 34–36.

Brown, Ashley. "Landscape into Art: Henry James and John Crowe Ransom," *Sewanee Review*, 79 (Apr.–June 1971), 206–13.

Burris, Shirley W. "The Emergency in Purdy's 'Daddy Wolf,' " *Renascence*, 20 (Winter 1968), 94–98.

Bush, George E. "James Purdy," *Bulletin of Bibliography*, 28 (Jan.– Mar. 1971), 5–6.

Coffey, Warren. "The Incompleat Novelist," *Commentary*, 44 (Sept. 1967), 98, 100–103.

Cook, Donald. "By the World Possessed," *New Republic*, 141 (Nov. 9, 1959), 26–27.

Cook, Roderick. "Books in Brief," *Harper's*, 235 (July 1967), 94.

Cott, Jonathan. "The Damaged Cosmos," in *On Contemporary Literature*, ed. Richard Kostelanetz. Freeport, N.Y.: Books for Libraries Press, 1971.

Crews, Frederick C. "Private Lives, Public Lives," *New York Review of Books*, 3 (Nov. 5, 1964), 13–15.

Curley, Thomas F. "The Sleep-Waker," *Commonweal*, 70 (Oct. 16, 1959), 80.

"Dame Edith Sitwell's Sad, Witty Farewell," *Life*, 58 (Apr. 30, 1965), 8, 12.

Demott, Benjamin. "The New Books," *Harper's*, 226 (Jan. 1963), 91–92.

French, Warren. "The Quaking World of James Purdy," *Essays in Modern American Literature*, 31 (1963), 112–22.

Gloag, Julian. "One Weary Savage," *Saturday Review*, 47 (Dec. 12, 1964), 50–51.

Gold, Herbert. "Dame Edith Was Right," *New Republic*, 143 (Oct. 3, 1960), 17.

Hatch, Robert. "Peering in with the Outsiders," *Harper's*, 230 (Jan. 1965), 90–91.

Herr, Paul. "The Small, Sad World of James Purdy," *Chicago Review*, 14 (Autumn–Winter 1960), 19–25.

Hicks, Granville. "Purdy, Humes, Ellis," *Saturday Review*, 42 (Sept. 26, 1959), 15.

Horchler, Richard. "Impending Revelations," *Commonweal*, 77 (Jan. 4, 1963), 393, 395.

Lewis, R. W. B. "Our Jaws Are Sagging After Our Bout with Existence," *New York Times Book Review*, Oct. 9, 1960, p. 5.

Lorch, Thomas M. "Purdy's *Malcolm*: A Unique Vision of Radical Emptiness," *Wisconsin Studies in Contemporary Literature*, 6 (Summer 1965), 204–13.

Malin, Irving. "Eustace Chisholm and the Works," *Commonweal*, 86 (July 28, 1967), 476–77.

Maloff, Saul. "James Purdy's Fictions: The Quality of Despair," *Critique*, 6 (Spring 1963), 106–12.

Morris, Robert K. "James Purdy and the Works," *The Nation*, 205 (Oct. 9, 1967), 342–44.

Pease, Donald. "James Purdy: Shaman in Nowhere Land," in *The Fifties: Fiction, Poetry, Drama*, ed. Warren French. DeLand, Fla.: Everett/Edwards, 1970.

Peden, William. "And Never a Silver Lining," *New York Times Book Review*, Dec. 29, 1957, p. 4.

———. "Mystery of the Missing Kin," *Saturday Review*, 43 (Nov. 26, 1960), 22.

———. "Out of Contrasts Two Fictional Worlds," *Virginia Quarterly Review*, 39 (Spring 1963), 345–48.

Pomeranoz, Regina. "The Hell of Not Loving: Purdy's Modern Tragedy," *Renascence*, 16 (Spring 1964), 149–53.

Prescott, Orville. "The Waste of a Small Talent," *New York Times*, Oct. 19, 1964, p. 31.

Rosen, Gerald. "James Purdy's World of Black Humor." Diss., University of Pennsylvania, 1969.

Schott, Webster. "James Purdy: American Dreams," *The Nation*, 198 (Mar. 23, 1964), 300–302.

Schwarzschild, Bettina, ed. *The Not-Right House: Essays on James Purdy*. (Missouri Literary Frontiers, no. 5.) Columbia, Mo.: University of Missouri Press, 1968.

Sheed, Wilfrid. "An Alleged Love Story," *New York Times Book Review*, May 21, 1967, pp. 4, 51.

Skerrett, Joseph Taylor, Jr. "James Purdy and the Works: Love and Tragedy in Five Novels," *Twentieth Century Literature*, 15 (Apr. 1969), 25–33.

Sloan, Gary Glenven. "The Fiction of James Purdy: Theme and Meaning." Diss., Texas Tech University, 1973.

Sontag, Susan. "Laughter in the Dark," *New York Times Book Review*, Oct. 25, 1964, p. 5.

Stetler, Charles. "Purdy's *Malcolm*: Allegory of No Man," *Critique*, 14, no. 3 (1973), 91–99.

Tanner, Tony. "Frames without Pictures (James Purdy)," in *City of Words: American Fiction 1950–1970*. New York: Harper & Row, 1971.

———. "Sex and Identity in *Cabot Wright Begins*," *Twentieth Century Studies*, 2 (Nov. 1969), 89–102.

Tucker, Martin. "All Ambivalent," *Commonweal*, 73 (Oct. 21, 1960), 99.

Weales, Gerald. "No Face and No Exit: The Fiction of James Purdy and J. P. Donleavy," in *Contemporary American Novelists*, ed. Harry Moore. Carbondale: Southern Illinois University Press, 1964.

Wilson, Angus. "Purdy Pushes Comedy past Blackness," *Life*, 62 (June 2, 1967), 8.

WORKS BY KEN KESEY

One Flew over the Cuckoo's Nest. New York: New American Library (Signet Classics), 1962.

Sometimes a Great Notion (1964). New York: Bantam Books, 1971.

WORKS ABOUT KEN KESEY

Allen, Henry. "A '60's Superhero, After the Acid Test," *Washington Post*, June 9, 1974, pp. L1–L3, cols. 4, 1–6.

Billingsley, Ronald Gregg. "The Artistry of Ken Kesey." Diss., University of Oregon, 1971.

Blaisdell, Gus. "SHAZAM and the Neon Renaissance," *Author & Journalist*, 48 (June 1963), 7–8.

Blessing, Richard. "The Moving Target: Ken Kesey's Evolving Hero," *Journal of Popular Culture*, 4 (Winter 1971), 615–27.

"Briefly Noted Fiction," *New Yorker*, 38 (Apr. 21, 1962), 182–83.

Falk, Marcia L. "A Hatred and Fear of Women?," *New York Times*, Dec. 5, 1971, p. 5.

Fiedler, Leslie A. "Making It with a Little Shazam," *Book Week*, Aug. 2, 1964, pp. 1, 10–11.

Field, Rose. "War inside the Walls," *New York Herald Tribune,* Feb. 25, 1962, p. 4.

Foster, John Wilson. "Hustling to Some Purpose: Kesey's *One Flew over the Cuckoo's Nest,*" *Western American Literature,* 9 (Summer 1974), 115–29.

Havemann, Carol Sue Pearson. "The Fool as Mentor in Modern American Parables of Entrapment: Ken Kesey's *One Flew over the Cuckoo's Nest,* Joseph Heller's *Catch-22* and Ralph Ellison's *Invisible Man.*" Diss., Rice University, 1971.

Hoge, James O. "Psychedelic Stimulation and the Creative Imagination: The Case of Ken Kesey," *Southern Humanities Review,* 6 (Fall 1972), 381–91.

Krupat, Arnold. "The Saintly Hero: A Study of the Hero in Some Contemporary American Novels." Diss., Columbia University, 1964.

Levin, Martin. "A Reader's Report," *New York Times Book Review,* Feb. 4, 1962, p. 32.

"Life in a Loony Bin," *Time,* 79 (Feb. 16, 1962), 90.

Martin, Terence. "*One Flew over the Cuckoo's Nest* and the High Cost of Living," *Modern Fiction Studies,* 19 (Spring 1973), 43–55.

Maxwell, Richard. "The Abdication of Masculinity in *One Flew over the Cuckoo's Nest,*" in *Twenty-seven to One: A Potpourri of Humanistic Material.* Ogdensburg, N.Y.: Ryan Press, 1970.

Mills, Nicholaus. "Ken Kesey and the Politics of Laughter," *Centennial Review,* 16 (Winter 1972), 82–90.

Peden, William. "Gray Regions of the Mind," *Saturday Review,* 45 (Apr. 14, 1962), 49–50.

Sassoon, R. L. Review of *One Flew over the Cuckoo's Nest,* *Northwest Review,* 6 (Spring 1963), 116–20.

Schopf, William. "Blindfolded and Backwards: Promethean and Bemushroomed Heroism in *One Flew over the Cuckoo's Nest* and *Catch-22,*" *Bulletin of the Rocky Mountain Modern Language Association,* vol. 26, pp. 89–97.

Sherman, W. D. "The Novels of Ken Kesey," *Journal of American Studies,* 5 (Aug. 1971), 185–96.

Sherwood, Terry G. "*One Flew over the Cuckoo's Nest* and the Comic Strip," *Critique,* 13, no. 1 (1972), 96–109.

Smith, William James. "A Trio of Fine First Novels," *Commonweal,* 75 (Mar. 16, 1962), 648–49.

Tanner, Stephen L. "Salvation through Laughter: Ken Kesey and the Cuckoo's Nest," *Southwest Review,* 57 (Spring 1973), 125–37.

Tanner, Tony. "Edge City (Ken Kesey)," in *City of Words: American Fiction 1950–1970*. New York: Harper & Row, 1971.

Waldmeir, Joseph J. "Two Novelists of the Absurd: Heller and Kesey," *Wisconsin Studies in Contemporary Literature*, 5 (Autumn 1964), 192–204.

Wallis, Bruce E. "Christ in the Cuckoo's Nest: or, the Gospel According to Ken Kesey," *Cithara*, 12 (Nov. 1972), 52–58.

Wegs, Joyce Markert. "The Grotesque in Some American Novels of the Nineteen-Sixties: Ken Kesey, Joyce Carol Oates, Sylvia Plath." Diss., University of Illinois, 1973.

Witke, Charles. "Pastoral Convention in Virgil and Kesey," *Pacific Coast Philology*, 1 (1966), 20–24.

Wolfe, Tom. *The Electric Kool-Aid Acid Test* (1968). New York: Bantam Books, 1969.

Zaskin, Elliot M. "Political Theorist and Demiurge: The Rise and Fall of Ken Kesey," *Centennial Review*, 17 (Spring 1973), 199–213.

WORKS BY PHILIP ROTH

"An Actor's Life for Me," *Playboy*, 11 (Jan. 1964), 84–86, 228–32, 234–35.

The Breast. New York: Holt, Rinehart and Winston, 1972.

"The Contest for Aaron Gold," *Epoch*, 7 (Fall 1955), 37–51.

"Courting Disaster (or, Serious in the Fifties)," *Esquire*, 75 (May 1971), 93–101.

"Every Inch a Man," *Esquire*, 79 (May 1973), 128–30, 208, 210, 212, 214.

"From the First 18 Years of My Life," *New York Times*, Oct. 24, 1971, sec. 2, pp. 1D, 3D.

Goodbye, Columbus and Five Short Stories (1959). New York: Bantam Books, 1970.

"Iowa: A Very Far Country Indeed," *Esquire*, 58 (Dec. 1962), 132, 240, 242–44, 247–48, 250.

Letting Go (1962). New York: Bantam Books, 1970.

"A Modest Proposal," *Look*, 34 (Oct. 6, 1970), 98–100.

"Novotny's Pain," *New Yorker*, 38 (Oct. 27, 1962), 46–56.

"On the Air," *New American Review*, 10 (1970), 7–43.

Our Gang. New York: Bantam Books, 1971.

"Philip Roth's Exact Intent," *New York Times Book Review*, Feb. 23, 1969, pp. 2, 23–25.

Portnoy's Complaint (1969). New York: Bantam Books, 1970.
"Positive Thinking on Pennsylvania Avenue," *New Republic*, 136 (June 3, 1957), 10–11.
"The Psychoanalytic Special," *Esquire*, 60 (Nov. 1963), 106, 108–9, 172, 174–76.
"Recollections from beyond the Last Rope," *Harper's*, 219 (July 1959), 42–48.
"Reflections on the Death of a Library," *Wilson Library Bulletin*, 43 (Apr. 1969), 746–47.
"Salad Days," *Modern Occasions*, 1 (Fall 1970), 26–46.
When She Was Good (1967). New York: Bantam Books, 1970.
"Which Writer under Thirty-five Has Your Attention and What Has He Done to Get It?," review of Alan Lelchuk's *American Mischief*, *Esquire*, 78 (Oct. 1972), 133, 198.
"Writing about Jews," *Commentary*, 36 (Dec. 1963), 447–52.
"Writing American Fiction," *Commentary*, 31 (Mar. 1961), 223–33.

WORKS ABOUT PHILIP ROTH

Amis, Kingsley. "Waxing Wroth," *Harper's*, 238 (Apr. 1969), 104, 106–7.
Barrett, William. "Let Go, Let Live," *The Atlantic*, 210 (July 1962), 111.
Baruch, Hochman. "Child and Man in Philip Roth," *Midstream*, 13 (Dec. 1967), 68–76.
Baumbach, Jonathan. Review of *When She Was Good*, *Commonweal*, 86 (Aug. 11, 1967), 498.
Bellow, Saul. "The Swamp of Prosperity," *Commentary*, 28 (July 1959), 77–79.
Bettelheim, Bruno. "Portnoy Psychoanalyzed: Therapy Notes Found in the Files of Dr. O. Spielvogel, a New York Psychoanalyst," *Midstream*, 15 (June–July 1969), 3–10.
Broyard, Anatole. "A Sort of Moby Dick," *New Republic*, 160 (Mar. 1, 1969), 21–22.
Cohen, Eileen Z. "Alex in Wonderland, or *Portnoy's Complaint*," *Twentieth Century Literature*, 17 (July 1971), 161–68.
Cooperman, Stanley. "Philip Roth: 'Old Jacob's Eye' with a Squint," *Twentieth Century Literature*, 19 (July 1973), 203–16.
Deer, Irving and Harriet. "Philip Roth and the Crisis in American Fiction," *Minnesota Review*, 6, no. 4 (1966), 353–60.

DeMott, Benjamin. "Jewish Writers in America: A Place in the Establishment," *Commentary*, 31 (Feb. 1961), 127–34.

Detweiler, Robert. "Philip Roth and the Test of Dialogic Life," in *Four Spiritual Crises in Mid-Century American Fiction*. Gainesville: University of Florida Press, 1963.

Ditsky, John. "Roth, Updike and the High Expense of Spirit," *University of Windsor Review*, 5 (Fall 1969), 111–20.

Donaldson, Scott. "Philip Roth: The Meanings of *Letting Go*," *Contemporary Literature*, 11 (Winter 1970), 21–35.

Dupree, Robert. "And the Mom Roth Outgrabe or, What Hath Got Roth?," *Arlington Quarterly*, 2, no. 4 (1970), 175–89.

Freedman, Seymour. "The American-Jewish Novel." Diss., Cornell University, 1968.

Freedman, William. "American Jewish Fiction: So What's the Big Deal?," *Chicago Review*, 19, no. 1 (1966), 90–107.

Friedman, Alan W. "The Jew's Complaint in Recent American Fiction: Beyond Exodus and Still in the Wilderness," *Southern Review*, 8 (Jan. 1972), 41–59.

Gilman, Richard. "Let's Lynch Lucy," *New Republic*, 156 (June 24, 1967), 19–21.

Goldman, Albert. "Wild Blue Shocker," *Life*, 66 (Feb. 7, 1969), 58B–58D, 58F, 61–64.

Greenfeld, Josh. Review of *Portnoy's Complaint*, *New York Times Book Review*, Feb. 23, 1969, pp. 1–2.

Greenway, John. "Philip Roth Emerges from the Men's Room, Hauriant," *National Review*, 23 (Dec. 17, 1971), 1389.

Grumbach, Doris. Review of *When She Was Good*, *America*, 116 (June 17, 1967), 857.

Guttmann, Allen. "The Conversion of the Jews," *Wisconsin Studies in Contemporary Literature*, 6 (Summer 1965), 161–76.

———. *The Jewish Writer in America: Assimilation and the Crisis of Identity*. New York: Oxford University Press, 1971.

Howe, Irving. "Philip Roth Reconsidered," *Commentary*, 54 (Dec. 1972), 69–77.

———. "The Suburbs of Babylon," *New Republic*, 140 (June 15, 1959), 17–18.

Hyman, Stanley Edgar. "A Novelist of Great Promise," in *On Contemporary Literature*, ed. Richard Kostelanetz. Freeport, N.Y.: Books for Libraries Press, 1971.

Isaac, Dan. "In Defense of Philip Roth," *Chicago Review*, 17, nos. 2 and 3 (1964), 84–96.

"Jewishness and the Younger Intellectuals," a symposium, *Commentary*, 31 (Apr. 1961), 306–59.

Kazin, Alfred. "Tough-minded Mr. Roth," in *Contemporaries*. Boston: Little, Brown, 1962.

———. "Up against the Wall, Mama!," *New York Review of Books*, 12 (Feb. 27, 1969), 3.

Kliman, Bernice W. "Names in *Portnoy's Complaint*," *Critique*, 14, no. 3 (1973), 16–24.

Landis, Joseph C. "The Sadness of Philip Roth: An Interim Report," *Massachusetts Review*, 3 (Winter 1962), 259–68.

Leer, Norman. "Escape and Confrontation in the Short Stories of Philip Roth," *Christian Scholar*, 49 (Summer 1966), 132–46.

Lelchuk, Alan, ed. "On Satirizing Presidents: An Interview with Philip Roth," *The Atlantic*, 228 (Dec. 1971), 81–88.

Leonard, J. "Life and Letters," *The Atlantic*, 231 (June 1973), 114–16.

Levine, Mordecai H. "Philip Roth and American Judaism," *CLA Journal*, 14 (Dec. 1970), 163–70.

Mademoiselle, an interview, 53 (Aug. 1961), 254–55.

Maloff, Saul. "Avenging Angel," *Newseek*, 69 (June 12, 1967), 94, 96.

———. "Tropic of Conversation," *Commonweal*, 90 (Mar. 21, 1969), 23–24.

McDaniel, John Noble. "Heroes in the Fiction of Philip Roth." Diss., Florida State University, 1972.

Meeter, Glenn. *Philip Roth and Bernard Malamud*. Grand Rapids, Mich.: William B. Eerdmans, 1968.

Mizener, Arthur. "Bumblers in a World of Their Own," *New York Times Book Review*, June 17, 1962, pp. 1, 28–29.

Noble, Donald R. "Dickinson to Roth," *American Notes & Queries*, 9 (May 1971), 150–51.

O'Connell, Shaun. "The Death of the Heart," *The Nation*, 205 (July 17, 1967), 53–54.

Plimpton, George. "Philip Roth's Exact Intent," *New York Times Book Review*, Feb. 23, 1969, pp. 2, 23–25.

Podhoretz, Norman. "The Gloom of Philip Roth," in *Doings and Undoings: The Fifties and After in American Writing*. New York: Farrar, Straus, and Giroux, 1964.

———. "Laureate of the New Class," *Commentary*, 54 (Dec. 1972), 4, 7.

Raban, Jonathan. "The New Philip Roth," *Novel*, 2 (Winter 1969), 153–68.

Shaw, Peter. "Portnoy & His Creator," *Commentary*, 47 (May 1969), 77–79.

Sheed, Wilfrid. "Pity for the Poor Wasps," *New York Times Book Review*, June 11, 1967, p. 5.

Sheppard, R. Z. "Name of the Game," *Time*, 101 (May 7, 1973), 69.

Solotaroff, Theodore. "Fiction," *Esquire*, 78 (Oct. 1972), 82, 84, 178.

——. "The Journey of Philip Roth," *The Atlantic*, 223 (Apr. 1969), 64–72.

——. "Philip Roth and the Jewish Moralists," *Chicago Review*, 13 (Winter 1959), 87 99.

Spacks, Patricia Meyer. "About Portnoy," *Yale Review*, 58 (June 1969), 623–35.

Tanner, Tony. "Fictionalized Recall—or 'The Settling of Scores! The Pursuit of Dreams!' (Saul Bellow, Philip Roth, Frank Conroy)," in *City of Words: American Fiction 1950–1970*. New York: Harper & Row, 1971.

Whitton, Steven Jay. "The Mad Crusader: The Quest as Motif in the Jewish Fiction of Philip Roth and Bernard Malamud." Diss., University of South Carolina, 1973.

Wisse, Ruth R. *The Schlemiel as Modern Hero*. Chicago: University of Chicago Press, 1971.

WORKS BY JOHN UPDIKE

Assorted Prose (1955–65). Greenwich, Conn.: Fawcett Publications, 1965.

Bech: A Book (1970). Greenwich, Conn.: Fawcett Publications, 1971.

The Centaur (1962). Greenwich, Conn.: Fawcett Publications, 1963.

"Commercial," *New Yorker*, 48 (June 10, 1972), 30–32.

Couples (1968). Greenwich, Conn.: Fawcett Publications, 1969.

"Henry Bech Redux," *New York Times Book Review*, Nov. 14, 1971, p. 3.

"Love: First Lessons," *New Yorker*, 67 (Nov. 6, 1971), 46–47.

Museums and Women and Other Stories. New York: Alfred A. Knopf, 1972.

The Music School: Short Stories (1966). Greenwich, Conn.: Fawcett Publications, 1967.

Of the Farm (1965). Greenwich, Conn.: Fawcett Publications, 1971.
On Meeting Authors. Newburyport, Mass.: Wickford Press, 1968.
Pigeon Feathers and Other Stories. Greenwich, Conn.: Fawcett Publications, 1962.
The Poorhouse Fair. Greenwich, Conn.: Fawcett Publications, 1958.
Rabbit Redux. New York: Alfred A. Knopf, 1971.
Rabbit, Run. Greenwich, Conn.: Fawcett Publications, 1960.
The Same Door (1959). Greenwich, Conn.: Fawcett Publications, 1971.
"The Tarbox Police," *Esquire*, 77 (Mar. 1972), 85–86.
"The Wait," *New Yorker*, 43 (Feb. 17, 1968), 34–46, 54, 57.

WORKS ABOUT JOHN UPDIKE

Adams, Robert Martin. "Without Risk," *New York Times Book Review*, Sept. 18, 1966, pp. 4–5.
Aldridge, John. "An Askew Halo for John Updike," *Saturday Review*, 53 (June 27, 1970), 25–27, 35.
Alley, Alvin D. "*The Centaur*: Transcendental Imagination and Metaphoric Death," *English Journal*, 56 (Oct. 1967), 982–85.
———, and Hugh Agee. "Existential Heroes: Frank Alpine and Rabbit Angstrom," *Ball State University Forum*, 9 (Winter 1968), 3–5.
Alter, Robert. "Updike, Malamud, and the Fire This Time," *Commentary*, 54 (Oct. 1972), 68–74.
Backscheider, Paula and Nick. "Updike's *Couples*: Squeak in the Night," *Modern Fiction Studies*, 20 (Spring 1974), 45–52.
Barr, Donald. "A Stone's Throw Apart," *New York Times Book Review*, Jan. 11, 1959, p. 4.
Bell, Vereen. "A Study in Frustration," *Shenandoah*, 14 (Summer 1963), 69–72.
Boroff, David. "You Cannot Really Flee," *New York Times Book Review*, Nov. 6, 1960, pp. 4, 43.
Brenner, Gerry. "*Rabbit, Run*: John Updike's Criticism of 'The Return to Nature,'" *Twentieth Century Literature*, 12 (Apr. 1966), 3–14.
Broyard, Anatole. "Updike Goes All Out at Last," *New York Times*, Nov. 5, 1971, p. 40.
Buitenhuis, Peter. "The Mowing of a Meadow," *New York Times Book Review*, Nov. 14, 1965, pp. 4, 34.

Burchard, Rachael C. *John Updike: Yea Sayings.* Carbondale, Ill.: Southern Illinois University Press, 1971.

Burgess, Anthony. "Language, Myth and Mr. Updike," *Commonweal,* 83 (Feb. 11, 1966), 557–59.

Burhans, Clinton S. "Things Falling Apart: Structure and Theme in *Rabbit, Run,*" *Studies in the Novel,* 5 (Fall 1973), 336–51.

Chester, Alfred. "Twitches and Embarrassments," *Commentary,* 34 (July 1962), 77–80.

Curley, Thomas. "Between Heaven and Earth," *Commonweal,* 78 (Mar. 29, 1963), 26–27.

Davenport, Guy. "Magic Realism in Prose," *National Review,* 13 (Aug. 28, 1962), 153–54.

DeBellis, Jack. "The Group and John Updike," *Sewanee Review,* 72 (Summer 1964), 531–36.

Detweiler, Robert. *John Updike.* New York: Twayne Publishers, 1972.

———. "John Updike and the Indictment of Culture-Protestantism," in *Four Spiritual Crises in Mid-Century American Fiction.* Gainesville: University of Florida Press, 1963.

———. "Updike's *Couples:* Eros Demythologized," *Twentieth Century Literature,* 17 (Oct. 1971), 235–46.

Doner, Dean. "Rabbit Angstrom's Unseen World," *New World Writing,* 20 (1962), 58–75.

Doyle, Paul A. "Updike's Fiction: Motifs and Techniques," *Catholic World,* 199 (Sept. 1964), 356–62.

Ducharme, E. R. "Close Reading and Teaching: Explication of 'Shillington,'" *English Journal,* 59 (Oct. 1970), 939–42.

Duffy, Martha. "Locked in a Star," *Time,* 98 (Mar. 8, 1971), 80–81.

Duncan, Graham H. "The Thing Itself in *Rabbit, Run,*" *English Record,* 13 (Apr. 1963), 25–27, 36–37.

Edelstein, J. M. "Down with the Poor in Spirit," *New Republic,* 143 (Nov. 21, 1960), 17–18.

———. "The Security of Memory," *New Republic,* 146 (May 14, 1962), 30–31, 146.

Edwards, A. S. G. "Updike's 'A Sense of Shelter,'" *Studies in Short Fiction,* 8 (Summer 1971), 467–68.

Edwards, Thomas R. "*Bech: A Book,*" *New York Times Book Review,* June 21, 1970, pp. 1, 38.

Enright, D. J. "Updike's Ups and Downs," *Holiday,* 38 (Nov. 1965), 162–66.

Epstein, Joseph. "Mother's Day on the Updike Farm," *New Repub-lic*, 153 (Dec. 11, 1965), 23–25.

Falke, Wayne. "*Rabbit Redux*: Time / Order / God," *Modern Fic-tion Studies*, 20 (Spring 1974), 59–75.

Finkelstein, Sidney. "Acceptance of Alienation: John Updike and James Purdy," in *Existentialism and Alienation in American Litera-ture*. New York: International Publishers, 1965.

———. "The Anti-Hero of Updike, Bellow and Malamud," *Ameri-can Dialog*, 7 (Spring 1972), 12–14, 30.

Fisher, Richard E. "John Updike: Theme and Form in the Garden of Epiphanies," *Moderna Sprak*, 56 (Fall 1962), 255–60.

Fitelson, David. "Conflict Unresolved," *Commentary*, 27 (Mar. 1959), 275–76.

Flint, Joyce M. "In Search of Meaning: Bernard Malamud, Norman Mailer, John Updike." Diss., Washington State University, 1969.

———. "John Updike and *Couples*: The WASP's Dilemma," *Re-search Studies*, 36 (Dec. 1968), 340–47.

Friedman, Ruben. "An Interpretation of John Updike's 'Tomorrow and Tomorrow and So Forth,'" *English Journal*, 61 (Nov. 1972), 1159–62.

Gado, Frank, ed. *A Conversation with John Updike*. Albany, N.Y.: Argus-Greenwood, 1971.

Galloway, David D. *The Absurd Hero in American Fiction: Updike, Styron, Bellow, Salinger*. Austin: University of Texas Press, 1966.

Gass, William. "Updike's *Couples*," *New York Review of Books*, 10 (Apr. 11, 1968), 3.

Geismar, Maxwell. "The American Short Story Today," *Studies on the Left*, 4 (Spring 1964), 21–27.

Gill, Brendan. "A Special Case," *New Yorker*, 47 (Jan. 8, 1972), 83–84.

Gilman, Richard. "A Distinguished Image of Precarious Life," *Com-monweal*, 73 (Oct. 28, 1960), 128–29.

———. "A Last Assertion of Personal Being," *Commonweal*, 69 (Feb. 6, 1959), 449–500.

———. "The Youth of an Author," *New Republic*, 148 (Apr. 13, 1963), 25–27.

Gindin, James. "Megalotopia and WASP Backlash: The Fiction of Mailer and Updike," *Centennial Review*, 15 (Winter 1971), 38–52.

Gingher, Robert S. "Has John Updike Anything to Say?," *Modern Fiction Studies*, 20 (Spring 1974), 97–105.

Gordon, David J. "Some Recent Novels: Styles of Martyrdom," *Yale Review*, 58 (Autumn 1968), 112–26.

Gordon, John. "Updike Redux," *Ramparts*, 10 (Apr. 1972), 56–69.

Gratton, Margaret. "The Use of Rhythm in Three Novels by John Updike," *University of Portland Review*, 21 (Fall 1969), 3–12.

Greenfield, Josh. "*Couples*," *Commonweal*, 88 (Apr. 26, 1968), 185–87.

Griffith, Albert J. "Updike's Artist's Dilemma: 'Should Wizard Hit Mommy?,' " *Modern Fiction Studies*, 20 (Spring 1974), 111–15.

Guyse, Hazel Sample. "The Lord Loves a Cheerful Corpse," *English Journal*, 55 (Oct. 1966), 863–66.

Hamilton, Alice and Kenneth. *The Elements of John Updike*. Grand Rapids, Mich.: William B. Eerdmans, 1970.

———. *John Updike: A Critical Essay*. Grand Rapids, Mich.: William B. Eerdmans, 1967.

Hamilton, Kenneth. "John Updike: Chronicler of the Time of the 'Death of God,' " *Christian Century*, 84 (June 7, 1967), 745–48.

Harper, Howard M., Jr. "John Updike: The Intrinsic Problem of Human Existence," in *Desperate Faith: A Study of Bellow, Salinger, Mailer, Baldwin, and Updike*. Chapel Hill: University of North Carolina Press, 1967.

Hertzel, Leo J. "Rabbit in the Great North Woods," *University Review* (Kansas City), 33 (Dec. 1966), 143–47.

Hicks, Granville. "John Updike," in *Literary Horizons*. New York: New York University Press, 1970.

Hiller, Catherine. "Personality and Persona: The Narrators in John Updike's Fiction." Diss., Brown University, 1972.

Howard, Jane. "Can a Nice Novelist Finish First?," *Life*, 61 (Nov. 4, 1966), 74–82.

Hyman, Stanley Edgar. "The Artist as a Young Man," *New Leader*, 45 (Mar. 19, 1962), 22–23.

———. "Chiron at Olinger High," *New Leader*, 46 (Feb. 4, 1963), 20–21.

———. "Couplings," *New Leader*, 51 (May 20, 1968), 20–21.

Kanon, Joseph. "Satire and Sensibility," *Saturday Review*, 55 (Sept. 30, 1972), 73, 78.

Kazin, Alfred. "Updike: Novelist of the New, Post-Pill America," *Book World*, Apr. 7, 1968, pp. 1, 3.

La Course, Guerin. "The Innocence of John Updike," *Commonweal*, 77 (Feb. 8, 1963), 512–14.

Larsen, Richard Bruce. "The Short Stories of John Updike." Diss., Emory University, 1973.

Lehmann-Haupt, Christopher. "Updike: A Mensch," *New York Times*, June 11, 1970, p. 43.

L'Heureux, John. "Centaur Tracks," *The Critic*, 24 (Dec. 1965–Jan. 1966), 64–65.

Locke, Richard. "*Rabbit Redux*," *New York Times Book Review*, Nov. 14, 1971, pp. 1–2, 12, 14, 16, 20.

Lodge, David. "Post-Pill Paradise Lost: John Updike's *Couples*," *New Blackfriars*, 51 (Nov. 1970), 511–18.

Lurie, Alison. "Witches and Fairies: Fitzgerald to Updike," *New York Review of Books*, 17 (Dec. 2, 1971), 6–11.

Lyons, Eugene. "John Updike: The Beginning and the End," *Critique*, 14, no. 2 (1972), 44–59.

Lyons, R. "A High E. Q.," *Minnesota Review*, 1 (Spring 1961), 385–89.

Mailer, Norman. "Norman Mailer vs. Nine Writers," *Esquire*, 60 (July 1963), 63–69, 105.

Malin, Irving. "Occasions for Loving," *Kenyon Review*, 25 (Spring 1963), 348–52.

Mano, Keith. "Every Inch an Updike," *Book World*, Oct. 22, 1972, p. 3.

Markle, Joyce B. *Fighters and Lovers: Theme in the Novels of John Updike*. New York: New York University Press, 1973.

McCoy, Robert. "John Updike's Literary Apprenticeship on *The Harvard Lampoon*," *Modern Fiction Studies*, 20 (Spring 1974), 3–12.

McKenzie, Alan T. "A Craftsman's Intimate Satisfactions: The Parlor Games in *Couples*," *Modern Fiction Studies*, 20 (Spring 1974), 53–58.

Meyer, Arlin G. "The Theology of John Updike," *The Cresset*, 34 (Oct. 1971), 23–25.

————, with Michael A. Olivas. "Criticism of John Updike: A Selected Checklist," *Modern Fiction Studies*, 20 (Spring 1974), 121–33.

Miller, Nolan. "Three of the Best," *Antioch Review*, 21 (Spring 1961), 118–28.

Mizener, Arthur. "The American Hero as High-School Boy: Peter Caldwell," in *The Sense of Life in the Modern Novel*. Boston: Houghton Mifflin, 1963.

———. "Behind the Dazzle Is a Knowing Eye," *New York Times Book Review*, Mar. 18, 1962, pp. 1, 29.

Muradian, Thaddeus. "The World of Updike," *English Journal*, 54 (Oct. 1965), 577–84.

Murphy, Richard W. "John Updike," *Horizon*, 4 (Mar. 1962), 84–85.

Myers, David. "The Questing Fear: Christian Allegory in John Updike's *The Centaur*," *Twentieth Century Literature*, 17 (Apr. 1971), 73–82.

Nadon, Robert J. "Urban Values in Recent American Fiction: A Study in the Fiction of Saul Bellow, John Updike, Bernard Malamud, and Norman Mailer." Diss., University of Minnesota, 1969.

Nichols, Lewis. "Talk with John Updike," *New York Times Book Review*, Apr. 7, 1968, pp. 34–35.

Novak, Michael. "Updike's Quest for Liturgy," *Commonweal*, 78 (May 10, 1963), 192–95.

O'Connor, William Van. "John Updike and William Styron: The Burden of Talent," in *Contemporary American Novelists*, ed. Harry T. Moore. Carbondale, Ill.: Southern Illinois University Press, 1964.

Overmyer, Janet. "Courtly Love in the A & P," *Notes on Contemporary Literature*, 2 (May 1972), 4–5.

Ozick, Cynthia. "Ethnic Joke," *Commentary*, 50 (Nov. 1970), 106–14.

Peden, William. "Minor Ills That Plague the Human Heart," *New York Times Book Review*, Aug. 16, 1959, p. 5.

Petter, H. "John Updike's Metaphoric Novels," *English Studies*, 50 (Apr. 1969), 197–206.

Podhoretz, Norman. "A Dissent on Updike," in *Doings and Undoings: The Fifties and After in American Writing*. New York: Farrar, Straus, and Giroux, 1964.

Poore, Charles. "Joey at 35, the House of Knopf at 50," *New York Times*, Nov. 20, 1965, p. 33.

Porter, M. Gilbert. "John Updike's 'A & P': The Establishment and an Emersonian Cashier," *English Journal*, 61 (Nov. 1972), 1155–58.

Raymont, Henry. "John Updike Completes a Sequel to *Rabbit, Run*," *New York Times*, July 27, 1971, p. 22.

Regan, Robert Alton. "Updike's Symbol of the Center," *Modern Fiction Studies*, 20 (Spring 1974), 77–96.

Reising, R. W. "Updike's 'A Sense of Shelter,'" *Studies in Short Fiction*, 7 (Fall 1970), 651–52.

Rhode, Eric. "Grabbing Dilemmas: John Updike Talks about God,

Love, and the American Identity," *Vogue,* 157 (Feb. 1, 1971), 140–41, 184–85.

Richardson, Jack. "Keeping Up with Updike," *New York Review of Books,* 15 (Oct. 22, 1970), 46–48.

Ricks, Christopher. "Flopsy Bunny," *New York Review of Books,* 17 (Dec. 16, 1971), pp. 7–9.

Rosa, Alfred F. "The Psycholinguistics of Updike's 'Museums and Women,'" *Modern Fiction Studies,* 20 (Spring 1974), 107–11.

Rotundo, Barbara. "*Rabbit, Run* and *A Tale of Peter Rabbit,*" *Notes on Contemporary Literature,* 1 (May 1971), 2–3.

Rowland, Stanley, Jr. "The Limits of Littleness," *Christian Century,* 79 (July 4, 1962), 840–41.

"Run from Rabbit," *America,* 104 (Nov. 19, 1960), 257.

Rupp, Richard. "John Updike: Style in Search of a Center," *Sewanee Review,* 75 (Autumn 1967), 693–709.

Samuels, Charles Thomas. "The Art of Fiction XLIII: John Updike," *Paris Review,* 45 (Winter 1968), 85–117.

————. *John Updike.* (Pamphlets on American Writers ser.) Minneapolis: University of Minneapolis Press, 1969.

————. "Updike on the Present," *New Republic,* 165 (Nov. 20, 1971), 29–30.

Sheed, Wilfrid, "Play in Tarbox," *New York Times Book Review,* Apr. 7, 1968, pp. 1, 30–33.

Sissman, L. E. "John Updike: Midpoint and After," *The Atlantic,* 226 (Aug. 1970), 102–3.

Sokoloff, B. A., and David E. Arnason. *John Updike: A Comprehensive Bibliography.* Norwood, Pa.: Norwood Press, 1973.

Spectorsky, A. C. "Spirit under Surgery," *Saturday Review,* 62 (Aug. 22, 1959), 15, 31.

Stafford, William T. " 'The Curious Greased Grace' of John Updike: Some of His Critics and the American Tradition," *Journal of Modern Literature,* 2 (Nov. 1972), 569–75.

Standley, Fred L. "*Rabbit, Run*: An Image of Life," *Midwest Quarterly,* 8 (Summer 1967), 371–86.

Stern, Richard G. "The Myth in Action," *The Spectator,* Sept. 27, 1963, p. 389.

Stubbs, John C. "The Search for Perfection in *Rabbit, Run,*" *Critique,* 10, no 2 (1968), 94–101.

Suderman, Elmer F. "The Right Way and the Good Way in *Rabbit, Run,*" *University Review,* 36 (Oct. 1969), 13–21.

Sullivan, Walter. "Updike, Spark, and Others," *Sewanee Review*, 74 (Summer 1966), 709–16.

Sykes, Robert H. "A Commentary on Updike's Astronomer," *Studies in Short Fiction*, 8 (Fall 1971), 575–79.

Tanner, Tony. "A Compromised Environment (John Updike)" in *City of Words: American Fiction 1950–1970*. New York: Harper & Row, 1971.

———. "The Sorrow of Some Central Hollowness," *New York Times Book Review*, Oct. 22, 1972, pp. 5, 24.

Tate, M. Judith. "John Updike: Of Rabbits and Centaurs," *The Critic*, 22 (Feb.–Mar. 1964), 44–47, 49–50.

Taylor, C. Clarke. *John Updike: A Bibliography*. Kent, Ohio: Kent State University Press, 1968.

Taylor, Larry E. *Pastoral and Anti-Pastoral Patterns in John Updike's Fiction*. Carbondale, Ill.: Southern Illinois University Press, 1971.

Thompson, John. "Other People's Affairs," *Partisan Review*, 27 (Jan.–Feb. 1961), 117–24.

———. "Updike's *Couples*," *Commentary*, 45 (May 1968), 70–73.

Todd, Richard. "Updike and Barthelme: Disengagement," *The Atlantic*, 230 (Dec. 1972), 126–32.

Trilling, Diana. "Updike's Yankee Traders," *The Atlantic*, 226 (Apr. 1968), 129–31.

Umphlett, Wiley L. "Theme and Structure in John Updike's *Rabbit, Run*," *Laurel Review*, 5 (Fall 1965), 35–40.

Vargo, Edward P. "The Necessity of Myth in Updike's *The Centaur*," *PMLA*, 85 (May 1973), 452–60.

———. *Rainstorms and Fire: Ritual in the Novels of John Updike*. Port Washington, N.Y · Kennikat Press, 1973.

Vickery, John B. "*The Centaur*: Myth, History, and Narrative," *Modern Fiction Studies*, 20 (Spring 1974), 29–43.

"View from the Catacombs," *Time*, 91 (Apr. 26, 1968), 66–74.

Walcutt, Charles Child. "The Centripetal Action: John Updike's *The Centaur* and *Rabbit, Run* and Wright Morris's *One Day*," in *Man's Changing Mask: Modes and Methods of Characterization in Fiction*. Minneapolis: University of Minnesota Press, 1966.

Waldmeir, Joseph. "It's the Going That's Important, Not the Getting There: Rabbit's Questing Non-Quest," *Modern Fiction Studies*, 20 (Spring 1974), 13–27.

Ward, John A. "John Updike's Fiction," *Critique*, 5 (Spring–Summer 1962), 27–41.

Weber, Brom. "*Rabbit Redux,*" *Saturday Review,* 54 (Nov. 27, 1971), 54–55.

Wood, Michael. "Great American Fragments," *New York Review of Books,* 19 (Dec. 14, 1972), 12–18.

Wyatt, Bryant N. "John Updike: The Psychological Novel in Search of Structure," *Twentieth Century Literature,* 13 (July 1967), 89–96.

Yglesias, Jose. "Coupling and Uncoupling," *The Nation,* 206 (May 13, 1968), 637–38.

Zylstra, S. A. "John Updike and the Parabolic Nature of the World," *Soundings,* 56 (Fall 1973), 323–37.

WORKS BY JOYCE CAROL OATES

"Background and Foreground in Fiction," *The Writer,* 80 (Aug. 1967), 11–13.

"Bloodstains," *Harper's,* 242 (Aug. 1971), 82–88.

"Building Tension in the Short Story," *The Writer,* 79 (June 1966), 11–12, 44.

By the North Gate. Greenwich, Conn.: Fawcett Publications, 1963.

"Concerning the Case of Bobby G.," *The Atlantic,* 231 (Feb. 1973), 84–88, 90–92.

The Edge of Impossibility: Tragic Forms in Literature. New York: Vanguard Press, 1972.

Expensive People. Greenwich, Conn.: Fawcett Publications, 1968.

"The Fact Is: We Like to Be Drugged," *McCalls,* 97 (June 1970), 69.

"A Far Countree," *The Critic,* 27 (Dec. 1968–Jan. 1969), 68–77.

A Garden of Earthly Delights. Greenwich, Conn.: Fawcett Publications, 1966.

"Henry James and Virginia Woolf: The Art of Relationships," *Twentieth Century Literature,* 10 (Oct. 1964), 119–29.

"How My Father Was Murdered," *The Atlantic,* 228 (Sept. 1971), 72–76.

"An Interior Monologue," *Esquire,* 71 (Feb. 1969), 84–85, 92–93.

"Joyce Carol Oates on Thoreau's *Walden,*" *Mademoiselle,* 76 (Apr. 1973), 96, 98.

"Man under Sentence of Death: The Novels of James M. Cain," in *Tough Guy Writers of the Thirties,* ed. David Madden. Carbondale: Southern Illinois University Press, 1968.

Marriages and Infidelities. New York: Vanguard Press, 1972.

"Other Celebrity Voices," *Today's Health,* 52 (May 1974), 31.

"Out of the Machine," *The Atlantic*, 218 (July 1971), 42–45.
"The Short Story," *Southern Humanities Review*, 5 (Summer 1971), 213–14.
"6:27 P.M.," *Redbook*, 138 (Dec. 1971), 82–83, 190–94.
them. Greenwich, Conn.: Fawcett Publications, 1969.
Upon the Sweeping Flood and Other Stories. Greenwich, Conn.: Fawcett Publications, 1966.
"What Herbert Brewer and I Did to Each Other," *McCalls*, 97 (Apr. 1970), 102–3, 143–46, 148, 154.
The Wheel of Love (1970). Greenwich, Conn.: Fawcett Publications, 1972.
With Shuddering Fall. New York: Fawcett World Library, 1964.
Wonderland. Toronto: Copp Clark, 1971.

WORKS ABOUT JOYCE CAROL OATES

Abrahams, William. "Stories of a Visionary," *Saturday Review*, 55 (Sept. 23, 1972), 76, 80.
Adams, Robert M. Review of *them*, *New York Times Book Review*, Sept. 28, 1969, pp. 4–5, 43.
Battersberry, Michael and Ariane. "Focus on Joyce Carol Oates," *Harper's Bazaar*, 106 (Sept. 1973), 159, 174, 176.
Bellamy, Joe David. "The Dark Lady of American Letters: An Interview with Joyce Carol Oates," *The Atlantic*, 229 (Feb. 1972), 63–67.
Bergonzi, Bernard. "Truants," *New York Review of Books*, 11 (Jan. 2, 1969), 40–41.
Bower, Warren. "Bliss in the First Person," *Saturday Review*, 11 (Oct. 26, 1968), 34–35.
Burwell, Rose Marie. "Joyce Carol Oates and an Old Master," *Critique*, 15, no. 1 (1973), 48–58.
Cassill, R. V. "Journey to the End of Suburban Night," *Book World*, Nov. 3, 1968, p. 5.
———. "Violence Can't Be Singled Out from an Ordinary Day," *Book World*, Nov. 23, 1969, p. 13.
Clemons, Walter. "Joyce Carol Oates at Home," *New York Times Book Review*, Sept. 28, 1969, pp. 4–5, 48.
———. "Joyce Carol Oates: Love and Violence," *Newsweek*, 80 (Dec. 11, 1972), 72–74, 77.
Dalton, Elizabeth. "Joyce Carol Oates: Violence in the Head," *Commentary*, 49 (June 1970), 75–77.

DeMott, Benjamin. "The Necessity in Art of a Reflective Intelligence," *Saturday Review*, 52 (Nov. 22, 1969), 71–73, 89.

"The Doomed and the Damned," *Time*, 92 (Nov. 1, 1968), 102.

Doyle, James. "Cather in the Raw," *The Critic*, (Feb.–Mar. 1968), 75–76.

Frankel, Haskel. Review of *By the North Gate*, *Saturday Review*, 46 (Oct. 26, 1963), 45.

Gilman, Richard. Review of *The Wheel of Love*, *New York Times Book Review*, Oct. 25, 1970, pp. 4, 62.

Gordon, Jan B. Review of *Wonderland*, *Commonweal*, 95 (Feb. 11, 1972), 449–50.

Grant, Louis T. "A Child of Paradise," *The Nation*, 207 (Nov. 4, 1968), 475.

Gray, Paul Edward. "New Novels in Review," *Yale Review*, 59 (Mar. 1970), 433.

Hayes, Brian P. Review of *Wonderland*, *Saturday Review*, 54 (Oct. 9, 1971), 38.

Hicks, Granville. "Fiction That Grows from the Ground," *Saturday Review*, 50 (Aug. 5, 1967), 23–24.

————. "What Is Reality?," *Saturday Review*, 51 (Oct. 26, 1968), 33–34.

Janeway, Elizabeth. "Clara the Climber," *New York Times Book Review*, Sept. 10, 1967, pp. 5, 63.

Joseph, Ellen. "Growing Up Assured," *Book Week*, Oct. 25, 1964, pp. 21, 23.

Kauffmann, Stanley. "O'Hara and Others," *New York Review of Books*, 3 (Dec. 17, 1964), 21–22.

————. "Violence amid Gentility," *New York Times Book Review*, Nov. 10, 1963, pp. 4, 61.

Kazin, Alfred. "Oates," *Harper's*, 243 (Aug. 1971), 78–82.

Knowles, John. "Nada at the Core," *New York Times Book Review*, Nov. 3, 1968, p. 5.

————. "A Racing Car Is the Symbol of Violence," *New York Times Book Review*, Oct. 25, 1964, p. 5.

Kuehl, Linda. "An Interview with Joyce Carol Oates," *Commonweal*, 91 (Dec. 5, 1969), 307–10.

L'Heureux, John. "Mirage-Seekers," *The Atlantic*, 224 (Oct. 1969), 128–29.

————. "Something New, Something Blue," *The Critic*, 27 (Fall 1969), 83–85.

Long, Robert Emmet. "A *Garden of Earthly Delights,*" *Common-weal,* 87 (Feb. 23, 1968), 630–31.

———. Review of *The Wheel of Love, Saturday Review,* 53 (Oct. 24, 1970), 36, 65.

McCormick, Lucienne P. "A Bibliography of Works by and about Joyce Carol Oates," *American Literature,* 43 (Mar. 1971), 124–32.

Oberbeck, S. K. "The Life Force Gone Wild," *Book World,* Oct. 10, 1971, pp. 4, 15.

———. Review of *Marriages and Infidelities, Book World,* Sept. 17, 1972, pp. 4, 10.

Pagones, Dorric. "Price of Survival," *Saturday Review,* 47 (Nov. 28, 1964), 39.

Price, Martin. "Reason and Its Alternatives: Some Recent Fiction," *Yale Review,* 58 (Mar. 1969), 468.

Ricks, Christopher. "The Unignorable Real," *New York Review of Books,* 14 (Feb. 12, 1970), 22–24.

Sale, Roger. "What Went Wrong?," *New York Review of Books,* 17 (Oct. 21, 1971), 3–4, 6.

Sheppard, R. Z. "Wilder Oates," *Time,* 98 (Oct. 18, 1971), 89–90.

Sissman, L.E. "The Whole Truth," *Saturday Review,* 45 (Dec. 6, 1969), 238, 241–42.

Sokolov, Raymond A. "Tobacco Boulevard," *Newsweek,* 70 (Oct. 2, 1967), 93–94.

Spector, Robert Donald. Review of *By the North Gate, Book Week,* Nov. 17, 1963, p. 32.

Stevens, Cynthia Charlotte. "The Imprisoned Imagination: The Family in the Fiction of Joyce Carol Oates, 1960–1970." Diss., University of Illinois, 1974.

Sullivan, Walter. "The Artificial Demon: Joyce Carol Oates and the Dimensions of the Real," *Hollins Critic,* 9 (Dec. 1972), 1–12.

Walker, Carolyn. "Fear, Love, and Art in Oates' 'Plot,' " *Critique,* 15, no. 1 (1973), 59–70.

Weeks, Edward. Review of *Wonderland, The Atlantic,* 228 (Nov. 1, 1971), 148, 150.

Wolff, Geoffrey. "Gothic City," *Newsweek,* 74 (Sept. 29, 1969), 120–22.

———. Review of *Wonderland, New York Times Book Review,* Oct. 24, 1971, pp. 5, 10.

"Writing as a Natural Reaction," *Time,* 94 (Oct. 10, 1969), 108.

Zimmerman, Paul D. "Hunger for Dreams," *Newsweek,* 75 (Mar. 23, 1970), 108, 110.

WORKS BY SYLVIA PLATH

Ariel. New York: Harper & Row, 1966.

The Bell Jar (1963, London). New York: Bantam Books, 1972.

"Context," *London Magazine,* 1 (Feb. 1962), 45–46.

"The Daughters of Blossom Street," *London Magazine,* 7 (May 1960), 34–48.

"The Fifteen-Dollar Eagle," *Sewanee Review,* 68 (Fall 1960), 603–18.

"The Fifty-ninth Bear," *London Magazine,* 8 (Feb. 1961), 11–20.

"Johnny Panic and the Bible of Dreams," *The Atlantic,* 222 (Sept. 1968), 54–60.

"The Mothers' Union," *McCalls,* 100 (Oct. 1972), 80–81, 126, 128, 130, 142.

"Sketchbook of a Spanish Summer," *Christian Science Monitor,* Nov. 5, 6, 1956, pp. 13, 17.

"The Wishing Box," *The Atlantic,* 214 (Oct. 1964), 86–89.

WORKS ABOUT SYLVIA PLATH

Adams, Phoebe. Review of *The Bell Jar, The Atlantic,* 227 (May 1971), 114.

Aird, Eileen M. *Sylvia Plath.* New York: Barnes and Noble, 1973.

Alvarez, A. *The Savage God: A Study of Suicide.* New York: Random House, 1971.

————. "Sylvia Plath: The Cambridge Collection," *Cambridge Review,* 90 (Feb. 7, 1969), 246–47.

Baro, Gene. "Varied Quintet," *New York Times Book Review,* June 26, 1966, pp. 10, 12, 14.

Birstein, Ann. "The Sylvia Plath Cult," *Vogue,* 118 (Oct. 1, 1971), 176.

"The Blood Jet Is Poetry," *Time,* 87 (June 10, 1966), 118, E9, 120.

Boyers, Robert. "Sylvia Plath: The Trepanned Veteran," *Centennial Review,* 13 (Spring 1969), 138–53.

Brinnin, John Malcolm. Review of *Ariel, Partisan Review,* 34 (Winter 1967), 156–57.

Claire, William F. "That Rare, Random Descent: The Poetry and Pathos of Sylvia Plath," *Antioch Review,* 26 (Winter 1966–67), 552–60.

Cox, C. B., and A. R. Jones. "After the Tranquillized Fifties: Notes on Sylvia Plath and James Baldwin," *Critical Quarterly,* 6 (Summer 1964), 107–12.

Davenport, Guy. "Novels in Braille," *National Review*, 33 (May 18, 1971), 538.

Davison, Peter. "Inhabited by a Cry: The Last Poetry of Sylvia Plath," *The Atlantic*, 218 (Aug. 1966), 76–77.

————. "Three Visionary Poets," *The Atlantic*, 229 (Feb. 1972), 105–6.

Dickey, William. "Responsibilities," *Kenyon Review*, 24 (Autumn 1962), 760–64.

Duffy, Martha. "Lady Lazarus," *Time*, 97 (June 21, 1971), 87–88.

————. "The Triumph of a Tormented Poet: The Growing Literary Boom for Sylvia Plath," *Life*, 71 (Nov. 12, 1971), 38A–38B.

Hardwick, Elizabeth. "On Sylvia Plath," *New York Review of Books*, 17 (Aug. 12, 1971), 3.

Holbrook, David. "R. D. Laing & the Death Circuit," *Encounter*, 31 (Aug. 1968), 35–45.

————. "Sylvia Plath and the Problem of Violence in Art," *Cambridge Review*, 90 (Feb. 7, 1969), 249–50.

Homberger, Eric. "I Am I," *Cambridge Review*, 90 (Feb. 7, 1969), 251–52.

Howe, Irving. "Sylvia Plath: A Partial Disagreement," *Harper's*, 244 (Jan. 1972), 88–91.

Howes, Barbara. "A Note on *Ariel*," *Massachusetts Review*, 8 (Winter 1967), 225–26.

Jones, A. R. "Necessity and Freedom: The Poetry of Robert Lowell, Sylvia Plath and Anne Sexton," *Critical Quarterly*, 7 (Spring 1965), 11–30.

Kalem, T. E. "Sylvia Plath," *Time*, 103 (Jan. 28, 1974), 77.

Kissick, Gary. "Plath: A Terrible Perfection," *The Nation*, 207 (Sept. 16, 1968), 245–47.

Klein, Elinor. "A Friend Recalls Sylvia Plath," *Glamour*, 56 (Nov. 1966), 168, 182–84.

Lerner, Laurence. Review of *The Bell Jar*, *The Listener*, 69 (Jan. 31, 1963), 215.

Libby, Anthony. "God's Lioness and the Priest of Sycorax," *Contemporary Literature*, 15 (Summer 1974), 386–405.

Locke, Richard. "The Last Word: Beside *The Bell Jar*," *New York Times Book Review*, June 20, 1971, p. 47.

Lowell, Robert. Foreword to *Ariel*. New York: Harper & Row, 1966.

Maloff, Saul. "Waiting for the Voice to Crack," *New Republic*, 164 (May 8, 1971), 33–35.

Melander, Ingrid. *The Poetry of Sylvia Plath: A Study of Themes.* Stockholm: Almqvist & Wiksell, 1972.

Moss, Howard. "Dying: An Introduction," *New Yorker,* 47 (July 10, 1971), 73–75.

Newman, Charles, ed. *The Art of Sylvia Plath: A Symposium.* Bloomington: Indiana University Press, 1970.

Oberg, Arthur K. "Sylvia Plath and the New Decadence," *Chicago Review,* 20, no. 1 (1968), 66–73.

Perloff, Majorie G. "Angst and Animism in the Poetry of Sylvia Plath," *Journal of Modern Literature,* 1, no. 1 (1970), 57–75.

———. " 'A Ritual for Being Born Twice': Sylvia Plath's *The Bell Jar,*" *Contemporary Literature,* 13 (Autumn 1972), 507–22.

Raven, Simon. "The Trouble with Phaedra," *The Spectator,* Feb. 15, 1963, p. 203.

Romano, J. "Sylvia Plath Reconsidered," *Commentary,* 57 (Apr. 1974), 47–52.

Rosenstein, Harriet. "Reconsidering Sylvia Plath," *Ms.,* 1 (Sept. 1972), 44–57, 96–98.

Rosenthal, M. L. "Metamorphosis of a Book," *The Spectator,* Apr. 21, 1967, pp. 456–57.

———. *The New Poets: American and British Poetry since World War II.* New York: Oxford University Press, 1967.

Scholes, Robert. Review of *The Bell Jar, New York Times Book Review,* Apr. 11, 1971, p. 7.

Simon, John. "More Brass than Enduring," *Hudson Review,* 15 (Autumn 1965), 464.

Skelton, Robin. "Britannia's Muse Revisited," *Massachusetts Review,* 6 (Autumn 1965), 834–35.

Smith, William Jay. "New Books of Poems," *Harper's,* 233 (Aug. 1966), 92.

Steiner, George. "In Extremis," *Cambridge Review,* 90 (Feb. 7, 1969), 247–49.

Zollman, Sol. "Sylvia Plath and Imperialist Culture," *Literature and Ideology,* 2 (1969), 11–22.

Index